D0388427

DECISIVE DAY

Also by Richard M. Ketchum

AUTHOR

Second Cutting: Letters from the Country

The World of George Washington

Will Rogers: His Life and Times

The Winter Soldiers

The Secret Life of the Forest

Faces from the Past

The American Heritage Book of Great Historic Places

Male Husbandry

What Is Communism?

The Borrowed Years 1938–1941

EDITOR

American Testament: Fifty Great Documents of American History

*The Original Water Color Paintings by John James Audubon
   for The Birds of America*

Four Days

The Horizon Book of the Renaissance

The American Heritage Picture History of the Civil War

The American Heritage Book of the Pioneer Spirit

The American Heritage Book of the Revolution

What Is Democracy?

Richard M. Ketchum

DECISIVE DAY

The Battle for Bunker Hill

AN EXPANDED AND
FULLY ILLUSTRATED
EDITION OF
THE BATTLE FOR
BUNKER HILL

ANCHOR BOOKS

Doubleday

NEW YORK LONDON TORONTO SYDNEY AUCKLAND

AN ANCHOR BOOK
PUBLISHED BY DOUBLEDAY
a division of Bantam Doubleday Dell Publishing Group, Inc.
666 Fifth Avenue, New York, New York 10103

ANCHOR BOOKS, DOUBLEDAY, and the portrayal of an anchor
are trademarks of Doubleday, a division of Bantam Doubleday
Dell Publishing Group, Inc.

Decisive Day was originally published as *The Battle for
Bunker Hill* by Doubleday in 1962 and published as *Decisive
Day* by Doubleday in 1974. This Anchor Books edition is
published by arrangement with Doubleday.

MAPS BY RAPHAEL PALACIOS

Library of Congress Cataloging-in-Publication Data
Ketchum, Richard M.   1922–
    Decisive day; the battle for Bunker Hill.
    "An expanded and fully illustrated edition of the battle
        for Bunker Hill   [1st ed., 1962]"
Bibliography: p.
1. Bunker Hill, Battle of, 1775. I. Title.
E241.B9K4 1974   973-3'312   73–14051
ISBN 0-385-41897-3

For my Mother and Father

Publisher's Note

This new edition of Richard Ketchum's book is revised, enlarged, and illuminated. It was published originally under the title *The Battle for Bunker Hill*. Now it has been retitled and more generously illustrated. This publication follows the recent much-admired work by Mr. Ketchum, *The Winter Soldiers*, an account of the pivotal battles of Trenton and Princeton. We believe that the two books, taken together, comprise a significant sequence in modern historical understanding of the American Revolution.

The Winter Soldiers, wrote Bruce Catton, causes the Revolution "to appear as a tale of men like ourselves who did their best in what looked like a failing cause and won a brilliant success." Orville Prescott called it "a superb military history of an intimacy and narrative power such as is rarely written." Of *Decisive Day*, in its original edition, Richard B. Morris, Gouverneur Morris Professor of History at Columbia University, wrote that it "should become the classic exposition of our greatest revolutionary battle."

Richard M. Ketchum is Senior Editor at American Heritage. As director of that company's book publishing, he edited many volumes, including *The American Heritage Book of the Revolution*, and he shared in the Pulitzer Prize Special Citation for *The American Heritage Picture History of the Civil War*. He is, said Bruce Bliven, Jr., "that rare combination, a scholar who knows how to tell a story." Mr. Ketchum makes his home in Dorset, Vermont.

CONTENTS

Publisher's Note   vii

Introduction   xiii

CHAPTER I

Our Elbows Must Be Eased   1

CHAPTER II

For the Security of This Colony   47

CHAPTER III

We Readly and Cheerfully Obeyed   85

CHAPTER IV

Raw Lads and Old Men Half Armed   105

CHAPTER V

A Most Awful, Grand and Melancholy Sight   137

CHAPTER VI

I Wish This Cursed Place Was Burned   185

A Note on Sources   228

Acknowledgments   234

Notes   237

Bibliography   269

Index   278

The day—perhaps the decisive day—is come, on which the fate of America depends.

ABIGAIL ADAMS

Introduction

For a battle that proved to be so decisive it was a curious one, in that neither side at first claimed to have won a victory. It was not a particularly large engagement; there were, after all, only about twelve hundred Americans arrayed against twice that many British. Ironically, people could not even agree on a name for it at the time. Battles are usually called after the place where they occur, but there was such widespread uncertainty about the location of the action that some referred to it as the battle of Charlestown, some as Bunker Hill, still others as Breed's Hill.

For those who like to imagine the ultimate drama of war in picture-book terms, this was one of the few genuine setpieces of the Revolutionary War—a pitched battle in which the pride of the British army, after being rowed across a body of water in full view of the mesmerized citizenry of Boston, lined up as if on parade and marched in precise order up a hill to storm a fort by direct, frontal assault. It was a scene difficult for novelist or filmmaker to surpass in terms of sheer pageantry.

War demands a final reckoning in human terms, however, and the casualties at the Battle for Bunker Hill were altogether staggering. Nearly half of the scarlet-coated regulars who stormed the redoubt fell in the attack, more than a third of the American defenders were killed, wounded, or captured, and in these grim statistics lies the true significance of the matter.

Under cover of darkness on June 16, 1775, the rebels had constructed an earthen fort directly opposite British-held Boston, and when General Thomas Gage saw it the next morning he recognized it for what it was—a challenge that could not possibly be ignored. The engagement that ensued was, quite literally, a fight to the death, signifying once and for all that both sides meant business—meant, in fact, to settle their differences through bloodshed instead of further talk. What occurred on the slopes of Breed's Hill differed substantially from the events of April 19, 1775, when British troops marched out into the countryside and were compelled to fall back in confusion from Lexington and Concord, pursued by bands of men who harried them, guerrilla-fashion, from the cover of trees and stone walls.

Two months separated Lexington and Concord from Bunker Hill, and during that period the rebellious Americans cobbled together an army of sorts—not a very well-organized or efficient one, to be sure, but an army nevertheless, and when several units marched from Cambridge to Charlestown peninsula on the night of June 16 they were the first of a long line of American expeditionary forces setting out to meet the foe in some sort of planned movement.

The Battle for Bunker Hill had a powerful effect on George III's government in London. Although further efforts would be made from time to time to reach a negotiated settlement with the Americans, those efforts were undertaken not in a spirit of conciliation, but as one enemy toward another. Bunker Hill, in other words, forced Great Britain to commit itself to war, and after the battle relationships between mother country and colonies were never the same again.

If the events of June 17 forced Britain's hand, they had a profound effect on America as well. Here were thirteen ill-assorted colonies, each tied more closely to London than to each other, and because two small armies met head to head in mortal combat they found themselves at war with the nation to which they owed allegiance. Suddenly there was an imperative need for the untried

Continental Congress to act, to take charge of events—to behave, in fact, like a real governing body, supplying a fragile unity and direction where little or none had existed before. Equally suddenly, individual Americans discovered that they had to take a stand, to choose between one side and the other for better or for worse.

Bunker Hill became a ray of hope to Congress and the various colonies, not because they thought the New Englanders had won, but because they had survived. Taken together with Lexington and Concord, the engagement demonstrated that the British army was not invincible after all and that an aroused citizenry was capable of resisting trained professional soldiers in red coats.

The lesson of Bunker Hill was not lost on Britain's military leaders. It is difficult to prove that a single battle affected the subsequent conduct of an army and its commanders, but the fact is that the British never again revealed quite the same aggressiveness after Bunker Hill. The recollection of the awful slaughter, where more British officers were killed than in any battle in memory, remained with General William Howe as long as he served in America. Not again did he risk a full-scale frontal assault on an entrenched rebel position.

None of these aftereffects was apparent to the men joined in battle in the fierce heat of June 17, 1775. Someone had ordered them to fight and most of them—British and American alike—did so with unsurpassed ferocity and courage despite the miscalculations of their commanders. The story of that decisive day, as the historian Allen French realized, was "a tale of great blunders heroically redeemed. Each side committed an unexplainable, inexcusable error in strategy; and each side paid in blood according to the magnitude of its mistake."

Dorset, Vermont
August 13, 1973

DECISIVE DAY

I. Our Elbows Must Be Eased

It had been a rough, unseasonable crossing. His Majesty's Ship *Cerberus* was thirty-four days out of Spithead when a lookout sighted Cape Ann through the lifting fog at dawn on May 25. Two hours later, as the vessel worked her way up the tortuous channel into Boston harbor, past low, wooded islands that lay mysterious and velvety green in the veiled morning sunlight, the crew and several military passengers were on deck early, eager for their first glimpse of land.

Two days before, when the *Cerberus* spoke a Salem fishing schooner, there had been an ominous hint of trouble around Boston; so when His Majesty's sloop *Otter* appeared out of the mist the men crowded to the rail and waited, silent and expectant, for any word she might carry. As the sloop came about and headed into the wind, a big, handsome man in the scarlet coat and epaulets of a British major general stepped to the quarterdeck rail of the warship, cupped his hands, and sang out impetuously: "What news is there?"

Across the water the *Otter's* skipper put a speaking trumpet to his mouth. There had been fighting between rebels and General Gage's troops, he shouted. More than a month ago. Nearly three hundred of the King's soldiers killed, wounded, or missing. Now Boston was surrounded by ten thousand country people.

Only the slap of sails, the creaking of spars, and the rush of water against the two ships' sides could be heard as the man's voice died away. Then the army officer called out again:

"How many regulars in Boston?"

"About five thousand," came the reply.

Another moment of silence; then the big man swung round toward his companions with a smile and exclaimed, "What! Ten thousand peasants keep five thousand King's troops shut up? Well, let *us* get in, and we'll soon find elbowroom!" A cheer went up aboard the man-o'-war at that, and as the sloop fell astern, heading for blue water, the men returned to their duties laughing at General John Burgoyne's little joke. He had a way of putting things, the general did; those rebels were for it when the *Cerberus* arrived.

There was no doubt that the big warship was carrying the most impressive array of military brass England could muster at that particular moment. On March 2, 1775, the Earl of Sandwich, First Sea Lord, had written Captain James Chads of the *Cerberus*, informing him that "The King having thought fit that the Major Generals Howe, Burgoyne & Clinton, should be employed upon His Majesty's Service in North America, and that they should repair as soon as possible to Boston," Chads should receive them on board his vessel "together with their Attendants, Servants & Baggage, and proceed with them without loss of time to Boston." Meanwhile Admiral Samuel Graves, Vice Admiral of the Blue, Commander of His Majesty's Ships and Vessels in North America at Boston, had been alerted to the major generals' arrival and told to expedite the return of the *Cerberus* to England with any dispatches they prepared after landing.

So the three men—William Howe, Henry Clinton, and John Burgoyne—the best England had to offer, had boarded ship and sailed west toward a destiny which was to alter the course of their lives. Of recent years this military trio had seen more fighting in Parliament than on the battlefield, but their departure was nevertheless an auspicious one, suggesting a bit of doggerel to a London wit:

"Behold the *Cerberus* the Atlantic plow,
Her precious cargo—Burgoyne, Clinton, Howe.
Bow, wow, wow!"

Of the three, Henry Clinton seems to have minded the crossing most. For nearly two weeks there had been fresh gales and squalls, and on May 7 a particularly hard blow carried away the ship's starboard main topsail sheet. Clinton had been thoroughly seasick (less so than on previous voyages, he observed—one result of being crowded into a tiny cabin with six others having been that he was on deck almost constantly). In his hours of misery he may have taken some solace from the thought of what it was like aboard the troop transports which had left before them, carrying reinforcements to North America. Clinton had sailed on transports, and knew how they heeled over even in mild weather, with the lee ports under water as often as they were out. Belowdecks was the awful stench of men packed like animals into filthy, almost airless quarters. The food was poor and insufficient, the water rotten, and at night the clanking of pumps kept the wretched landsmen tossing sleeplessly on their pallets of rancid straw. First they succumbed to seasickness, then to boils from exposure to salt water, then to scurvy—and on older ships the dread ship-fever often raged. They got no pity from the sailors, either, who had a saying, "A messmate before a shipmate, a shipmate before a stranger, a stranger before a dog, a dog before a soldier." As one British noncom described his voyage to America: "There was continued destruction in the foretop, the pox aboveboard, the plague between decks, hell in the forecastle, the devil at the helm."

No, the *Cerberus* was bad, but the transports were worse, and fortunately for Clinton the weather had turned fair after the first fortnight. Now the sight of Boston's outlying islands, with rolling green countryside beyond, brought a lift to the spirits and set a major general to thinking of the future that lay ahead. Burgoyne's "elbowroom" jest had been typical of the man, but it was a fairly accurate summary of what Henry Clinton felt, too. Off to the left of the roadstead he could see Castle William, mounting a hundred guns or more; ahead, above the silhouette of Boston, the masts of the Royal Navy swayed against the sky; in the city itself were five thousand regulars under General Thomas Gage, with more on the way from Ireland. It was inconceivable that any number of untrained, ill-equipped, poorly led provincials could hold out for long against that kind of strength.

In a sense this was a homecoming for Clinton, although the thought may not have occurred to him in just that way. He was the only son of a British admiral and had been born in America in 1738. Before going "home" to England, he had had a taste of militia training in the colonies; he obtained a lieutenant's commission in the 2nd Foot Guards at the age of thirteen; and by thirty-four he was a major general, after campaigning on the continent during the Seven Years' War. But if his youth and rank suggested brilliance, there was little to justify it. Clinton was a colorless, short, rather paunchy man with a round face, a large nose, and a sensitivity to criticism that was almost a disease. Although he was an intelligent, reasonably competent soldier who might have gone far, his tendency to suspect everyone, to look behind every remark and gesture for an affront, made him mistrust even himself in the end.

Clinton was the youngest of the three major generals on the *Cerberus*, but the second in rank. The senior man was William Howe, reputedly a distant cousin of the King and therefore marked for advancement, but for all that a soldier of unquestioned talent and ability. He too had served in America, at the capture of Louisbourg in '58, and the following year at the storming of Quebec. There the great James Wolfe, who had called Howe the best officer in the King's service, picked him to lead the detachment that scaled the Heights of Abraham. Howe's older brother was the admiral, "Black Dick" Howe, and another brother, George Augustus, third Viscount Howe, had been one of the most popular figures in America a generation earlier. He was

The querulous, self-centered Henry Clinton—shown in a contemporary engraving—was no easy subordinate, as General Thomas Gage discovered. His military judgments were often well founded, but he pressed them so assertively and tactlessly that he only succeeded in irritating his superiors. (*Emmett Collection, New York Public Library*)

Whether or not William Howe's subsequent lack of aggressiveness may be laid to the memory of the carnage he witnessed on Breed's Hill, his record after succeeding Thomas Gage as commander in chief was one of missed opportunities, of objectives never fully realized. One such was the incomplete victory at Long Island, for which he received the Order of the Bath he wears in this print. (*Anne S. K. Brown Military Collection, Providence*)

killed in Abercromby's hopeless frontal assault on the French at Ticonderoga, and the New Englanders who had served with him loved him so well that they placed a monument in Westminster Abbey as a reminder of "the affection their officers and soldiers bore to his command." It was more than most officers of that age received, and George III, in giving William his appointment, may have recognized that the name Howe still held some magic in the colonies. Against this, of course, was the matter of William Howe's politics. He was a staunch Whig, and as a member of Parliament had assured his Nottingham constituents in 1774 that he would accept no command which meant fighting Americans. When his appointment arrived he is said to have asked if it was a request or an order, and only when assured it was the latter did he comply, explaining that he "could not refuse without incurring the odious name of backwardness to serve my country in distress." (Henry Clinton would take pains to make the same point, many years after the Revolution. "I was not a volunteer in that war," he wrote. "I was ordered by my Sovereign and I obeyed.")

But if his politics were suspect in some quarters, Howe's professional skill was recognized by friends and enemies alike. Lord George Germain, the Secretary of State for the colonies, had not spoken to Howe's brother, the admiral, for seventeen years. (Germain was the same man who, as Lord Sackville, had been pronounced "unfit to serve his majesty in any military capacity whatsoever" as a result of misconduct in the Seven Years' War, but who was now deemed capable of handling one of the most critically important jobs in the kingdom.) After receiving the news of Lexington and Concord, Germain wrote to a friend, comparing those battles with Braddock's defeat, recalling the lessons in Indian fighting which the British army had learned as a result, and concluding that "Nobody understands that discipline so well as General Howe . . . who will, I am persuaded, teach the present army to be as formidable as that he formerly acted with."

Major General William Howe was a large, dark-complexioned man of forty-six, whose soldierly bearing had begun to lose ground to the high living he enjoyed so thoroughly. He was an inveterate gambler; in fact, his debts unquestionably influenced his decision to come to America, for he needed the money which active duty would bring him. He had the mind, the qualities of leadership, and all the opportunities a soldier might wish for, yet Howe was doomed to years of disappointment and criticism in the colonies. In all of the complaints leveled against him—that he was a Whig, that he drank too much, that his attentions to an American mistress kept his mind off campaigning, that he was lazy, lacked initiative, and sympathized with the rebels—in all these charges there were varying degrees of truth. Yet it is worth mentioning that no man who served with Howe or against him ever questioned his courage on the battlefield.

The third man of the triumvirate, Major General John Burgoyne, was by all odds the most singular personality. He was junior to both Howe and Clinton, despite his fifty-three years, but this was because he had entered the army at the advanced age of twenty-two, had sold his commission three years later, and had not rejoined until 1756. He was the colorful commander of the 16th Dragoons, known as "Burgoyne's Light Horse," which the King was fond of reviewing, and in the Portugal campaign of 1762–63 had received much praise for capturing Valencia with cavalry alone. Burgoyne's theories on the treatment of troops were far in advance of his age. Among his proposals was the radical notion that soldiers should be treated like intelligent human beings, that they should not be subjected to brutal corporal punishment, that they should not be trained "like spaniels by the stick"; and at the same time he urged that officers read books, learn to write accurate reports, and study mathematics. Because he practiced these precepts himself, he was extremely popular with his men, who nicknamed him "Gentleman Johnny."

The nickname fit in every respect. Burgoyne came from an old Lancashire family of some repute, and he was a graceful-mannered, dashing figure, handsome in the ruddy-faced, full-fed style of the period. Like Howe, he was a heavy gambler, and was also promi-

Sir Joshua Reynolds' portrait (done about 1766) captures the flamboyance that was such a part of John Burgoyne's makeup. Vain, boastful, and self-seeking, he was forever maneuvering for political advantage with authorities in London, but when the opportunity for personal glory finally came in 1777 the result was the disaster at Saratoga that led to France's entry into the war. (*Copyright The Frick Collection, New York*)

nent in London high life as a member of Parliament, man of fashion, wit, and playwright (David Garrick brought out his play *Maid of the Oaks* shortly before Burgoyne received his appointment to the American command).

Upon learning that he was to be posted to America, Burgoyne had begun putting his friendship with highly placed persons to use. Always one to turn a nice phrase in public, he put himself firmly on the side of the Ministry by asking boldly, "Is there a man in England—I am sure there is not an officer or soldier in the King's service—who does not think the Parliamentary rights of Great Britain a cause to fight for—to bleed and die for?" And at the same time, privately dissatisfied with his assignment and anxious for his future (he was quick to see that he would be junior to three other generals in Boston), he began seeking the command in New York. He approached Lord North, Germain, Lord Dartmouth, Lord Rochford, and even Howe himself, to no avail. As a last ·resort he persuaded Lord North to set before the King a proposal that he might return to England by fall if he did not receive an important command, and he sailed for America with George III's approval of this plan.

All in all, the three major generals seem to have gotten on well during the voyage. Not long after they landed Clinton wrote a friend, confiding that "At first (for you know I am a shy bitch) I kept my distance [and] seldom spoke till my two colleagues forced me out. . . . I could not have named two people I should sooner wish to serve with in any respect."

At 10 A.M. on May 25, 1775, the *Cerberus* took a pilot aboard, and soon afterward passed His Majesty's ships *Mercury, Nautilus,* and *Falcon* lying at anchor in Nantasket Roads. After saluting the admiral she dropped anchor in seven fathoms of water about a half mile offshore where, according to the log, the watch officer "found riding . . . the *Preston, Boyne, Somerset, Glasgow & Marlin.*" Boats were lowered—one carrying to Samuel Graves his promotion to Vice-Admiral of the White—and the three major generals, their attendants, and baggage were rowed across the water toward the docks, where a crowd had already collected to greet them on this historic occasion.

Boston was a very different city from the one Howe, Clinton, and Burgoyne had expected to find when they left England on April 21. So far as they knew then, it was the seat of most of the colonial troubles, a hotbed of radicalism—but that was no more nor less than it had been for five years. The guns fired at Lexington and Concord two days before their departure had changed all that, and just now Boston was for all the world like a medieval castle under siege. The cheers that went up when their boat touched Long Wharf were from Tories, from men and women loyal to the Crown who believed pathetically that the arrival of these three would somehow change everything, rid them of the plague that had settled over the countryside, and set things to rights again. Even the army had taken hope from the rumors of their arrival. As Lieutenant John Barker of the King's Own wrote on May 1: "We are anxiously awaiting the arrival of the Genl. Officers and Troops that are expected; we want to get out of this coop'd up situation. We cou'd now do that I suppose but the G—— [Gage] does not seem to want it; there's no guessing what he is at; Time will shew."

Many a man loyal to the Crown had been unable to guess what Gage was at, had failed to understand why he and his men had not put a quick end to the trouble long before now. Only a month earlier the Earl of Sandwich had risen in the House of Lords and with some heat taken to task a member of the Opposition who described the conquest of America as "impracticable." "Suppose the colonies do abound in men," Sandwich had cried, "what does that signify? They are raw, undisciplined, cowardly men. I wish instead of 40,000 or 50,000 of these brave fellows, they would produce in the field at least 200,000, the more the better, the easier would be the conquest; if they did not run away, they would starve themselves into compliance with our measures." A similar opinion was held by virtually every officer now serving in the colonies. It might be a nasty business, fighting against men who were, after all, Englishmen of a sort; but even though it would only be a brief affair, one could hope that there might be some opportunity for glory and recognition.

Whatever their thoughts on this subject, it must have been a high moment for the three major generals—a little pageant right out of the Crusades, with the valiant knights resplendent in scarlet and gold come to do battle against the infidel. As they left Long Wharf and climbed into the carriage which the governor had sent for them, crowds lined either side of King Street and a procession formed behind them to do homage. There were cheers and waving handkerchiefs and tears of relief as they clattered by. Somewhere along the route Burgoyne's "elbowroom" remark was repeated, caught fire, and spread from one man to the next, evoking outbursts of joy and pride at each new telling. At the head of King Street they went by the Town House, rattling over cobblestones which had run red with the blood of five men killed on a March night of 1770, in what the rebels called "the Massacre." Here they turned left into Cornhill, passing Old Meeting and the bookstores which abounded in that section, then past Christ Church, Old South, and then turned right into the entrance to Province House. Far back from the road, fronted by a majestic sweep of green lawn, ancient shade trees, and flowering shrubs, was the three-story brick mansion that housed the royal governor of Massachusetts. There was something incongruous about the huge, gilt-bronzed figure of an Indian, with drawn bow and arrow, that surmounted the cupola of the building; but there was no mistaking the authority of the elaborately carved coat of arms over the doorway, which informed visitors that here dwelt the representative of George III. With the noise of the crowd still ringing in their ears, the three generals climbed the stone steps and went inside to pay their respects to Thomas Gage, Captain-General of His Majesty's forces in North America, and military governor of the Massachusetts Bay Colony.

Gage would have heard those cheers all the way from the waterfront, and they must have been a galling reminder of his

Although this view was painted after the war, it shows the heart of Revolutionary Boston essentially as Burgoyne, Clinton, and Howe saw it upon their arrival in May 1775. On the cobbled street in front of the Old State House (center)

and the red brick Custom House (right) the Boston Massacre took place in 1770. The British Coffee House (right, behind carriage) was a favorite haunt of English officers who were stationed in town before the war. (*Massachusetts Historical Society*)

failure here in Boston. Exactly a year ago he had received the same kind of ovation when he succeeded Thomas Hutchinson as governor, but the sweet wine of popularity had turned to vinegar in remarkably short order.

His present situation, while scarcely of his own making, was not what a man would choose to end a distinguished career. He had fought the French in Flanders in '41, served as an aide-de-camp to the Duke of Albemarle in the bloody battle of Fontenoy, marched against Bonnie Prince Charlie in the campaigns that ruined the Young Pretender, and was at the rout of the Scottish clans at Culloden. For the past twenty years Gage had soldiered in America, fighting for the colonials, taking their side as his own. On a fierce, hot July day in 1755 he had led the three-hundred-man advance party of General Edward Braddock's army across the Monongahela River, and as his scarlet grenadiers marched in line of battle into the dense green forest they were the first to be hit by a withering fire from French and Indians. Within a few minutes Gage had bullet holes in his hat and a wound in his stomach, and with most of his officers killed or wounded he kept bellowing commands to the demoralized men, urging Braddock to make "one bold attack," but for naught. He had seen a thousand brave men fall that day, of fifteen hundred who went into action, and without sighting more than one or two of the hidden enemy; yet he had gone back for more later, under Generals James Abercromby and Amherst. Out of his wilderness experience had come, in 1757, a proposal for disciplined troops trained in irregular warfare; and the formation of the 80th Regiment, as Gage's "chausseurs" were designated, was a landmark in military history. It was the first light-armed regiment in the British army, an outfit that combined discipline and special training with rapidity of movement. In 1760 Gage was made governor at Montreal and three years later he took command of the British forces in North America from Amherst.

Thomas Gage was an even-tempered, persistent man who saw his duty and followed it to the best of his ability, and so far as he knew, he had been patient and reasonable at every turn. Certainly his record in the colonies spoke for itself, he was married to an American woman—the beautiful Margaret Kemble—and he had tried to be impartial in every action he took as governor in Massachusetts. The previous June 1 it had been his personal misfortune but his duty to put the Port Bill into effect by closing the port of Boston—an event greeted by tolling bells, fasting, prayer, and the public display of mourning—and since that moment he had had to cope with every piece of legal trickery, political chicanery, and general cantankerousness known to the Yankee. Lord knows Gage had tried everything—argument, persuasion, and recently force—and now he was worn out with his task, disgusted with the people he had honestly hoped and tried to serve, and possibly hopeful that the arrival of Howe, Clinton, and Burgoyne meant an end to his present command. For it was truly an impossible situation. His own soldiers and the loyalists considered him far too mild-mannered, ridiculing him as "Tommy, the old woman," while the rebels for their part called him "monster."

He could so easily have imposed martial law on Boston, yet he had not. Instead, he permitted the town's residents almost complete freedom; he made no move to censor or suppress the scurrilous local press, though it was constantly full of attacks on the government he represented or his own person; he allowed the rabble-rousers to come and go as they pleased and to hold their meetings; while all around him, in the outlying towns, provincial militiamen drilled on every village green and collected supplies and ammunition for war. To set an example of justice to civil authorities who were totally lax in punishing political offenders, he had listened to every complaint by selectman or citizen against drunken soldiers, and followed them with public floggings —to such extent that the army complained that the Liberty Boys were exempt while loyal subjects were harassed and British troops whipped in the presence of their enemies for minor offenses. He had prohibited his men from wearing side arms in public, only to have them grumble that this would encourage the populace in their "licentious and riotous disposition." And he had ordered his patrols to seize any military men involved in any disturbance, whether they were aggressors or no, and to hold them until an investigation could be made. With what result? That his men complained (only too properly), accused him of unfairness, and lost confidence in him. And all the while he was caught on the horns of this local dilemma he was being torn asunder by the hardening policies of George III and the intransigence of colonial fire-eaters. Thomas Gage had known for some time that the day of reckoning was not far off.

Unfortunately he could not make policy; the government had to do that. But Gage had seen the unhappy results of the government's unwillingness or inability to take a firm stand and assert its authority. Again and again he had written home, suggesting that the policy toward the colonies must be to "lop them off as a rotten limb from the empire, and leave them to themselves, or take effectual means to reduce them to lawfull authority." It had to be one or the other. Leniency would not work; force and action would—even though war with America, if it came to that, would be a desperate affair.

Happily for Gage's peace of mind, a few of his friends recognized his dilemma for what it was worth and offered him solace. In September of 1774 he had a letter from Colonel James Abercromby saying, "I am extreamly sorry that you are so situated, for little honor or credit is to be got, but your all is at stake. . . ." And from Holland came word from Sir Joseph Yorke, an old friend who was now ambassador to The Hague: "The eyes of all Europe are upon you at present, & tho' I trust you will be able to save both countries, yet I cannot look upon the arduous scene you are employ'd in without anxiety. . . ."

Yorke understood the problem. Above all else Gage had tried to avoid an open breach until he was ready for it. Like a good diplomat, he had endeavored to keep the situation fluid, leaving room for negotiation; for Gage the governor could never forget the responsibilities of Gage the commander-in-chief, who knew

Thomas Gage—honest, honorable, loyal servant to his king—shows no sign of the torment he underwent in Boston in this serene portrait by John Singleton Copley. The most powerful official in the colonies, Gage found himself cast as villain by the colonists and scapegoat by George III for his efforts to cope with an all but impossible situation. When he was recalled in disgrace in October 1775, some of his countrymen suggested that he be hanged. (*Thomas Agnew & Sons, London*)

that his little army of four thousand could not put down a determined rebellion. Time and again he had written home for reinforcements. "If force is to be used at length, it must be a considerable one," he had argued, "for to begin with small numbers will encourage resistance, and not terrify; and will in the end cost more blood and treasure." And again: "If you will resist and not yield, that Resistance should be effectual at the Beginning. If you think ten thousand Men sufficient, send Twenty, if one Million [in pounds sterling] is thought enough, give two, you will save both Blood and Treasure in the end. A large Force will terrify, and engage many to join you, a middling one will encourage Resistance, and gain no Friends." This last was written to Lord Barrington, the secretary of state in charge of the army, in November of 1774, the same month that George III had decided that "the line of conduct seems now chalked out." To Lord North the King wrote: "the New England governments are in a state of rebellion, blows must decide whether they are to be subject to this country or independent."

Ironically, Gage's requests for reinforcements caused his prestige to sink lower and lower with the King and his ministers, who were angered by what seemed a cautious, conciliatory attitude on the one hand and repeated pleas for an increased military force on the other. Gage recommended that there be no coercion until he was fully prepared, with the result that government officials clamored for his recall. In the end it was decided to retain Gage as governor but to send Amherst back to America as commander-in-chief. When Amherst refused to take on this unpleasant task, the government turned to the triumvirate of Howe, Clinton, and Burgoyne.

Once Gage became aware that the die was cast, that the King intended to use force, he urged Barrington again to send him "a sufficient Force to command the Country, by marching into it. . . ." On February 10, 1775, he decided that "To keep quiet in the Town of Boston only, will not terminate Affairs; the Troops must March into the Country." On April 14 he received a dispatch ordering him to act decisively, to use force if necessary, and to arrest the principal rebels—even at the risk of bringing on hostilities. So on the night of April 18 the troops had marched, with what disastrous result only Gage knew so well.

There is no record of that first encounter between Thomas Gage and the newly arrived major generals, but their conversation must have turned around the situation in Boston. A glance at the map would have told all they needed to know about the military picture. Boston itself was shaped much like a pollywog, the city proper occupying the body, with a long tail connecting it to the mainland at Roxbury. To all intents and purposes the town was virtually an island, and indeed high tides and storms often surged across the narrow isthmus, isolating it completely from the higher mainland to the south. Along the eastern or seaward side of the pollywog was a great, crescent-shaped bay which, until June 1, 1774, when the port was closed, had been the very lifeblood of the town. Here, where the major generals had landed, Long Wharf reached out to greet incoming vessels. Nearly half a mile long, it could accommodate the biggest ships in the world, even at low tide. On its north side were the now empty warehouses and countinghouses of merchants, while the south portion was left clear for ships.

Immediately after the battles of Lexington and Concord on April 19, Gage had devoted his efforts to strengthening the bastion within which he was confined, and his principal concern was with Boston Neck—that narrow strip of land leading to Roxbury. On the twenty-fourth, Lieutenant Barker described these defenses in his diary: "There is an *Abbatis* in front of the left Bastion, and across the road is a triple row of chevaux de frise. . . . Another Battery is erecting for four guns close under the Blockhouse to command the Marsh to the left of the Dyke." This strongpoint would now accommodate ten twenty-four-pounders. The city was studded with steep hills and one of them, Fort Hill, commanding the lower edge of the crescent-shaped bay, had been a stronghold for a century or more. Gage had also fortified Barton's Point, to

A VIEW OF PART OF THE TOWN OF BOSTON IN NEW

1. Beaver   5. Mermaid
2. Senegal 6. Romney
3. Martin   7. Launceston
4. Glasgow 8. Bonetta

On friday Sept! 30th 1768, the ships of War, armed Schooners, Transport
a Spring on their Cables, as for a regular Siege. At noon on Saturday Oct
and Train of Artillery, with two pieces of Cannon, landed on the Long
playing, and Colours flying, up KING STREET. Each Soldier having rec

Boston's main artery to the outside world was the Long Wharf, where the three major generals disembarked in May 1775. This view was engraved by Paul Revere, who showed British troops landing in 1768 to garrison the town. From the wharf they marched up King Street, Revere noted, "with insolent Parade." (*Courtesy, The Henry Francis du Pont Winterthur Museum*)

the northwest, just opposite Lechmere's Point on the mainland. While these efforts, in combination with the protection offered by ships of the Royal Navy, provided rather tenuous guardianship of the northern, southern, and eastern sides of Boston, the whole western flank of the city—along the Common and the foot of Beacon Hill—lay exposed, open to attack. In this area the water was so shallow that no warship could anchor, and it invited a night assault by boat from the mainland. It was true that the regiments camped on the Common had erected a few small batteries there, but Gage had also begun another redoubt, atop Beacon Hill, which Lieutenant Barker described as "a temporary thing of Casks fill'd with earth and fraised," which meant that pointed stakes were driven into the ground around it.

Gage's visitors could hardly have taken exception to these positive steps; but it would be interesting to know if he informed them of a far more fateful decision he had made in the fading hours of April 19—in a very real sense a negative step which would affect profoundly the future activities of the British in Boston. When Lord Percy led the badly beaten and completely demoralized remnants of the British army back from Concord toward the safety of the city on April 19, he had decided not to cross the Charles River and return via the Neck (most fortunately, since the rebels had torn up the bridge over the river), but to proceed by land to Charlestown, whence the troops could be ferried easily and quickly across the quarter mile of water to Boston. There his retreat was covered by the guns of the *Somerset*, lying in the river; the usually inactive Admiral Graves landed his ship's marines in Charlestown as a protective measure; and Gage sent General Pigot over to Charlestown peninsula with reinforcements from Boston. While Percy's exhausted men were ferried back to the city, Pigot took charge in Charlestown, and Captain Montresor of the engineers began throwing up a redan, or small pointed earthwork, on a high point of land known as Bunker Hill, which commanded Charlestown Neck and protected the defeated army's rear.

While all this was going on, Samuel Graves went to Gage with a plan that was intelligent, daring, and since the admiral's lack of initiative was almost a byword, startlingly out of character. It was curious for another reason, too: Graves—who was a bully and a grafter in addition to being notoriously incompetent—had once had a nasty quarrel with Gage's father, and from the beginning of their association in Boston took his enmity out on the son. All of which made his sensible proposal the more surprising. Let us, he suggested, burn the towns of Charlestown and Roxbury and seize Bunker Hill and Roxbury Heights. A look at a contemporary map shows immediately that the only points of high land from which Boston or the admiral's ships could be threatened by bombardment were Bunker or Breed's Hills at Charlestown, and Dorchester Heights. Since Bunker Hill commanded the strip of land leading onto Charlestown peninsula, and since Dorchester Heights dominated the peninsula southwest of Boston, the admiral's scheme would have given the British the two positions they needed to assure the safety of the town. But Gage, already undone by the turn of events that bloody day, and fearful that Boston's townspeople might rise against him if he attempted the unquestionably tough job of seizing Roxbury, rejected Graves's plan as "too rash and sanguinary," and ordered all his troops back to Boston as fast as possible. The wonder is that he did not elect to hold Charlestown and Bunker Hill, which were already his. Had he done so, the history of the first year of the war might have been quite different.

Before leaving Gage's office, the admiral did secure permission to accomplish one objective. Graves was mightily concerned about the safety of the *Somerset*, swinging at anchor there in the Charlestown ferry-way, "unable to be removed except upon a flood tide and then only by warping," and he was determined to protect her at all cost. So with Gage's acquiescence, and to the astonishment of the entire British army, Graves's seamen and marines began building a redoubt on Copp's Hill on the morning of April

23. According to the admiral's estimates, Copp's Hill was of "equal height with Bunkershill," and he had a good idea that the twenty-four-pounders his men were dragging up there would stand him in good stead one day. They would indeed, but as the admiral wryly observed, before that day came, "The erection of this battery by the Commander at Sea afforded much pleasantry to the Garrison, particularly among those who did not readily perceive the intent; it was christened soon by the name of the Admiral's battery and always spoken of with a smile." As it turned out, the one British fort which played a part in any action during the siege of Boston was the one built and armed by Admiral Samuel Graves.

Since the commanding general and the admiral, in the tradition of such relationships, were not on the best of terms, it is entirely possible that Gage neglected to tell his guests of Graves's role in fortifying the city. Whatever briefing he gave them, it is certain that their next few days in Boston made them aware of that town's painful predicament. For over a month now the army had been licking the wounds of Lexington and Concord, and while it was, for an army of that day, a good one, rather well officered and equipped, its strength and morale had suffered much as a result of April 19. Before that date Gage had ordered frequent marches into the countryside. "This practice is conducive to the health of the troops; and may enable the General to send Regiments or Detachments to particular parts of the Country without occasioning so much alarm as would otherwise take place," Lieutenant Frederick Mackenzie of the Royal Welch Fusiliers had observed. But now there could be no more of them, and the army, restricted to the narrow confines of Boston, poorly housed, inactive, and with a growing shortage of fresh provisions, suffered from sickness and poor spirits. As though they lacked troubles enough of their own, they were by turns an object of contempt and a joke at home. Chatham characterized Gage's establishment in Boston as "an impotent general and a dishonoured army, trusting solely to the pickaxe and the spade for security against the just indignation of an injured and insulted people." Another critic put his thoughts into verse:

> The saints, alas! have waxen strong;
> In vain your fasts and godly song
> To quell the rebel rout!
> Within his lines skulks valiant Gage,
> Like Yorick's starling in the cage
> He cries, "I can't get out!"

The experience of April 19 had been a baffling one for many a British redcoat, trained to the open field of battle where two armies faced each other in well-ordered ranks. Instead, their retreat from Concord had been as confused and degrading as it was costly, with an enemy skulking behind walls and houses, almost never out in the open, and firing on them nearly at will. Some who suffered through that day agreed with Captain Evelyn of the King's Own, who branded the rebels "the most absolute cowards on the face of the earth," but a few wiser heads had learned a lesson. "Whoever looks upon them as an irregular mob will find himself much mistaken," Lord Percy wrote. "For my part, I never believed, I confess, that they would have attacked the King's troops, or have had the perseverance I found in them yesterday. . . . They have men amongst them who know very well what they are about." And the commanding general, who had witnessed this kind of fighting on the western frontier, was seriously concerned over the British position. "The situation these wretches have taken in forming the blockade of this town is judicious and strong," Gage admitted to Lord North. Not only did they have a numerical superiority already under arms, but "upon the alarm being given, they come far and near, and the longer the action lasts, the greater their numbers grow." As for their method of fighting, he pointed out their aptitude in "getting behind fences and every sort of covering, firing from thence; then retire and

The redcoat's lot was not an easy one, as a sympathetic British cartoonist suggested in this 1775 engraving. For his services in America against the hostile rebels (at right, wearing headbands reading "Death or Liberty") the soldier was so badly underpaid that he could not support his family; his wife and children went hungry, the artist indicated, while fat, prosperous Englishmen (at left) enjoyed their ease at home. So difficult was it to obtain recruits for the war in America that the former age limits of eighteen and thirty had been increased to sixteen and fifty. Even so, the ranks were filled with jailbirds, vagrants, and country lads tricked into enlisting. (*Chicago Historical Society*)

load under cover and return to the charge; or take another situation from whence they fire." What made this so dangerous in Gage's opinion was that "The country for 30 miles round is amazingly well situated for their manner of fighting, being covered with woods and small stone wall inclosures, exceedingly uneven and much cutt with ravin. . . ." If ever a man understood what he was up against, it must have been the founder of Gage's "chausseurs." And it was precisely his anxiety on this score that had made him urge his superiors repeatedly for reinforcements.

At the outset of fighting in April he had considerably less than four thousand troops fit for duty—and with these he had to man his lines, build or strengthen fortifications, resist any attack made on him from outside the city, and quell a possible insurrection of the citizens inside it. Early in May four companies of the 65th Regiment had arrived from Halifax, and during that month six hundred marines landed; but when the major generals disembarked, Gage was still waiting for reinforcements who should have sailed in March, and was completely unaware that the usual delays had put off their departure until the end of April. The men he had available were, for the most part, recruits from jails and slums, for this was an era when men and boys who would be dismissed nowadays with a fine ran the risk of the hangman for minor offenses. There were nearly two hundred crimes which incurred the death penalty, and the harshness and cruelty of society in general was reflected in the treatment of the men in the ranks. Wellington, more than thirty years later, was to call them "the scum of the earth," not a particularly unusual opinion. No one had a good word for the King's uniform, but the recruit soon discovered that the scorn of his countrymen was as nothing compared to the terrors of the service—a service that involved not only fighting his nation's enemies, but a maiming lash wielded by hardened noncoms, food that was notoriously poor, inadequate and often brutally callous medical care, killing diseases such as typhus, scurvy, rheumatic fever, and pneumonia. During the Seven Years' War, for example, only 1512 men were killed in action, while 134,000 were lost to disease, mismanaged wounds, and desertion! And by way of recompense the private soldier received a weekly four shillings and sixpence, from which sixpence was withdrawn for a uniform, medicine, and armorer's charges, plus a halfpenny each for the regimental quartermaster and surgeon. Every man had to provide out of his annual pay a pair of shoes, long black cloth gaiters, shirts, socks, mittens, a black stock, forage cap and knapsack, shoe brushes, and the various articles required for clubbing or pigtailing his hair. The only possible consolation for the soldier was that he was, in a time of general poverty and misery, slightly better off than most men of his class. He was fed, clothed, housed, and, in a fashion, looked after, and in his shortage of spending money he was simply like almost everyone else.

Yet in spite of all that may be said against conditions in the British army, the quality of Gage's force—especially in comparison with his opponents—was remarkably high. For one thing, his troops were much better organized, equipped, and trained than their foes. Components of this army had been based in Boston for some time; they knew the city and the outlying area, and their supply lines were well organized and functioning smoothly. Beyond this, they had the incalculable advantage of drill and discipline and of having worked together over long periods of time as a team.

Far worse than the state of the army was the state of Boston's citizenry. For a year and more a steady stream of refugees had been pouring into the city from the Massachusetts countryside —men, women, and children whose principal crime against their neighbors had been to recognize openly the authority of King and Parliament. They brought with them stories of persecution, threats, economic and social boycotts, and physical intimidation by mobs; they had been attacked in the public press, ostracized by former friends, and often, threatened with tarring and feathering, forced to recant and apologize in the newspapers. "You who have seen mobs, generous ones compared to these," Captain

Evelyn wrote to his father in England, "may have some idea of the wretched situation of those who were known or suspected to be friends to the King or government of Great Britain." That was in 1774, months before the outbreak of armed violence.

On the night of April 19, 1775, in the wake of the British retreat from Concord, the outskirts of Boston had been a confused bedlam of frightened people, all trying to pass through the funnel of the Neck. On horseback, by wagon, and on foot they came, seeking safety under the British guns, bringing with them all the belongings they could carry. Questioned at every crossroad by a rebel militia officer, the pitiful groups of women and children huddled together for protection while the men waited, silent and watchful, wondering if they would have to fight their way through. Off in the darkness, surrounding them, were throngs of armed men, some on mysterious errands, most of them crouched around campfires as if they were attending some monstrous picnic, laughing, cursing, shouting to one another about the day's events. Filling the air along with the hum of thousands of voices were the smells of roasting meat and of wood smoke from the long lines of campfires, while the noise of alarum and excursion, the galloping to and fro of messengers, and sudden hoarse cries pierced the night.

Once they arrived in Boston and passed through the fortifications at the Neck, the refugees breathed a sigh of relief, and for a time threw off the weight of their troubles as they felt the protection of the King's troops. But inside the city their problems had only begun. The town was crowded already with other refugees, with the British garrison dumped willy-nilly on top of the normal population. While many patriots had left the city, thousands of Boston Whigs were too poor, too involved with their own business affairs, or just too stubborn to go away. Every shade of political opinion could still be met in Boston, and on all sides the new refugees received the dark looks of patriots who had not departed, or of moderates and other loyalists concerned by the overcrowding. Night after night mobs roamed the dusty streets,

When the British troops arrived in Boston in 1768 the lack of housing made it necessary for numbers of them to pitch tents on the Common, as shown in an engraving after Christian Remick's water color, and it may be assumed that the sight of the King's regiments drilling in front of his mansion (right, rear) tried

the patience of the owner, John Hancock. In 1775 the housing problem was exacerbated by a flood of loyalist refugees pouring into the city. (*The I. N. Phelps Stokes Collection, Prints Division, The New York Public Library*)

and day after day more displaced persons came in. The rebels had cut off all supplies from the countryside, and horses, lacking fodder, grew scrawny and unkempt, and children who had been there through the winter had the white, pinched look of malnutrition. Lieutenant Barker said "the worst of it is we are ill off for fresh provisions, none to be bought except now and then a little pork."

The refugees with goods piled into wagons and carts and wheelbarrows were scarcely recognizable as the officials, the merchants, the landowners and clergy who represented most of the Massachusetts aristocracy. Just now they were women in dirty, wrinkled silks, helping servants drag or carry the family silver and portraits to safety; they were men in dusty clothes who had the look of a frightened animal about their faces. Yet these had been the voices of authority in their communities, the people who had created a little section of England in America. Many were American born, but they had remained English in feeling and temperament, had moved naturally into the English-fed officialdom, and had wanted quite naturally to keep things as they were. They were men like Peter Oliver, who had only now received a letter from his brother in England, by the *Cerberus*. Oliver was the son of the former chief justice, the nephew of the former lieutenant governor, and an obvious heir to the ruling Hutchinson-Oliver clique, yet when he learned that his brother had given up all thought of returning to Boston he could only rejoice.

"Our situation here," he wrote by return mail, "without any exaggeration, is beyond description almost; it is such as eye has not seen nor ear heard, nor hath it ever entered into the heart of man to conceive Boston ever to arrive at.

"We are besieged this moment with 10 or 15000 men, from Roxbury to Cambridge; their rebell sentrys within call of the troops' sentry on the Neck. We are every hour expecting an attack by land or water. All marketing from the country stopt ever since the battle. Fire and slaughter hourly threatened . . ."

As for the Oliver property in Middleborough, it had been "exposed to the ravage of a set of robbers." Peter had been unable to get any word about the women and children on the estate, and confessed that he did not even know if they were alive. He had heard that his brother's wife was in Plymouth, "yet we can't get any intelligence of her, good or bad."

"Good God!" he pleaded. "Do thou avert the impending calamity that threatens this former happy land."

Another troubled resident of Boston, Richard Reeve, writing to his patron Sir George Howard, M.P., gave a clear picture of the situation and the hopes and fears of the citizenry. He had fully expected, "from the pitch of Madness and frenzy to which the Minds of the People had been wrought," that Boston would be attacked shortly after the nineteenth of April. Had the rebels intended to carry out such a desperate scheme, they should have seized the opportunity that very night, he thought, or the next day, "when they were flushed with the triumph of a supposed Victory, and when part of the Troops were greatly harassed and fatigued with their long March from Concord & Lexington, and the rest with double Duty in their absence." Apparently a good many Boston residents believed that the Americans had actually planned a surprise attack on the town for April 24 (the festival of St. George, when most British officers and other gentlemen "would have made too free with the Glass") and that the only thing that prevented it from coming off was the march of the King's troops to Lexington and Concord. Lest Sir George Howard think that Boston was the only trouble spot, Reeve ticked off the unhappy state of affairs in other colonies: in Connecticut, despite the efforts of moderates to halt the rush of events, "a considerable body of People" had joined the rebel army; from Rhode Island came word that growing numbers were under arms; in New York "Things were as bad as we could possibly suppose them . . . the Liberty Party having gained a Compleat ascendancy over those who were called the Friends of Government." There was no news from Philadelphia or the southern colonies, "all communication by land having been stopped for some time, and no Vessels have arrived from those parts." Reeve fully expected that the Continental Congress would make matters worse by adopting "the most violent measures"; certainly those two Massachusetts trouble-makers, John Hancock and Samuel Adams, would "use their best endeavours to throw Things into the utmost confusion."

What little information filtered into Boston through the lines failed to improve Reeve's disposition; among other things, he heard that the besieging army was rolling in provisions and food of all kinds, brought to camp by farmers in return for some vague promise of future payment. He understood that the Provincial Congress, sitting at Watertown, had issued a proclamation permitting loyalists from the country to come into Boston, "but it is supposed that Secret and insiduous Arts have been made use of to intimidate them, as very few are come yet."

Richard Reeve, asking himself what had brought America to "such an alarming & fatal dilemma," concluded that "the Poison has lain deeper than most People imagine—it was certainly no want of Liberty, it will perhaps be found to be owing to an Excess of it, which like strong Drinks has drove the People to a State of intoxication." And there seemed to be only two alternatives: "Great Britain must now Subdue the Colonies by Force of Arms, or relinquish her Authority over them, for all appearance of Accomodation appears to be now at an End."

In the happier days of the 1760s, Jamaica Plain had been a pleasant little community about five miles beyond Boston Neck. Here was the estate of Sir Francis Bernard while he was royal governor, which was occupied after 1769 by Sir William Pepperrell; beautiful Shirley Place, built about 1748; the handsome Auchmuty house; and within a radius of a few miles were other establishments of comparable rank and wealth. One was that of Commodore Joshua Loring, who had gone to sea as a boy, privateered against the French in the forties, and later served as a captain in the Royal Navy in Amherst's campaign against Quebec. The Commodore had married well, and in 1760 he moved his wife and children into their new mansion, recently completed on sixty acres of fine land in Jamaica Plain. It was a large house of more than twelve rooms, and the estate included several outbuildings, a coach house and stables, another dwelling with its own barn and meadow land, and Loring had acquired twenty-three acres of woodlot in Roxbury, a house near Boston Common, and five acres of salt meadow near the Neck. His first son, Joshua the Younger, married Elizabeth Lloyd in 1769; a daughter Hannah married Joshua Winslow; and one of the twin sons, Benjamin, was second in the Class of 1772 at Harvard—the last year in which students were listed in the order of family prestige. All things considered, the Lorings had done about as well as anyone could in eighteenth-century Massachusetts, but the sands were beginning to run out.

For years members of the Governor's Council had been elected by the representatives of the people, but in 1774, after he took office as military governor, Gage took an entirely different view of the matter, threw out the elected Council, and placed in their stead his own slate of so-called "Mandamus Councillors"—including Commodore Joshua Loring of Jamaica Plain. According to Mrs. Loring, Junior, who filed a petition for a pension from the Crown in 1789, her father-in-law's acceptance of this appointment "rendered him [so] obnoxious to the People that he was repeatedly mobbed and otherwise ill treated in such manner as to oblige him to leave his House as early as 31 August 1774 and to fly for Refuge to Boston, and put himself under the Protection of the Kings Troops, from which time untill the Evacuation of the Place (which was more than eighteen Months) he was confined to the Town, and never saw his House nor any part of his Estate afterwards, which was taken possession of by the American troops on the 19th April 1775 (being allotted them for Quarters) who plunder'd it of the Furniture, Stock, and Stores." Mrs. Loring calculated the loss at nearly £5000—the equivalent of something like $125,000 in today's money. By way of temporary recompense, Gage made her husband, Joshua the Younger, "sole vendue master and auctioneer in and for the town of Boston," as well as sheriff. It was in the latter job that he showed such a remarkable talent for maltreating rebel prisoners taken at Bunker Hill, and subsequently he became Commissary of Prisoners, a role that seems to have been admirably suited to his mean and brutal disposition.

It was probably soon after the arrival of the *Cerberus* that the wandering eye of Major General William Howe fixed on the handsome Elizabeth Lloyd Loring, and it is a real key to the character of Joshua Loring, Junior that, even after his wife became the general's mistress, he was so intent on the personal profit he might extract from the relationship that he traveled with the army wherever she went. Some attempts have been made to credit Elizabeth with making Howe neglect his duties so completely that he lost the war for England. While this is scarcely credible, some of her ribald contemporaries did their best to saddle her with that distinction. Francis Hopkinson, in "The Battle of the Kegs," told how

> Sir William, he, snug as a flea,
> Lay all this time a-snoring;
> Nor dreamed of harm, as he lay warm
> In bed with Mrs. ——.

And she was the heroine of at least one British verse, written during Howe's inactivity during the Philadelphia campaign:

> Awake, arouse, Sir Billy,
> There's forage in the plain.
> Ah, leave your little Filly,
> And open the campaign.

A loyalist, Justice Thomas Jones of New York, described the arrangement this way: "Joshua had a handsome wife. The General . . . was fond of her. Joshua made no objection. He fingered the cash, the General enjoyed Madam."

Whatever her follies and faults, it is agreeable to note that the petition which Elizabeth Loring filed in England after the death of her husband in 1789 was endorsed by a gentleman who signed himself "W. Howe."

If, at this time, Mrs. Loring was beginning to cause some consternation in the upper echelons of the British army, another lady of quality had recently given their foes a great deal of difficulty. Every schoolboy in Boston had known and snickered over the story of Sir Charles Henry Frankland, descendant of Oliver Cromwell and Collector of the Port, and his infatuation with the Marblehead serving girl, Agnes Surriage. Sir Charles had brought her to his great three-story brick house in the North End of town to "educate" her, and later married her out of gratitude when she saved his life in a Lisbon earthquake. In mid-May Lady Frankland, now widowed and living comfortably in Hopkinton, decided that she wanted to go to England, and wrote to Doctor Joseph Warren, president of the Provincial Congress and chairman of the Massachusetts Committee of Safety, requesting a pass through the Roxbury lines on Thursday, May 18. With her letter she enclosed a list of "things necessary for her voyage to England"—six trunks, one chest, three beds and bedding, six wethers, two pigs, one small keg of pickled tongues, some hay, and three bags of corn. Permission was granted, and on the eighteenth she appeared at the lines with what appeared to be an extraordinary number of belongings, carried in a procession of chaises, carts, and a phaeton. This was too much for the sentries, including one named Craft, and for the crowd which had assembled at sight of this remarkable caravan; harsh words were exchanged, some of Lady Frankland's possessions seem to have been filched, and a messenger was sent clattering off to the Provincial Congress at Watertown for further instructions while Lady Frankland and her servants cooled their heels and tried to ignore the taunts of their tormentors. The messenger informed the Congress that Lady Frankland had not been entirely truthful in declaring her belongings. To be precise, she had far more than she ever had listed, including "one gun, one pistol, and one sword, one flask, with a small quantity of powder and lead."

To its credit, Congress acted with dispatch, calling before it the unhappy Craft, who was "politely admonished" for his failure to honor Lady Frankland's pass. After all, Congress had issued that pass and the scolding given Mr. Craft was essential to preserve congressional "dignity and power over the military." At the same time a guard of six men was sent off to escort Lady Frankland through the lines, which they did after relieving her of her arms and ammunition, plus six oxen, two horses, two carts, five sheep, and one swine—none of which were considered essential for the voyage to England.

The war had not yet reached a stage where civilians in Boston lost touch with the world on the mainland. Over in Cambridge, Mrs. Ralph Inman had remained on their large farm even though her husband had long since fled to the security of Boston, and these two not only corresponded regularly, but arranged occasional meetings in Charlestown, where Mrs. Inman seems to have given him food to take back to the city. There were many others not so fortunate, however, among them Henry Pelham, the miniature painter and surveyor, who wrote his half-brother John Singleton Copley, the artist, that "We have been obliged to live intirely upon salt provisions and what stores we have in the house, and I think we are very fortunate. . . . It is inconcivable the Distress and Ruin this unnatural dispute has caused to this town and its inhabitants. Almost every shop and store is shut. No buisness of any kind going on . . . the Cloaths upon my back and a few Dollers in my pocket are now the only property which I have the least Command of."

"The tories lead a devil of a life," one soldier wrote during the summer of 1774; many of them had lost hope entirely and, like Lady Frankland, had decided to return to England at the first opportunity. Anne Hulton, the sister of the town's Customs Commissioner, had seen the handwriting on the wall as early as 1770, when she began writing to friends in England about her dangerous situation, "the want of protection, the perversion of the Laws, & the spirit of the People inflamed by designing men." She had been troubled deeply by the sight of bands of men roaming around the Hulton country place in Brookline, "disguised, their faces blacked, with white Night capts & white Stockens on, one of 'em with Ruffles on & all with great clubs in their hands." In Boston her brother had been attacked in his own house on at least one occasion; and she often thought wistfully of the "little genteel Town about 4 Miles off calld Cambridge, where a number of Gentlemens Familys live upon their Estates." She had watched helplessly as Boston was split down the middle into two violently opposed factions, with what she called the people of property and sense and character on the one side, the leaders of faction on the other; and although the arrival of General Gage and more troops from England gave her a flicker of hope, there had been at least one act of horror in 1774 that made her resolve to return to England.

On a bitter winter's night an old man named Malcolm, a Tory, was attacked by a mob, stripped naked, coated with tar and feathers, and then, "his arm dislocated in tearing off his cloaths, he was drag^d in a Cart with thousands attending, some beating him wth clubs & Knocking him out of the Cart, then in again. They gave him several severe whipings, at different parts of the Town. This Spectacle of horror & sportive cruelty was exhibited for about five hours." According to Miss Hulton, the poor wretch was tortured further in an attempt to make him curse the King and the governor, but he continued to defy them, crying "Curse all Traitors!" It was, she said, the second time old Malcolm had been tarred and feathered.

One of the last letters she wrote before returning to England described the events of April 19, as she heard the account from returning troops. At the end of that black day, in the Boston she loved so well, "a Solemn dead silence reigns in the Streets," and "we are now cut off from all communication with the Country &

A Boston Tory's existence was hazardous, to say the least, for there was no telling when Sam Adams' Liberty Boys might take it into their heads to rough him up, or worse. This British cartoon shows an unfortunate tax collector, who has been tarred and feathered, being forced to drink boiling tea. (*The John Carter Brown Library, Brown University*)

many people must soon perish with famine." It was all she could bear, and before the year was out she sailed for England.

Of the loyalists who remained, most tried to make the best of things as they found them. One man who was going nowhere just now was George Harris, a philosophical captain of a grenadier company in the 5th Regiment, who seems to have been delighted when warm weather arrived and the army moved into tents. His was located on the Common, and from it he looked out across a mile of water, sparkling in the spring sunshine, toward a prospect of tumbling green hills and valleys, interspersed here and there with villages and an occasional church spire that peeped through the trees. It was a pity, he thought, that "these infatuated people cannot be content to enjoy such a country in peace. But, alas! this moment their advanced sentinels are in sight."

As the last days of May turned toward June, inactivity and boredom were beginning to tell on the army in general, and particularly on two of the three warriors who had arrived on the *Cerberus*. A few days after landing, Henry Clinton found himself deeply disturbed by the commanding general's lack of initiative and by the army's morale. A foray into the countryside, some vigorous action would fix things, if Clinton was any judge, and almost before he knew it he was trying out Burgoyne's phrase, finding that he liked it, and muttering that "our elbows must be eased." He was horrified to learn that no decent maps were available, but he did not need one to tell him that their first objectives—the keys to Boston's safety—were the heights of Charlestown and Dorchester. An attack, preferably by night, would "shake those poor wretches" on the mainland.

Idleness was bothering John Burgoyne too, but in a different fashion. He found himself in a "motionless, drowsy, irksome medium, or rather vacuum, too low for the honour of command, too high for that of execution," and for want of something better to do he began writing to some of his highly placed friends in England, complaining about the situation in general and about Gage in specific. It would be impossible to describe his feelings,

MEDFORD

Ten Hills Farm

Mystic River

Plowed Hill

Penny Ferry

Winter Hill

MONTRESOR'S REDAN

CHARLESTOWN NECK

Bunker

ROAD TO LEXINGTON AND CONCORD

CHARLESTOWN COMMON

MILL POND

Prospect Hill

CHARLESTO

Fort No.3

Lechme Point

WILLIS CREEK

Pillon Bridge

Lechmere's Farm

Christ Church

Hastings House

Inman Farm

Vassall House
Lechmere House
Lee House

COMMON

Harvard College

Fairweather House

Fort No.2
Cobble Hill

Oliver House

TORY ROW

CAMBRIDGE

Fort No. 1

Charles River

ROAD TO WATERTOWN

N

E

W

S

ROAD TO WATERTOWN

BROOKLINE

0 Scale 1/2   1 miles 1½

map by palacios

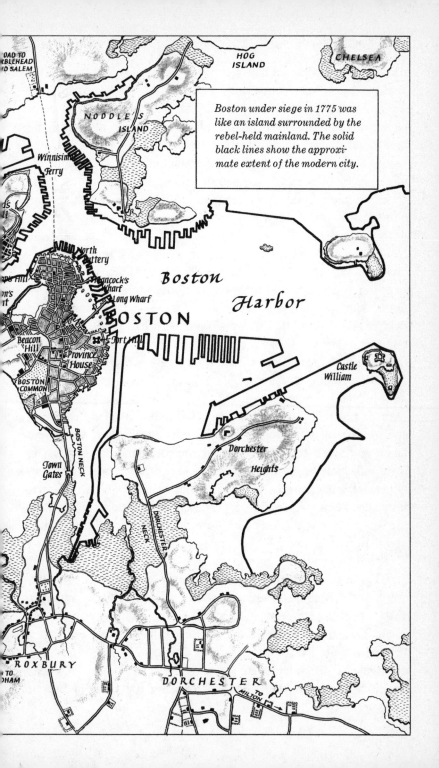

HOG ISLAND

CHELSEA

ROAD TO MARBLEHEAD AND SALEM

NODDLE'S ISLAND

Winnisimet Ferry

Boston under siege in 1775 was like an island surrounded by the rebel-held mainland. The solid black lines show the approximate extent of the modern city.

North Battery

Hancock's Wharf

Long Wharf

BOSTON

Boston Harbor

Beacon Hill

Province House

Fort Hill

Castle William

BOSTON COMMON

BOSTON NECK

Town Gates

Dorchester Heights

DORCHESTER NECK

ROXBURY

TO DEDHAM

DORCHESTER

TO MILTON

he said, about what he had seen upon his arrival. The town was invested by a "rabble in arms" who had insolently posted their sentries within pistol shot of the British outposts, and in all companies of the army (and this included both officers and men) he had found "a sort of stupefaction" caused by the events of April 19. Now the men were angry or despondent, and with good reason. Had Gage acted earlier; had he appropriated the rebels' arms or seized their leaders, Hancock and Adams; had he taken the normal precautions of readying his troops for combat, of establishing outposts in the countryside, of erecting proper fortifications around the city and the harbor, or of securing his sources of supply—had he, in fact, made any such preparations, none of the resulting "perplexity and disgrace" need have followed. What was more, Burgoyne pointed out ruefully, there was no money, and neither he nor the other two major generals had received the five hundred pounds equipage promised them. Far worse from the military standpoint, no money meant no spies, with the result that they were totally ignorant of what the rebels might be planning on a hill half a mile away. Hardly a man in the Provincial Congress or the militia could not be bought, Burgoyne stated flatly, and all it took was proper management. Speaking of which, he had a few more words to say about the commanding general. "It is no reflection to say that he is unequal to his present situation, for few characters in the world would be fit for it," he wrote carefully and, he may have thought, modestly. "It requires a genius of the very first class, together with firm resolution and a firm reliance upon support at home."

Having done his best to undermine his chief (it might be added that Howe and Clinton were doing much the same in their letters home), Burgoyne then proceeded to call on Gage and talk him into issuing a proclamation which did both of them irreparable harm in England and in the colonies. Perhaps Gage was uncertain of his ability to write, but in any case he permitted the distinguished litterateur and playwright to compose a document for his signature. It was intended to bolster the army in Boston at the same time it frightened the rebels, and it was duly published on June 12, 1775; but it was so flamboyant, so ridiculously verbose, that none of its readers—no matter what their allegiance —could possibly take it seriously. "Whereas the infatuated multitudes," it began, "have long suffered themselves to be conducted by certain well-known incendiaries and traitors" into a state of open rebellion, "it only remains for those who are invested with the supreme rule . . . to prove they do not bear the sword in vain." It went on to mention the atrocities committed by the rebels, to warn of the chastisement that was coming, and in the course of its wanderings to attack the leaders of the revolt, the patriot press, and the ministers who preached sedition. The author of the proclamation laughed hollowly at the rebels, "who with a preposterous parade of military arrangement, affected to hold the Army besieged," and concluded by declaring martial law and offering pardons to all but John Hancock and Samuel Adams, in order to avoid further bloodshed.

When this diatribe arrived in London it was greeted mainly with guffaws for Gentleman Johnny, whom most wits recognized as its author, and one critic put his finger on the heart of the matter: "They *affect* to hold the army besieged . . . they do not affect it, they actually do besiege ye, in spite of your teeth; and the next time you write to your friends, say in plain English that the Americans *effected* the siege."

Indeed they had, and if the British high command would not admit it in public, they were privately coming to grips with the problem. The rebels were digging trenches in Roxbury and Cambridge, and it could not be long before they moved onto the nearer hills. It was beginning to be a question of prudence as well as a matter of honor to take some action, and with the restless Clinton and Burgoyne spurring him on, Thomas Gage called a council of war and discovered that there was surprising unanimity about what they should do. Howe outlined the plan in a letter written on June 12 to his brother, the admiral. First, a detachment would move out against Dorchester Neck, throw up two redoubts there, and then attack the rebel post at Roxbury. Once Boston was safe from attack in that direction, Howe would take a large force to Charlestown Heights and either attack the Americans in Cambridge or outflank that post, which would accomplish the same purpose. "I suppose the Rebels will move from Cambridge," Howe added confidently, "and that we shall take and keep possession of it."

The attack was set for June 18. It would begin with an assault on Dorchester Heights, with Howe landing the transports down on the Point, southeast of Boston, Clinton in command of the center, and Burgoyne responsible for bombarding the rebels from the British fortifications on the Neck. It was a promise of action at last, and as John Burgoyne left the meeting and made his way back to his quarters he could not help thinking that the whole operation was going to be remarkably easy.

II. For the Security of This Colony

The Americans learned of the British plans almost accidentally. Early in June a nameless New Hampshire resident was visiting in Boston, where he had "frequent opportunity of conversing with the principal officers in General Gage's army," and on Friday, June 9, he left for home. He seems not to have been overly disturbed by the information he had gleaned, and in his own good time arrived in New Hampshire, imparted his news to someone in authority there, and as abruptly and anonymously as he appeared on the stage, made his exit. But the events so casually set in motion began to gather speed. On June 13 the Committee of Safety in Exeter, New Hampshire, sent off a fast express to the Provincial Congress in Massachusetts, repeating the information they had received from this "gentleman of undoubted veracity." There was talk around British headquarters, they understood, that as soon as the expected reinforcements arrived, "General Gage will secure some advantageous posts near Boston, viz: Dorchester and Charlestown." The New Hampshire committeemen knew nothing of the importance of those places, they were sorry to say, "but if this hint should be in any degree useful, it will give us pleasure."

The Provincial Congress knew precisely how important both of those objectives were. These were tidings of the utmost significance and danger. True, there had been earlier warnings of a somewhat similar nature: on May 8 an "old Campaigner" had gotten word out of town that a stroke was planned, possibly that very night, against Dorchester Neck; and on May 10, Elijah Shaw heard some British officers say that "they shall soon come out"—probably toward Dorchester. These rumors had occasioned flurries of excitement, and a resolve to strengthen the defenses around the perimeter of the siege lines, but very little else.

The report from New Hampshire was taken far more seriously, not because its source was that gentleman of undoubted veracity, but because it was confirmed by so many similarly phrased portents seeping through the lines. There seems to have been as much loose talk by the British soldiery in early June as there had been in mid-April before the march to Concord, and scores of innocent-looking patriots walking the narrow streets of Boston made it their business to listen, to digest, and to report their conclusions to the Provincial Congress in Watertown. Numerous avenues of communication still existed between beleaguered Boston and the world outside, and there were farmers and professional men, fisherfolk and ferryboatmen, all with some legitimate and approved errand to perform, who could be relied upon to get a message to the proper destination. Burgoyne himself, as well as a number of "inferior Officers," had been heard telling of the plan, and letters written to London on June 12, 13, and 14 made no secret of the "preparations for going out of the Town in a few days."

But the question was, what to do about it? Fortunately the Americans had had more than six months in which to patch together a governmental organization of some efficiency and authority. When Gage dissolved the Great and General Court of Massachusetts in the autumn of 1774, its members promptly formed themselves into a Provincial Congress, and this body, on October 26, had adopted a plan for organizing the militia, maintaining it, and calling it out when circumstances rendered it necessary. Military stores were collected, and a thirteen-man executive authority, called the Committee of Safety, was created as a sort of emergency action group which could function on short notice and without waiting for the deliberations of the more cumbersome Congress. The Committee was now responsible for directing the operations of the army. Needless to say, George III and the British government considered this organization and its activities completely illegal, as they did the affairs of the Continental Congress now meeting in Philadelphia. But both bodies continued to function, more or less in concert with one another, and what had appeared to be little more than ripples of dissension six months earlier had now become a gathering tide of insurrection threatening the entire structure of His Majesty's colonies in North America.

However, any proposal for any sort of action had to be considered against the fact that there was, as yet, no real desire for an irrevocable break with the mother country, at least among more reasonable men. It was still a matter of loyal protest. Writing to Arthur Lee in London, Dr. Joseph Warren, president of the Provincial Congress and chairman of the Committee of Safety, put it in these terms: "One thing, I can assure you, has very great weight with us; we fear, if we push this matter as far as we think we are able—to the destruction of the troops and ships of war—we shall expose Great Britain to those invasions from foreign powers which we suppose it will be difficult for her to repel." This was a strange thought coming from a man the British considered a ringleader of rebellion, yet Warren obviously had the interests and future of England very much in mind. Britain must have "a change of men and measures, or be ruined," he wrote, and for his part, he promised to do "Every thing in my power to serve the united interest of Great Britain and her colonies"—scarcely the ideas of one who felt the breach was irreconcilable, despite the blood spilled on April 19.

But always, in the background and behind the voices of reason, there were rumblings of impending trouble, growing ripples of fear that played on Americans like nervous flashes of heat lightning. A Captain Thompson, arriving in New York from Ireland, reported that six regiments of redcoats had sailed for Boston and four for New York, that thirty thousand Prussians were "ready, at a minute's warning," to embark. In Westminster, New York, the people were sufficiently disturbed by the thought of what "Regulars, Roman Catholicks, and the Savages at the northward" might do that they requested formation of a regiment to defend themselves. There was talk of Parliament arming Negro slaves to rise against their masters, and along the frontier families shuddered and barred their doors more securely at night against Indian attacks that might be unleashed at any moment.

Across the land Americans were preparing for something. What it was to be, or what form it might take, they could not say, but they knew it was coming and they planned to be ready. In Lancaster County, Virginia, members of the militia pledged themselves to protect their fellow volunteers of Hanover, the "worthy Captain Patrick Henry," and all other friends to American liberty. In New York a recently arrived Scotsman named Donald McLeod asked permission to form a company of Highlanders, men already equipped with guns, swords, pistols, and dirks, requesting only that he be allowed to command them, since some of them could not speak the English language. Far down the Atlantic coastline in Charleston, South Carolina, the Provincial Congress voted to raise two regiments, listing among their officers such men as Christopher Gadsden, Isaac Huger, William Moultrie, and the Horrys. And Massachusetts' own Provincial Congress, suddenly reminded of potential allies to the west, sent off a flowery letter to the Stockbridge Indians, telling how "friends of the wicked counsellors of the King" had been defeated and shut up in the great town called Boston, and stating their hope that the redmen would smoke their pipes, speak with their Indian brothers toward the setting sun, and if some of their young men "should have a mind to see what we are doing here, let them come down and tarry among our warriors." Two, it would seem, could play at rousing the Indians.

Against the day of reckoning, the patriots were preparing in another way—by purging their ranks of the enemy within, by testing the loyalties of friend and neighbor, forcing them to conform or suffer the consequences. In every colony the public prints and records of committees were filled with the statements of recanters, with ugly episodes of terror. In Stamford, Connecticut, Silvanus Whitney confessed his guilt in buying and selling Bohea Tea and asked the public to forgive his transgression; in Londonderry, New Hampshire, John Prentice renounced an address he had written to the "late Governour Hutchinson, so universally and so justly deemed an enemy to American liberty"; in Charleston, loyalists Laughlin Martin and James Dealey were tarred and feathered, hauled through the streets in a cart, and put aboard a ship bound for Bristol for protesting that they had a right to bear arms; in Maryland, the crier of the Worcester County court was declared an enemy of his country and forbidden to carry on any dealings with true Americans after volunteering the suggestion that members of the Baltimore Committee of Safety were a parcel of damned rascals who ought to be "hang'd up"; the selectmen of Lancaster, Massachusetts, were writing to the Provincial Congress, respectfully inquiring what was to be done with the estates of men who had fled to Boston.

Confused and fragmented as the picture was, it nevertheless bore all the signs of an inevitable conflict which would pit neighbor against neighbor in that most tragic and desperate of all struggles, civil war. Despite all the avowed good intentions of men such as Joseph Warren, the fuse of rebellion and strife had been lighted, and the powder keg which would blow everything to kingdom come was a lot nearer than anyone believed during those early weeks of June, 1775.

For their part, the men who were desperately trying to control the reins of government in Watertown had their hands too full to see much beyond the thousand and one tasks of the moment. Over them all hung the looming specter of an army—the shapeless mass of fifteen or twenty thousand men who had unexpectedly converged on a little corner of Massachusetts during and after the day of Lexington and Concord. Not one of those legislators had ever seen a body of men this size in one place before, and not one of them had anything more than the vaguest notion of what this army was supposed to do, how it was to be fed and housed and clothed and supplied, and how in God's name it was to be kept under some sort of discipline and control. If it was a monster that filled their nightmares and occupied nearly all their deliberations by day, it is worth remembering that nothing quite like it had ever been seen on the North American continent before; and if the members of Congress appeared to be overwhelmed by the magnitude of the situation in which they found themselves, they deserve nothing but credit and respect for the degree of integrity and wisdom with which they handled an immensely difficult and totally foreign problem.

When Paul Revere and Billy Dawes set out to call the men of Massachusetts to arms, they set in motion a chain reaction that spread out across New England, and the crash of British muskets at Lexington Green had been echoed by messengers riding toward the Sound, across the Hudson, on into Philadelphia and Maryland, down to Virginia, the Carolinas, and Georgia. Out into Kentucky the news went, prompting men building a new community there to call it Lexington in honor of the event. Most of the patriots beyond the Hudson Valley stayed near home and readied themselves for a fight they knew was coming, but the angry, determined men and boys of New England, assembling with a speed which was nothing short of miraculous, streamed into Massachusetts and laid siege to the port of Boston with an efficiency and on a scale which neither General Thomas Gage nor the patriot leaders had dreamed possible. As dusk deepened into night on April 19, a great arc of campfires ringed the city; in Roxbury and in Charlestown guards were posted with commendable foresight, the sound of drums and thousands of voices filled the night, and all through the hours of darkness the steady tramp of marching companies could be heard coming into camp. The next day it continued. Men came in the clothes they had on their backs, with what food they had been able to stuff into pockets, bearing weap-

One of the most effective pieces of propaganda issued by the rebels was this list of American casualties on April 19, published in Boston. One purpose of the broadside was to enlist the support of those whose loyalty to the mother country was weak or wavering. (*Library of Congress*)

A LIST of the Names of the PROVINCIALS who were Kil led and Wounded in the late Engageme nt with His Majesty's Troops at *Concord,* &c.

KILLED.

Of *Lexington.*
* Mr. Robert Munroe,
* Mr. Jonas Parker,
* Mr. Samuel Hadley,
* Mr. Jona\. Harrington,
* Mr. Caleb Harrington,
* Mr. Isaac Muzzy,
* Mr. John Brown,
Mr. John Raymond,
Mr. Nathaniel Wyman,
Mr. Jedediah Munroe.

Of *Menotomy.*
Mr. Jason Russel,
Mr. Jabez Wyman,
Mr Jason Winship.

Of *Sudbury.*
Deacon Haynes,
Mr. —— Reed.

Of *Concord.*
Capt. James Miles.

Of *Bedford.*
Capt. Jonathan Wilson.

Of *Acton.*
Capt. Davis,
Mr. —— Hosmer,
Mr. James Howard.

Of *Woburn.*
* Mr. Azael Porter,
Mr. Daniel Thompson.

Of *Charlestown.*
Mr. James Miller,
Capt. William Barber's Son.

Of *Brookline.*
Isaac Gardner, Esq.

Of *Cambridge.*
Mr. John Hicks,
Mr. Moses Richardson,
Mr. William Massey.

Of *Medford.*
Mr. Henry Putnam.

Of *Lynn.*
Mr Abednego Ramsdell,
Mr. Daniel Townsend,
Mr. William Flint,
Mr. Thomas Hadley.

Of *Danvers.*
Mr. Henry Jacobs,
Mr. Samuel Cook,
Mr. Ebenezer Goldthwait,
Mr. George Southwick,
Mr. Benjamin Daland, jun.
Mr. Jotham Webb,
Mr. Perley Putnam.

Of *Salem.*
Mr. Benjamin Peirce.

WOUNDED.

Of *Lexington.*
Mr. John Robbins,
Mr. John Tidd,
Mr. Solomon Peirce,
Mr. Thomas Winship,
Mr. Nathaniel Farmer,
Mr. Joseph Comee,
Mr. Ebenezer Munroe,
Mr. Francis Brown,
Prince Easterbrooks,
    (A Negro Man.

Of *Framingham.*
Mr. —— Hemenway.

Of *Bedford.*
Mr. John Lane.

Of *Woburn.*
Mr. George Reed,
Mr. Jacob Bacon.

Of *Medford.*
Mr. William Polly.

Of *Lynn.*
Joshua Feit,
Mr. Timothy Munroe.

Of *Danvers.*
Mr. Nathan Putnam,
Mr. Dennis Wallis.

Of *Beverly.*
Mr. Nathaniel Cleaves.

MISSING.

Of *Menotomy.*
Mr. Samuel Frost,
Mr. Seth Russell,

Those distinguished with this Mark [*] were killed by the first Fire of the Regulars.

Sold in Queen Street.

ons which had been closest at hand, all driven by some wondrous compelling force to meet a common danger.

As many as two thousand New Hampshire men hurried south immediately, and were among the first to arrive from outside Massachusetts. Hollis and New Ipswich and Nottingham sent about one hundred men each, other towns less, and when Andrew McClary of New Hampshire wrote home on April 23 he reported that many more men were still on the way. The news of Lexington reached Connecticut on April 20, and classes at Yale were temporarily suspended as students departed for Massachusetts. Individuals set off singly and in little groups, and militia companies had to be restrained from leaving until they received official orders. A New Haven company was denied powder by the town authorities until its commander, Benedict Arnold, threatened to break open the magazine. They marched on April 24. The Connecticut Committee of Correspondence wrote John Hancock that "The ardour of our people is such, that they can't be kept back," and that colony's assembly began enlisting militiamen into an army, offering ten shillings to every one who provided himself with a "good gun, well fixed with a bayonet and cartouch box."

The Massachusetts men, who were nearest and therefore first to arrive, included members of regular militia companies, in which every man between the ages of sixteen and sixty was expected to serve; younger and more active men drawn from the militia units and formed into minute companies—so called because they were to be ready at a "minute's warning"; and reserve groups known as alarm companies, composed of young boys, old men, ministers, and other town officials. During the chaotic days following April 19 the task of assembling this mass of volunteer soldiers into manageable shape fell to the military leaders of Massachusetts, principally the two men who had assumed command upon their arrival —Artemas Ward and John Thomas.

The latter was a doctor by profession, whose warm letters reveal a devotion to family exceeded only by a love of country. He had served capably in the French and Indian Wars, and although he was now fifty years old, there were few better officers than John Thomas. He and Ward divided the army between them, with Thomas setting up a virtually independent command in Roxbury, separated by the Charles River and several miles of land from Ward's Cambridge headquarters.

When he heard the alarm on April 19, Artemas Ward had been sick in bed in Shrewsbury, suffering from a bladder stone which plagued him off and on for years, but he immediately saddled his horse and rode down to Cambridge to take command. He was a man of medium height, with a long, sharp nose and pointed chin. Although he was a little too stout for his forty-seven years, in his powdered wig, long, silver-buttoned coat, knee breeches, and riding boots, Ward presented a rather imposing figure. By turns a farmer, politician, and volunteer soldier, Ward was deeply religious, quiet, and thoughtful. Physically he was energetic, but he was a slow, heavy thinker and unhappily lacking in precisely the kind of aggressive leadership which the patriot army would need desperately in the imminent future.

The very haste with which the militiamen had descended on Boston was the chief factor in their sudden departure from the scene of action—an exodus which rapidly began to assume alarming proportions. Almost as soon as the army had assembled it began to waste away, first by handfuls, then by the scores and hundreds, forced to leave by the very meagerness of clothing and provisions, and the untended responsibilities at home. Most of these men were farmers, and there were fields to be plowed and harrowed and planted, arrangements to be made for wives and children and hired hands which took precedence over soldiering once the first emergency was over. It began to look as though Thomas Hutchinson, back in England, was right in his prediction that "unless fanaticism got the better of self-preservation" the rebels "must soon disperse, as it was the season for sowing their Indian corn, the chief subsistence of New England." To keep as many men as possible in camp, to maintain the blockade of Boston, to repel another British attack, and somehow to forge an army out of the confused mass of volunteers was the formidable task now facing Ward. Fortunately the general did not have to do it alone. Advising and counseling him at every turn was a remarkable and very nearly tireless group of men known as the Committee of Safety. Ward's headquarters was the Jonathan Hastings house in Cambridge, a fat, comfortable, dignified residence where the Committee of Safety also held its meetings, acting always as a committee of the Provincial Congress, which sat five miles away in Watertown, but acting promptly and, in the main, judiciously. The chief figure on the Committee, and in fact the principal leader of the rebellion now that John Hancock and Samuel Adams had left to take part in the Second Continental Congress in Philadelphia, was Dr. Joseph Warren.

Of the great triumvirate of Adams, Hancock, and Warren, this thirty-four-year old Boston physician was by far the most attractive and winning personality. In many respects Warren was a more impassioned leader than the other two, but he was also kind and friendly, completely open and frank in everything he said and did, as scrupulously fair and humane in his dealings with enemies as he was with friends, and a believer in the restoration of colonial rights without separation from England. Warren was a good-looking man of medium height, with large, wide-set eyes, a full mouth, rather long, straight nose, and in his portrait by Copley there is a hint of fullness to the face, just the faintest suggestion that he was beginning to add a little too much weight. Two years ago his young wife had died, and he had taken the four children to their grandmother's house to live so that he could devote his days to practicing medicine and his nights to politics.

Until now he had been prominent chiefly within the town of Boston, as a gifted writer and speaker and counselor for the cause. The last patriot leader to remain in the city, Warren had dispatched Paul Revere and William Dawes on their errands on the night of April 18, and since that day he had given up his busy medical practice and devoted all of his remarkable energies to the public service. Characteristically, he had rushed to the scene of

In many respects the ablest rebel leader in Boston was Joseph Warren, whose portrait was painted by John Singleton Copley in 1775, when Warren was thirty-four. Nothing about the dignified physician's appearance suggests that he was, as a British officer called him, "the greatest incendiary in America." (*Courtesy, Museum of Fine Arts, Boston*)

action on the nineteenth, narrowly missed death during the British retreat from Concord, and then headed for Watertown, where he found himself virtually in charge of the affairs of Massachusetts. As president of the Provincial Congress, the doctor was leader and spokesman for the farmers, artisans, tavern-keepers, and businessmen who largely made up its membership. In the turn affairs had taken, this body of men suddenly found itself charged not only with the routine affairs of a peacetime government, but with the myriad details and problems confronting a society at war. Massachusetts was not only the leader of the rebellion—it *was* the rebellion—and members of Congress were forced to consider every decision, every act, in the light of their possible effect upon twelve other colonies that were not yet in the fight. Theirs was a heavy responsibility, and there is clear evidence that the legislators felt it.

Just now the question weighing most heavily on the minds of Congress and the Committee of Safety was how they were going to keep control of the military. History was full of disasters brought on by allowing an army to get out of hand, and they had no intention of permitting this Frankenstein creature to be anything but a servant of the civil government. To their credit, they recognized almost immediately that they had no real army—that it was nothing but a disorganized, undisciplined conglomeration of men which, if nothing was done to preserve and to shape it into a force capable of maintaining the siege, would rapidly melt away before their very eyes. One man who visited the camp early in May said the army was in "such a shifting, fluctuating state as not to be capable of a perfect regulation. They are continually coming and going." And poor Artemas Ward warned Congress that if they did not permit him to enlist men immediately into a more permanent force, "I shall be left all alone."

In response to Ward's urgent plea, Congress voted to print enlisting papers for the first twenty regiments, set up a schedule of pay, and requested the Committee of Safety to appoint field officers recommended by the generals. It was to be an army of thirty thousand men, with 13,600 of them from Massachusetts, the balance from other colonies. Despite the complete practicality of this matter, the Puritan leaders of revolt were very conscious of the underlying moral issues, and although they were desperate for every man they could enlist, the Committee of Safety resolved that only "Freemen" should be included in the forces to be raised. Anything else, they decided, would be "inconsistent with the principles that are to be supported, and reflect dishonour on this Colony." Slaves would not be admitted into the army "upon any consideration whatever."

Each regiment, commanded by a colonel, was to contain ten companies of fifty-six men and three officers, but unhappily, this scheme for the appointment of officers ran afoul of a tradition dear to the heart of every militia company. For generations these companies had been formed locally, with the men electing their own officers, and as soon as they learned that this system was to be scrapped, a hue and cry went up from all ranks. The men of Newbury, learning that they were to be annexed to Colonel Gerrish's regiment, wanted no part of him—they wanted their own colonel or they were heading for home. Men from York County refused to serve under Alexander Scammell, because he "lives in New Hampshire, and has no property in Berwick of the County of York"; while certain troops in Nixon's regiment who found themselves shifted to Gardner's command protested that it was "contrary to our inclination, and repugnant to the promise made us at our enlisting." As Amos Farnsworth confided to his diary, most of three days—April 26, 27, and 28—were taken up by "a Strugling with the offisers which shold be the hiest in offist." This ardent spirit of localism, which was to plague civilian and military leaders through the entire course of the Revolution, the Provincial Congress was powerless to override. At this juncture it desperately needed an army, and it would have to take it on whatever terms it had to make. So the colonels distributed enlistment papers to eligible captains, and the captains went off to beat the countryside for fifty-six men who would serve with them.

While this went on, the army was shrinking steadily. Over in Roxbury, John Thomas saw his forces dwindle from six thousand men to twenty-five hundred, and of these nearly one-third were from Connecticut. When he requested reinforcements from Ward, the commander reported his ranks so thin that he could not possibly spare them, so the resourceful Thomas began marching his men round and round Roxbury hill, creating an illusion of numbers that thoroughly deceived the watchful British. Fortunately, on May 23, Thomas was strengthened by the arrival of fourteen hundred Rhode Islanders who came into camp behind their brigadier general, Nathanael Greene. As a curious illustration of the hatred of Parliament and allegiance to the King which prevailed just now in the colonies, these men had signed up to serve "in His Majesty's Service, and in the pay of the Colony of Rhode Island, for the preservation of the Liberties of America." Rhode Island made one of its greatest contributions to the war in Nathanael Greene, who was to demonstrate that he was second only to Washington in his ability to manage men, to conserve resources, and yet to risk all on one brilliantly planned maneuver. It was surprising that Greene had received the command, for his only knowledge of war seems to have come from what he had studied or read in books—a good many of which he had obtained from Henry Knox, the Boston bookseller who was interested in the same course of study. But the Rhode Island Assembly had somehow spotted in Greene those abilities which were to become so apparent later on, and the immediate result of their choice was a Rhode Island Corps which was the best disciplined outfit in the American army. Greene was a lot tougher on his boys than most other commanders, and although he was a long way from being satisfied with the results just yet, early in June he was forced to admit that "they are under much better government than any troops round about Boston."

By this time the Massachusetts quota of 13,600 men was still a mythical figure on paper; only two of Connecticut's six regiments of one thousand men, plus a spare company or two, were due to come into camp before mid-June; and New Hampshire had but fourteen hundred men ready for action, in two regiments of the three promised. All of this gave the Provincial Congress something between ten and twelve thousand enlisted men, plus a scattering of militia companies whose men were still unwilling to serve under this or that colonel. It was a long way from the hopeful total of thirty thousand, and the members of Congress, weighed down by the burden of problems and responsibilities, began appealing to a higher power. After all, four New England colonies were carrying the entire American cause, and it was clear that unless other means of support were found, and found at once, the rebellion was going to founder as rapidly as it had begun. To the Second Continental Congress, now sitting in Philadelphia, the Provincial Congress of Massachusetts poured out its tale of woe. Revealing their fears at having an army—even one comprised of their own countrymen—without a strong civil power to maintain and control it, the Massachusetts legislators appealed to the delegates in Philadelphia not only for advice, but since the army was for the defense of all America, they asked them to take over the assembled troops. From now on, the correspondence between Watertown and Philadelphia would show a mounting note of reliance on the Continental Congress, a willingness of the local people to put their faith and trust in the representatives of all thirteen colonies.

But whatever aid, comfort, and responsibility the Continental Congress might proffer was, during the early weeks of June, 1775 as illusory as the thirty thousand men who were supposed to be in camp, and until assistance was forthcoming, the Provincial Congress would have to take matters in hand as best they could. Over and over, it was the problem of the army. The military stores were totally inadequate for a force of any size. There were not enough arms or camp utensils, provisions, blankets, or tents. And powder was the most critical shortage of all. On the fourth of June, Ward, Joseph Warren, and Moses Gill, who was chairman of the Committee of Supplies, had written letters to the Continental Congress and to several colonial assemblies, saying, "We suffer at present the greatest inconvenience from a want of a sufficient supply of powder; without this, every attempt to defend ourselves or annoy our enemies must prove abortive." Already they had requisitioned for the general magazines all that could be spared by individual towns (Charlestown, closest to the British and presumably in the greatest danger, had forwarded what seems to have been its entire supply), but occasional skirmishes had seriously diminished that little stock. Civilians had done their utmost to smuggle powder out of Boston—hidden in wagons under piles of manure, hay, or household goods—but Gage had learned of this and immediately put a stop to it. An appeal to New York brought forth at first the response that that colony was "destitute of ammunition"; then, on June 10, the New York Congress reported to Governor Trumbull of Connecticut that they had been successful in obtaining a quantity which they could spare "the brethren of the Massachusetts-Bay," and asked Trumbull to forward 650 pounds from his own supply to Boston, which New York would then replace. In case Connecticut did not have any to spare, the shipment would come direct to Boston, but not until June 12 did Alexander McDougall write Joseph Warren, saying that two wagons, guarded by four or six "trusty men," had left that day, to travel only by night.

On May 15 there was only one box of paper for cartridges in or around Cambridge, and on the following day the Committee of Safety, learning that a British prisoner held at Worcester was a papermaker, ordered him taken to James Boice's "Manufactory" at Milton. Most of the men who responded to the Lexington alarm had brought their own guns with them, but those who left camp for home, even temporarily, often left their weapons with their families in case they were needed there. In purely financial terms the contribution of a gun and bayonet was considerable. Their value was estimated at about £2 by the Provincial Congress—an amount which would buy approximately seven cords of wood, or pay a laborer for a week's work, or purchase some twenty-five bushels of coal. As late as June 14, the Congress found it necessary

ADVERTISEMENT.

Any Gun-smith or Lock-maker,
within the County of *Windham*, who is willing to
supply the Colony with any number of Fire Arms,
to be compleated by the 20th Day of *October* next,
of the same Dimension, as prescribed by an Act of
the General Assembly in *April* last, except the addition of two Inches to length of the Bayonet, may
apply to the Subscriber in *Lebanon*, who is by said
Assembly appointed a Committee for said County,
to procure the same ; and be informed of the Bounty
and Encouragement they may be intitled to, in addition to the Value of such Guns and Locks. Who,
also desires to be soon informed, how many, he may
engage, and depend on.
  June 1st. 1775.   WM. WILLIAMS.
  It is probable the whole Number wanted, will
soon be undertaken for.
  WILLIAM HILLHOUSE, Esq; is a Committee for
the same Purpose in *New-London* County.

Advertisements of this kind were common in every colony during 1775, when it
became apparent how critical the shortage of weapons and ammunition really
was. (*The Connecticut Historical Society*)

to appoint a committee "to consider some way and means of furnishing those who are destitute of arms in the Massachusetts Army," and on the following day—two days before the battle for Bunker Hill—certain towns were ordered to have their inhabitants deposit firearms with the town treasurers—each piece to be paid for. The total set forth in this quota was 1065 muskets.

For an army which was supposedly besieging a fair-sized town, the number of cannon available to this one was laughable. By mid-May the depot established in Cambridge had succeeded in collecting only twenty-four guns of assorted size; but without any real quantity of powder and ball, they were virtually useless. On hand were a fair number of digging tools—some 460 pickaxes, 23 hatchets, 190 spades, and 156 axes being "under the care of Captain Foster" in Cambridge—but medical supplies were in woefully short supply. There were two medicine chests available for the entire army, one at Cambridge and one at Roxbury, and all other surgeons were to be given "free recourse" to these until more were received.

Thus far, at least, food had not been a serious problem. There had been temporary shortages of certain items, but what was lacking more than anything else was a commissary system capable of supplying the right amounts of certain kinds of food to an enormous number of men. On June 10, a daily allowance for each man was set at one pound of bread, half a pound of beef, and half a pound of pork. Once a week he was to get fish instead of meat. If milk was available, he was to have a pint a day; if not, he was to receive rice in its place; and the orders stipulated a quart of good spruce or malt beer daily, beans or peas, and a weekly ration of butter and vinegar, if they could be had. Last but not least, there was to be "one pound of good common Soap for six men per week."

At the outbreak of hostilities, a good many residents had moved out of houses in the area, and the troops had been barracked in these homes, in those of loyalists who had departed earlier, and in vacated Harvard College buildings in Cambridge; yet there did not begin to be adequate facilities for the men. A few of the better-equipped outfits, such as the Rhode Islanders, had tents, and more had been made from the sails of vessels from various harbors, but there was an urgent need to get more of the men under cover of some sort. Early in May, Joseph Trumbull sent his father, the Connecticut governor, a doleful description of the camp: "The Houses are all full, and the Provincial Troops are not yet in Tents, and uncertain when they will be." The overcrowding was so bad, he said, that the men "are growing Sickly and daily dying out of the Barracks."

What effect this had on morale and discipline can be imagined. Despite all efforts of the Provincial Congress, "The want of government, and of a certainty of supplies, had thrown everything into disorder," Nathanael Greene reported. When a few companies threatened to march home, Greene "made several regulations for introducing order and composing their murmurs; but it is very difficult to limit people who have had so much latitude."

With the exception of an occasional prostitute, such as the two "fire Ships" Samuel Haws saw "drumed out of the rhodisland company" on June 11, the Americans had no women in their camp, as the British did, to do the washing and mending. Rather than lower himself to chores of this sort, the average American went ragged and filthy, and one visitor observed that they chose "to let their linen, etc., rot upon their backs than to be at the trouble of cleaning 'em themselves." On June 13, Lieutenant Joseph Hodgkins was writing to his wife in Ipswich asking for a new shirt, "for the weather is hot & shirts Durttey verry fast."

In Medford, tough John Stark was having his problems. He had come down with the New Hampshire militia, and now he was attempting to enlist a regiment. There had been some difficulty over his commission, Stark being a contrary sort who was curiously unwilling to accept one from his own colony, but he had gone ahead recruiting men nonetheless. By the end of May he had acquired arms for nearly all of his men, but there were serious deficiencies in other quarters, as he told the New Hampshire Congress. Many of his soldiers were entirely without blankets, and suffering terribly from the damp, cold nights. And unless some money was forthcoming soon, neither officers nor soldiers would have any choice but to return home. He strongly urged that a sutler be supplied, and "would likewise be glad there might be a chest of medicine procured for the Regiment, and forwarded, as it is wanted very much, and also armourer's tools."

Joseph Warren, who had witnessed all the troubles of army and Congress alike, and who had done his level best to find solutions to them, somehow had also found time to do a little abstract thinking on the whole chaotic situation. In a thoughtful letter to his friend Sam Adams, now with the Continental Congress, he urged "the necessity of establishing a civil government here . . . such a government as shall be sufficient to control the military forces not only of this colony, but also such as shall be sent to us from the other colonies. The continent must strengthen and support with all its weight the civil authority here; otherwise our soldiery will lose the ideas of right and wrong, and will plunder, instead of protecting, the inhabitants." Once again, a voice was being lifted in favor of a government for *all* the colonies on the theory that one strong organization could control all the pieces far better than the pieces could handle themselves. And what kind of government should it be? One, Warren believed, which would "give every man the greatest liberty to do what he pleases consistent with restraining him from doing injury to another."

From the Provincial Congress, too, another communiqué went off by special messenger to Philadelphia, cataloguing the embarrassments, delays, and disappointments which had resulted from the "want of a settled civil polity or government," mentioning renewed apprehensions over Gage's reinforcements, and once more urging the Continental Congress to send advice and then to consider the possibility of moving somewhere "not so far distant," so that their help would be less difficult to come by. Not that the delegates in Philadelphia had neglected the matter; they had listened sympathetically to the requests and pleas that poured in from the north, they had rounded up what tangible aid they could put their hands on, they had lent support to the argument that Massachusetts no longer owed obedience to any governor refusing to observe its charter. But as to leading the bewildered men of Massachusetts out of their present predicament, there was to date only a good deal of backing and filling and dragging of feet, mostly because the whole confused situation was so unprecedented. On June 9 a resolution signed by President John Hancock was dispatched to Watertown, suggesting in roundabout fashion that the assembly do the best it could with what it had, and in fact dumping the whole matter back in the laps of Joseph Warren and his colleagues until further notice.

Which is just where it had been right along, and where it would remain for the next few weeks. In the two months which had elapsed since Wednesday, April 19, the Provincial Congress and Committee of Safety had been smothering brush fires wherever any sparks took hold, and although there was complete agreement that the volunteer fire department at their disposal was inadequately equipped and poorly organized, there was also a reasonable certainty that it was not going to be caught napping, and that its enthusiasm partially made up for a lot of serious flaws. At the end of the first week in May, on the heels of rumors that Gage would make an attempt upon Roxbury, several thousand militia had turned out from nearby towns to meet "our restless enemies" in case they ventured forth. On May 21 a real threat had developed, and the Americans had every reason to believe they had met it quickly and effectively. Gage, cooped up in Boston, had reached the conclusion that he had to do something, even before reinforcements arrived, and he had ordered a small detachment to Grape Island to seize a quantity of hay for his horses and livestock. "It was," according to waspish Lieutenant John Barker of the King's Own Regiment, "the most ridiculous expedition that ever was plan'd," for there were neither enough men nor enough guns on the sloop which carried them to keep off predatory rebels; but Gage seems to have needed not only hay but the tonic of a little activity. Grape Island was just off Weymouth, on the south shore of the enormous, island-spattered bay that constitutes greater Boston harbor, and since this came under the jurisdiction of the American right-wing commander, John Thomas dispatched three companies from his "No-Man's Land" in Roxbury to lend a hand. A party of provincials—including Joseph Warren, who with characteristic vigor hurried to the spot—put out in boats, but the regulars escaped from one end of the island just as they were landing at the other. The redcoats had their hay, but the patriot leaders were encouraged nevertheless by the speed with which the emergency was met. As Abigail Adams described it to her husband John, down in Philadelphia, "The alarm flew like lightning, and men from all parts came flocking down, till two thousand were collected." We expect, she went on, "to be in continual alarms, till something decisive takes place," and this state of nerves was as hard on the civilians as it was on the army—"Soldiers coming in for a lodging, for breakfast, for supper, for drink, etc. Sometimes refugees from Boston, tired and fatigued, seek an asylum for a day, a night, a week. You can hardly imagine how we live."

The lesson of Gage's incursion was not lost on the patriot leaders, who reasoned that the British commander might reach out at any moment, by means of boats, to other islands on which other supplies lay unguarded. To prevent him from doing so they determined to remove them.

Half a mile east of Boston lay Noddle's Island, an open, low-lying farm where prosperous Henry Williams grazed his cows and sheep. Beyond it was Hog Island, where more animals were pastured. Since Hog Island was separated from the mainland of Lynn by a narrow channel which was fordable at low tide, and since a similarly shallow body of water lay between the two islands, the Committee of Safety reasoned that the stock could be gotten off without much difficulty, and directed Colonel John Nixon to handle the job. Amos Farnsworth was one of Nixon's men, and he and some two or three hundred others set out under cover of darkness on May 26, headed down through Mystic, Malden, and Chelsea to Hog Island, and the next morning drove off all the horses, cattle, and sheep they could locate. So far the little raiding party was unobserved and unhindered, but early in the afternoon the British detected signs of activity and swung into action. Admiral Graves, who had a depot of irreplaceable stores on Noddle's Island, ordered the schooner *Diana*, commanded by his nephew Thomas, to cut off the provincials' retreat, and at the same time landed a party of marines to attack the marauders. The Americans retired in good order, having burned the buildings and what hay they found and driven off or killed all the stock, reached Hog Island, and there turned to face their pursuers. Amos Farnsworth and about fourteen others "Squated Down in a Ditch on the mash" and exchanged "a hot fiar untill the Regulars retreeted." There were no casualties in the brisk little engagement, although "the Bauls Sung like Bees Round our heds," and the British headed back to Boston, resigned to the fact that the damage had been done. And there the affair would have ended, had the wind not died and had the tide not shifted.

The sun was setting when the *Diana* found herself in this embarrassing situation. Thomas Graves began warping her down the creek by means of a kedge and signaled his uncle, who sent off a dozen barges to tow her, backed by the armed sloop *Britannia*. But by now, word of the *Diana's* plight had reached the American lines, and in short order about a thousand men hurried to the scene and began collecting along the low bluffs above the river. Joseph Warren was on hand, and the senior officer present was Israel Putnam, one of the most picturesque characters in the rebel, or any other, camp. Putnam was fifty-seven years old, a powerfully built five-foot-six, with a round, open face and a jaw so square it appeared that he had fallen on his chin and mashed it into a flat line. Within his own lifetime he had become a folk hero, a man to whom impossible feats were attributed because the facts were so extraordinary. In the French and Indian Wars he had escaped almost miraculously from a party of Indians who were

The best likeness of Israel Putnam is this pencil sketch by John Trumbull. When he was appointed a major general by the Continental Congress, Old Put was fifty-eight years old—a powerfully built man five feet six inches tall with the face of a cherubic bulldog. Regarded by his countrymen as something of a folk-hero, he was a superb leader on the battlefield but—as later events were to reveal—something less than a brilliant general. (*Wadsworth Atheneum; lent by the Putnam Phalanx, Hartford*)

preparing to burn him at the stake; he had been shipwrecked off Cuba, served in the Pontiac War, ascended the Mississippi on an exploring trip, and after his retirement from military affairs had returned to farm his lands near Pomfret, Connecticut. When the port of Boston was closed, Old Put had driven a herd of sheep all the way from Connecticut and presented them to the beleaguered citizens. He was working in the field on the morning of April 20 when the news of Lexington reached him; immediately he saddled up, rode off to alarm the officers of his militia company, and shouted orders for them to collect their men and follow him. According to tradition he arrived in Concord at sunrise the next morning, still on the same horse, and there is an entry in Artemas Ward's orderly book for April 21 stating: "This day, General Putnam, of Connecticut, attended the Council of War."

In 1767, Putnam had married for the second time, to a widow of some affluence who began exposing him to a newer and higher social circle; but her efforts had little effect on the jovial, outspoken, almost illiterate Put; the rough edges of the farmer and tavern-keeper had not rubbed off, and he was still the hero of those small farmers who had pushed out beyond the eastern seaboard onto the frontier. As one of his contemporaries said, "He does not wear a large wig, nor screw his countenance into a form that belies the sentiments of his generous soul; he is no adept either at politics or religious canting and cozening; he is no shake-hand body; he therefore is totally unfit for everything but fighting." Richard Reeve, describing Putnam, said he had "the character of being of a most violent and impetuous make, fit to lead them on to any desperate enterprize," and hinted that Putnam was one of the American hotheads who had advocated taking Boston by storm. No one had the slightest doubt that if fighting came, Put would be in the thick of it, and one of the thornier problems confronting the Committee of Safety was how in the world to hold him back. His Connecticut men were stationed near Cambridge, and already he had thrown up Forts Number One, Two, and Three to block the road the British might take out of Boston.

He had been one of the first to get news of the *Diana's* predicament, and like an old warhorse the fiery, impatient campaigner had pelted down Charlestown Road in the gathering dusk, sniffing action all the way.

By the time Putnam and his men arrived, Admiral Graves had landed three guns on Noddle's Island, and Gage had sent two twelve-pounders and eighty marines to protect the *Diana*. Put, never one to waste time, hailed the schooner, demanded that she surrender, and was promptly answered by a blast from her guns. The provincials replied with two fieldpieces they had brought along —the first cannon to be used in the war—and Putnam led his men waist-deep out into the water, closing in on the vessel with musket fire. The twelve-pounders on Noddle's Island began thundering ominously and there was more firing from the *Diana* and *Britannia*, but the forces of nature were working a lot faster than the British artillery could remedy matters. As the night wore on, the tide ebbed so fast that the schooner was grounded and in real danger of tipping over. Putnam's men were firing almost blind in the darkness, but they cut down some of Lieutenant Graves's seamen before the tide took charge and won their battle. The *Diana* fell over on her beam-ends, young Graves sent his wounded off to the *Britannia*, and when his men could no longer stand on the sloping deck or bring the guns to bear, he abandoned ship. With a shout the Americans swarmed onto the helpless schooner, and after carrying off four guns and a number of swivel pieces, set her afire. About three in the morning the *Diana* blew up, and Old Put led his tired and happy men back to camp. Still soaked to the waist, he encountered Ward and Warren in Cambridge and, grinning, said he wished there were more of this sort of work to do every day.

So that, if the Americans greeted Gage's bombastic Proclamation of June 12 with combined derision and anger, they did so with a feeling of awakening strength, a realization that they had on several occasions taken the best the redcoats had to offer and given a little better than they had got, that they *did* have Gage corked up in Boston, and that if he wanted out it would be on their terms, not his. But the formality of the times required a bit more than public outcry and scorn, and on Tuesday afternoon, June 13, the Provincial Congress selected a committee of Joseph Warren, Colonel Palmer, James Warren, Mr. Sever, and Doctor Taylor "to consider the subject-matter of a late extraordinary Proclamation of General Gage." On Friday two more men were added to the drafting committee, possibly because Joseph Warren suddenly found himself very, very busy with other matters.

Unbeknownst to the Congress, the game was not going to be played with words any more—and all because that "gentleman of undoubted veracity" had overheard some British officers talking in Boston and reported their remarks to a Committee of Safety in New Hampshire, who sent a rider galloping back down to Watertown with the news. It was a roundabout way for the end of an era to arrive, but the sound of British troops preparing to march again could mean only that. In a curious sense, the day of Lexington and Concord had not quite spelled finish; there was too much accident about it, too much of the improbable, and not enough preparedness on the part of either side. There was still some breathing room in the eight tense weeks that followed—narrow, to be sure—but room nevertheless for some extraordinarily bold and imaginative men to have put a stop to things, to have patched up the family fight so that the dark stain might fade away with the passage of years. Indeed, there were a few such men on both sides of the water, and some did what they could to avert the avalanche; but everything conspired against them as spring spilled over into summer of 1775. What confounded the very best of intentions was the enormous distance between England and America—a gulf concocted both of time and misunderstanding; in addition to which, the opposing protagonists had passed their respective points of no return, exceeding the outermost limits of patience and endurance and willingness to compromise. And so, even if the battle of April 19 had not been the final, irrevocable deed, it had succeeded in creating a shrouded maze of tension and suspicion and fear, in which two fighters with drawn knives were groping about, ready to lash out the moment they heard a hostile footstep in the dark.

The heightening nervousness was reflected in the June 13 decision of the Committee of Safety to keep all of its deliberations "a profound secret" until further notice. What the Committee did not guess was that this edict would succeed just now only because one member was absent on a mission to Philadelphia. That respected member—Doctor Benjamin Church—who was in the heart of Whig councils and who had always seemed the most ardent of patriots, was performing double duty, by serving as General Thomas Gage's principal informer. Probably Church had been betraying patriot plans for two years or more, and in recent months he had passed to Gage all important decisions of Congress and the Committee of Safety, providing him with detailed estimates of American strength and military prospects; yet not until September of 1775 would he be apprehended, and not for one hundred and fifty years would the full extent of his treachery be uncovered by scholars. But in a stroke of sheer luck, Church had been appointed, to his private "vexation," to carry dispatches to the Continental Congress, which meant that he was not present in Cambridge when the Committee of Safety met on June 15 to discuss urgent business.

North of the college buildings in Cambridge, and fronting on the Common, was the Hastings house, occupied until April 20 by Jonathan Hastings, the Harvard steward. It was a handsome, gambrel-roofed dwelling in which Artemas Ward had set up his headquarters, and here, in a comfortable room to the right of the front hall, the Committee of Safety and the Council of War held their sessions. On Thursday, June 15, the energetic Committee turned its attention immediately to the arrival of British reinforcements, to Gage's "very extraordinary Proclamation," and to various accounts of his plans to "penetrate into the country." Pressing the Provincial Congress to increase the size of the army and to see that all soldiers without arms received them without delay, the

Committee urged that militiamen be instructed to march "on the shortest notice, completely equipped, having thirty rounds of cartridges per man," and that civilians "go to meeting armed on Lord's day," for Sunday, June 18, was the date scheduled for Gage's attack on Dorchester Heights. Before the session broke up, a historic decision was made:

"Whereas, it appears of Importance to the Safety of this Colony, that possession of the Hill, called Bunker's Hill, in Charlestown, be securely kept and defended; and also some one hill or hills on Dorchester Neck be likewise Secured. Therefore, Resolved, Unanimously, that it be recommended to the Council of War, that the abovementioned Bunker's Hill be maintained, by sufficient force being posted there; and as the particular situation of Dorchester Neck is unknown to this Committee, they advise that the Council of War take and pursue such steps respecting the Same, as to them shall appear to be for the Security of this Colony."

Bunker Hill and Dorchester Heights, those two strategic points of land which loomed so large in Gage's plans, had hardly been ignored by the Americans until now—quite the contrary. Back in early May, when reports of an impending British attack on Charlestown were received, Colonel Richard Gridley, Richard Devens, and Colonel Henshaw had been sent off to reconnoiter the ground, and returned with a recommendation that breastworks be erected near Prospect Hill to guard the Charlestown Road, and redoubts constructed on Winter Hill and on Bunker Hill, the highest point of land on Charlestown peninsula. When these works were completed, the report stated confidently, "we apprehend that the country will be safe from all sallies of the enemy in that quarter." There was a good deal of sense to this, of course, but it provoked a heated debate among rebel leaders, dividing them sharply into two schools of thought. The first, whose chief spokesmen seem to have been Israel Putnam and Colonel William Prescott, argued in favor of immediate action, their theory being that a fort on Bunker Hill

Richard Byron, an English naval officer and great-uncle of Lord Byron, painted this water color of Boston and the nearby countryside in 1764. The large land mass in the foreground is the peninsula occupied by the town—much of it still pastures and meadows, particularly in the vicinity of the Common. In the middle distance is the long Neck, across which all traffic to and from the mainland

had to move. The town gates were here and the road, which led to Roxbury (off toward the right), was fortified by the British. In the background, to the right of the church steeple and beyond the Neck, is the hill known as Dorchester Heights. (*The Bostonian Society, Old State House*)

would draw the British out of Boston into the open. Old Put was deeply troubled by the American army's inactivity, and he had full confidence in the militia's ability to fight under certain conditions. They are "not afraid of their heads," he argued, "though very much afraid of their legs"; therefore, if you put them in trenches or behind breastworks, "they will fight forever." Joseph Warren and Artemas Ward agreed that the construction of works on Bunker Hill would indeed lure the British into battle, but they were equally certain, in mid-May, that their own forces had neither the organization nor the cannon nor the powder to hold this exposed position. They were, in short, in no condition to risk a general engagement. Overruling Putnam, they decided to put off any activities on Bunker Hill and Dorchester Heights until the troops were better organized, better supplied, and able to defend the two points which lay directly under the enemy's nose.

Then, in what must have been complete defiance of his superiors, the impetuous Old Put decided to have a go at the project himself, and on May 13 he led two thousand Connecticut men into Charlestown, marching them up and down Bunker and Breed's Hills in full view of the British Navy and the Boston garrison. The purpose, as Amos Farnsworth surmised, was "to Shoe themselves to the Regulars," and it had its effect. Lieutenant Barker, watching the demonstration from the Boston side of the water, saw the Americans enter Charlestown, parade boldly along the waterfront, and then, "after giving the War-hoop opposite the Somerset, return as they came." Barker wished mightily that they had fired on the Somerset, for "she had everything ready for Action, and must have destroyed great numbers of them, besides putting the Town in Ashes." But in mid-May the time was not ripe for that; not for another month would Putnam have his way; and beyond his erection of a few defensive posts, and Loammi Baldwin's request for some "mathematical instruments" from Harvard for surveying "of the ground between us and our enemies," things were quiet in the direction of Charlestown.

Joseph Warren, who managed to strike an excellent balance between the impatience of Putnam and the caution of Ward, was concerned lest the Connecticut fire-eater act rashly and somehow involve all of them prematurely in a situation from which there would be no turning back. After the engagement at Noddle's Island, Warren called Putnam aside and told him, "I admire your spirit, and respect General Ward's prudence. We shall need them both, and one must temper the other." And there matters had stood until the dark warnings of a British attack left Ward and Warren and the other more conservative leaders with no choice but to act.

Since the Committee of Safety's resolution of June 15 left the problem of Dorchester Heights completely up in the air, Putnam and two other officers, along with Joseph Palmer and Benjamin White of the Committee, hurried over to Roxbury to sound out John Thomas. General Ward might have told them what kind of reaction they would get, for on June 6 he had gone out to have a look at the lay of the land with Thomas, Joseph Spencer, and William Heath, and their appearance on the heights had immediately provoked three shots from the alert British gunners. Besides, Thomas was too concerned with the state of his Roxbury defenses to undertake any offensive move; on the fourteenth, after ordering his men to be ready for anything, he had kept them busy all day hauling logs for fascines and breastworks. Evidently he and his staff vetoed any stroke against the Heights of Dorchester, for Putnam and the others returned to Cambridge knowing that the right wing of the army was not yet ready to move.

That put the problem squarely in Artemas Ward's generous lap. On paper, at least, he had more than enough men to take Bunker Hill even without Thomas. In the Massachusetts regiments there were over six thousand privates, plus 1581 officers, sergeants, and drummers; and he also had Putnam's Connecticut regiment and the New Hampshire troops under Stark, Reed, and Sargent. Exclusive of the right wing, he had two thousand more troops than Gage could muster, and in many respects he was ideally situated for operations against Charlestown. His main body was in and

Commander in chief of the Massachusetts troops was Artemas Ward, a slow, heavy-bodied man whose health had been permanently impaired by his service in the French and Indian War. Sneered at as no more than a "church warden" by Charles Lee, he did lack ingenuity and brilliance, but the fact that the rebel army remained intact outside Boston until he was superseded by Washington was largely Ward's doing. This portrait was painted by Charles Willson Peale. (*Independence National Historical Park Collection, Philadelphia*)

around Cambridge; Putnam was at the Inman Farm, even closer to the objective; Stark was at Medford, only three miles from Charlestown; and by the happiest combination of luck and poor management, Reed's regiment was right there at Charlestown Neck. When James Reed and his men arrived in Cambridge on June 12, Ward had told him that the town was hopelessly over-crowded and suggested as tactfully as possible that he find lodgings elsewhere. Reed hustled his regiment over to Medford, where Stark gave him the same story; so Reed, having had enough of marching fruitlessly to and fro, appealed again to Ward, who told him to quarter his men in the houses near Charlestown Neck, to post guards between the barracks and the ferry, and to push sentries out onto Bunker Hill. Although he was bothered by the fact that he had no "apothecary," little medicine, and no chaplain, Reed seems to have had all of the more important matters of discipline and training well in hand; already his men were being drilled twice a day, and they were under strict orders not to damage any house or grounds in the vicinity, not to leave camp without permission, not to make any noise after nine o'clock at night, not to permit anyone through the lines without a pass or countersign, and not to go swimming on the Sabbath ("nor any other day to stay in the water any longer than is necessary to wash themselves."). As Colonel Israel Gilman reported to the New Hampshire Committee of Safety, the regiment was completely of-ficered and "good harmony" prevailed. It was "still times with the Regular Troops at present," Gilman observed, but he ventured an opinion which everyone else in the army apparently held—that the British would soon make a push for Bunker Hill or Dorchester Neck. Which was just what was worrying Ward, de-spite the seventy-five hundred troops he had on paper.

There was a frightening disparity between those returns and the actual count of men fit for duty; he could not have had much more than five thousand effectives after the sick and the absent were deducted, and of these, many lacked firearms or were short of am-munition. But what concerned Ward most was the safety of Cambridge, or more accurately the center of his army, which he was determined to preserve at all costs—even at the expense of the force he was about to assign to take Bunker Hill. Most of the details which should have been handled by a competent staff Ward had to think of himself, which meant that many of those details were not even contemplated, or were forgotten in the confusion of planning and organizing and making up his mind just how deeply he would commit himself. These things are a lot easier to see in retrospect than they were at the time, and in fairness it must be said that Ward had no staff in the true sense, that he had far too many problems for any one commander to cope with; but beyond this, it must also be remembered that Ward's immediate experience had been in building an army, in collecting every last man and piece of equipment he could lay his hands on, in husbanding every available resource; so that he was understandably reluctant to risk a major part of that carefully nurtured army in battle. There was a stubborn streak in Ward, too, and once he had decided to preserve the bulk of his strength in Cambridge, it meant that the contingent which would march against Bunker Hill would go off without enough men, without proper equipment, without plans for a sufficient relief force, and without adequate cannon, ammunition, powder, or even food and water.

What Ward's instructions were to Colonel William Prescott, or whether Prescott protested the inadequacy of his detachment and of the commanding general's plans, no one knows; but at some time on June 16 Prescott received orders to proceed to Bunker Hill and erect a fort.

At last the die had been cast. Israel Putnam headed over to the Inman Farm to make his preparations, and Joseph Warren, after scrawling a hasty note to William Heath, intimating that Heath had a good chance of being made a brigadier soon, rode off to Watertown to attend to some last minute affairs of the Provincial Congress. Just two days earlier the members had appointed him the second major general of the Massachusetts Army, in addition to all his other duties, and even though he had not yet received his commission Warren suspected that he might be needed on the morrow at Bunker Hill. There was so much to be done before morning, and he planned to work long into the night after dining with Joseph and Elizabeth Palmer. In the years to come Elizabeth would recall the brief visit he paid them; Warren wore a tie wig, she remembered, and "had a fine color in his face and light blue eyes."

III. We Readyly and Cheerfully Obeyed

About seven o'clock on the evening of June 16, the side door of the Hastings house swung open and the Reverend Samuel Langdon made his way toward the troops assembling across the road on Cambridge Common. Langdon, the president of Harvard College, was a stern, stately-looking man, known to everyone in the vicinity as an ardent patriot and the preacher of some of the longest sermons on record. He had been a classmate of Sam Adams's at Harvard, and he was one of that influential New England group which the recently deposed chief justice, Peter Oliver, described contemptuously as James Otis's "black regiment, the dissenting clergy."

Apart from his patriotism and the business immediately at hand, Dr. Langdon had a great deal on his mind. Since the day of Lexington and Concord, the once-orderly, lovely village of Cambridge had been in a state of absolute chaos. All the students had been sent away, out of the combat zone, and now their rooms in Stoughton, Harvard, and Massachusetts Halls were overflowing with militiamen from the surrounding countryside. Christ Church, whose parishioners were mostly Tories, now served as a barracks; officers and their staffs had taken over the houses vacated by loyalists fled to the safety of Boston; the Provincial Congress had provided eleven hundred tents—every one at its disposal—and agents of the commissary general were even now collecting sails from vessels forced into port by the Royal Navy. But still men were sleeping in the open. General Ward was begging the Congress for more tents, men were growing sick and actually dying in barracks because of overcrowding, and the lack of sanitation was appalling. Not until two weeks after the battle of April 19 had latrines been dug, and the filth and stench of the huge, makeshift camp were beyond description.

Then there was the matter of the men's morals, for which Langdon, as chaplain of the Massachusetts Army, felt a heavy responsibility. Regimental orders required that "Every officer and Soldier Strickly Attend Prayers," and warned against "Profane Cusing or Swearing"; while general orders issued two days ago directed the men to attend prayers both morning and evening—armed and ready to march in case of alarm. Yet while the camps, as a Connecticut soldier, James Coggswell, wrote on June 15, "abound with Clergymen," there was still a distressing amount of profanity. "I see no kind of seriousness," Coggswell complained to a friend back home, "but on the contrary my ears are filled with the most shocking oaths and imprications; and the tremendous name of the great God is taken on the most trifling occations."

Fortunately the Provincial Congress had a strong sense of moral obligation, and had appointed one committee to see what could be done about violations of the Sabbath, and another to "bring in a Resolve for a Day of Fasting and Prayer." The first group made two tries before it came up with a report satisfactory to the sinconscious members of Congress, while the second was actually admonished for its recommendation, and told sharply that it would do well to mention the following items: "blessing on the Continental Congress, unity of the Colonies, health, fruitful seasons, &c, &c." Religion and politics went hand in hand these days, and the Puritan spirit, in some quarters at least, was still evident.

As if his other problems were not enough, Dr. Langdon had to worry over the affairs of a college which had virtually ceased to exist. Only the day before, members of the Corporation and Board of Overseers had met at his house to compose a letter to

Congress. After a tactful reference to "the present difficult situation of publick affairs," the overseers informed the legislators that it was no longer possible for them to meet regularly, and, with a wistful reminder of the "approaching season of the annual Commencement," stated their intention of conferring degrees on as many qualified candidates "as may offer themselves" on that once-happy occasion.

In fact, the only bright spot in Samuel Langdon's day had been the removal of his precious College library to a place of safety. This had come about quite suddenly, and he was not entirely certain why, except for an uneasy feeling that something momentous was about to happen. Shortly before his meeting with the overseers on Thursday, a communication had arrived from the Provincial Congress at Watertown, urging that the "Library, apparatus and other valuables of Harvard College be removed, as soon as may be, to the Town of Andover." Dr. Langdon's grateful approval had been immediate, and all morning workers had trudged in and out of Harvard Hall, loading the books into wagons. The president had been warned to carry out this operation "with the greatest safety and dispatch," and it may have occurred to Langdon, as he joined the soldiers on the Common, that their presence there and the removal of the library were somehow related.

For several hours the men in the ranks had known that something was up. This had been one of those perfect New England days, the sort that happens now and again in that all too brief season between the long winter and onrushing summer, when the sun is just warm enough, and all of nature seems to stand out with an early-morning freshness. The morning had begun like every other one in recent weeks, and while the novelty of soldiering and life in camp had scarcely worn off for most of the men, they were beginning to grow accustomed to the strange sound of drums beating reveille at four, to company parades at sunrise for morning prayers, to officers no better than they were inspecting a man's own musket, to guard duty and more guard duty, to pick and

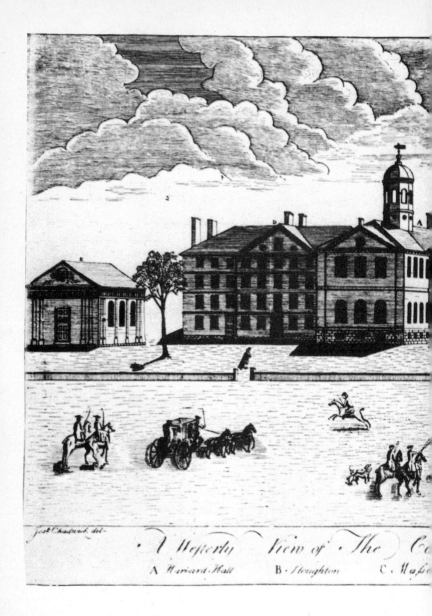

Jos. Chadwick del.

A Westerly View of The Co

A Harvard Hall   B Stoughton   C Masse

s in Cambridge New England

D. _Hollis_   E. _Holden Chapel_

This charming engraving of Harvard College, the first institution of higher learning in the colonies, was made by Paul Revere in 1767. In those happy times no one could have guessed that the buildings—including the chapel at far left—would house colonial troops of an army besieging Boston. (_Courtesy, American Antiquarian Society_)

shovel work on the entrenchments going up around Cambridge. By midafternoon most of their duties were complete, and the bawl of sergeants and the steady tramp of soldiers drilling had given way to the drowsy hum of insects, chirping birds, and desultory conversation. Relaxing after the day's activities, men sat around making cartridges, dozed under shade trees, noted homely details in a diary, or laboriously traced out the words a man away from home writes to his wife. Those who had been shoemakers or makers of breeches or hats two months ago were haggling now over the price of clothing they had made for a comrade, or bartering the products of their hands for the fresh produce a farm boy had brought into camp. Those few who had stayed with the army since April 19 considered themselves seasoned veterans now, and were inclined to look with scorn on new arrivals in camp—"The Long Faced People," one such old-timer called the raw recruits.

Yet somehow, as the hours of June 16 ticked off, the sum total of things that happened or that did not happen began falling together like pieces in a puzzle, and by late afternoon the whole camp knew, with the unerring sixth sense armies always have, that a movement was afoot. An early indication had been the flurry of activity in and around the Hastings house the day before, with the Committee of Safety and the top commanders in long and apparently urgent session. Another portent of the sort that impresses soldiers was the simple but noteworthy fact which Corporal Amos Farnsworth of Groton recorded in his diary for Friday, June 16: "Nothing done in the forenoon." And it is probable—this being the kind of news that travels fastest through an army—that word had reached Cambridge of a resolution passed in Watertown that morning, permitting generals of the Massachusetts Army to draw on the commissary for liquor, whenever the men were on "extraordinary duty."

Details marching past the rose-brick quadrangle of college buildings took note of workmen hurrying in and out of the library, their arms loaded with books for the waiting wagons. Colonel Richard Gridley's newly organized battalion of artillery sweat and cursed over the mysteries of limbering up their six fieldpieces and the guns taken from the schooner *Diana* on May 27. And Captain Thomas Foster's company began loading wagons with the entrenching tools in its care.

That afternoon orders reached several regimental headquarters, and quill pens scrawled notations into orderly books: "Frye's, Bridge's, and William Prescott's regiments to parade this evening, at six o'clock, with all the intrenching tools in this encampment." Over by the Inman house, not quite a mile east of Cambridge, where most of the Connecticut troops were bivouacked, Captain Chester's orderly recorded: "Special orders; Draught from Capt Chesters Comp^y 1 Sub^n 1 Serg^t & 28 privates, and appear on the grand Parade equiped with ammunition, Blankets and one days provision at 5 o'clock P.M." Rumor, founded and unfounded, passed from one man to another, from one company to the next, and before long the whole camp knew about the impending march.

When Experience Storrs, lieutenant colonel of Israel Putnam's Connecticut regiment, received a draft for thirty-one men from his own company, it hardly came as a surprise. "Expecting an engagement soon," he had jotted in his diary—an entry he had been anticipating ever since June 3, the day his company marched into Cambridge. As soon as he had seen them settled at Mr. Fairweather's house he presented himself at headquarters, and General Ward had recommended their "being emediately provided for Action."

Like a good many other officers and men with whom he was now thrown together, Eph Storrs was having difficulty adjusting to the business of war and soldiering. Not two months ago, at home in Mansfield, Connecticut, he had been going about his spring chores in the raw cold—plowing, mending stone walls, sowing rye—but the "Mallencolly Tidings" received there on April 20 had changed everything. From that day to this it had been a nightmare of activity—organizing the militia, sandwiching Committee of Safety meetings in between stepped-up sessions of the legislature, attending to the endless details of getting his men ready to march, outfitting them with arms, powder, balls, and flint—and with what little room there was left in his brain trying to decide what he, Eph Storrs, should do. Every step of the way, uncertainty had nagged at him. When the first Connecticut companies set out for Massachusetts, all the officers had urged him to come along, but Eph decided then that "Providence calls Lowder on me to Return to the Assembly at Hartford," and did not go. Then they heard a rumor of seventeen thousand regulars being shipped to America, of seventy-two thousand British muskets being sent to arm Canadians and Negroes, and still Storrs had wavered. On April 29 John Hancock arrived in Hartford, having left Lexington hurriedly in the wee hours of April 19, and that day the Connecticut assembly seriously considered "Makeing a Declaration of the Ocasion of our Makeing warlike preperations & publishing it to the World"—something the Second Continental Congress would be debating just as seriously a year later.

By mid-May the weather in Connecticut was "Something Dry," Eph Storrs had made his decision, and on May 29, after prayers and a sermon, his company set off for Cambridge. Life in camp, he found, had its difficulties too. First off, he was nervous about taking command of the guard—a new experience for him. Then he came down with a bad cold, a result of the long march and too little sleep. When it came right down to it, he had not had a good night's rest so far, what with drunken soldiers roistering about, the unfamiliar sounds of the darkened camp, and frequent assignments to night duty. He was quartered at the Fairweather house in Cambridge, and this had proved an awkward situation at best. One morning when he came in off duty, hoping to get a few hours' sleep, there had been the devil to pay; Mr. Fairweather had returned home in foul humor the night before—the aggravations of sharing his house with Storrs's company having brought his temper to an understandable boil—and it had required all the lieutenant colonel's friendliness and tact to placate him.

Along with everything else, none of his men had enough beer

or soap, there had been a regular parade of visitors from Connecticut drifting into camp and taking up his time, his cold had developed into a bad cough, and Storrs began to wonder if his portly constitution was strong enough for a campaign. He suspected he would find out soon enough.

If any man had a right to complain of his health, it was Colonel James Frye, confined to his quarters on June 16 by an excruciatingly painful attack of gout. There was a strong fighting tradition in the Frye family, the colonel's brother Joseph having served in the last two French wars—as commander of the Massachusetts forces in '57. That year Joseph was captured by Indians at Fort William Henry, stripped naked, and gashed with tomahawks; but he lived through it and afterward his officers had presented him with a fine piece of plate for his courage. James had been through the fight on April 19 and was present at General Ward's first council of war the day following, but just now his disposition was not improved by the knowledge that his regiment would march tonight without him. He had turned over command temporarily to Lieutenant Colonel James Brickett, adding testily that he would join on the morrow.

Whatever else the men in the ranks may have guessed about their assignment, it seems certain that none knew their objective. Peter Brown, a young company clerk in Colonel Prescott's regiment, made that plain when he wrote to his mother nine days later. "Frydy the 16th of June," he reported, "we were ordered to parade at 6 o'clock with one day's provisions and blankets ready for a march somewhere, but we did not know where. So we readly and cheerfully obeyed, the whole that was called for, which was these three, Col. Prescotts, Frys and Nicksons regiments. . . ." (He was confused—it was Bridge's, not Nixon's, regiment that reported for duty that night.)

To the steady rattle of drums, something over eight hundred men from three Massachusetts regiments marched onto Cambridge Common soon after six o'clock, the cadenced thud of tramping feet muted by green turf, the bawled commands of officer and sergeants confined by arching elms overhead. As the ranks halted there was a self-conscious wriggling back and forth of the lines as farmers and shopkeepers still raw to the mysteries of close-order drill dressed on the men to their left, then came to uncertain attention.

An eyewitness of that assembly recalled that all the men wore small-clothes (trousers which fastened below the knee), long stockings, and cowhide shoes. In the main, their coats and waistcoats were overlarge, "with colors as various as the barks of oak, sumach and other trees of our hills and swamps could make them." The tricorn was not yet in vogue, and most of the men wore hats with a large round crown and broad brim. Glancing down the ranks, the observer could see almost as many types of weapons as there were men—"here an old soldier carried a heavy Queen's arm, with which he had done service at the Conquest of Canada twenty years previous, while by his side walked a stripling boy with a Spanish fusee not half its weight or calibre, which his grandfather may have taken at Havana, while not a few had old French pieces that dated back to the reduction of Louisbourg." The officers' swords had mostly been made by local blacksmiths, and while they were serviceable they were also heavy and ungainly. The only other fact worth noting was that almost no one carried a bayonet.

It is doubtful if the thought occurred to any of the men standing at awkward attention on that soft June evening, but in their own peculiar fashion they were the first of a long, long line of American battle contingents to be sent forth against an enemy in some kind of planned movement. To be sure, soldiers on this side of the Atlantic had been fighting Indians or Frenchmen or both as far back as they could remember, but until two months ago, they had not fought strictly as Americans. Before Lexington and Concord they had been soldiers of the King—not in the same sense as his redcoated regulars, but nevertheless fighters in his name and for his causes. And while April 19 was the first occasion on which men of this land had taken up arms on their own behalf, that day they were reacting to a situation forced upon them—

reacting in a manner largely unplanned, unordered, and very nearly uncomprehended until the smoke of battle had cleared. What was happening now was quite different, and whether they knew it or not, the results of their action would take on a significance totally unguessed at, its effects spreading out in ever-widening circles, like the rippled surface of a pond, until everything in their world and that of their contemporaries was touched by the thing they had begun.

The town of Cambridge itself—particularly that part of it which lay behind the men on the green—had already been affected deeply by the tide that had brought them here. Just west of the Common, bordering the long, gentle S-curve of the Watertown Road, were the great houses and estates of the landed gentry, the loyalists who had fled to the British garrison in Boston with what possessions they could carry with them. Back of Christ Church, what was known as Tory Row began with the Brattle estate, whose magnificent gardens stretched down to the slow-moving Charles. Until a few short months ago, William Brattle had been a pillar of the community—theologian, preacher, physician, lawyer, politician wrapped into one—but he had known what to expect if he remained in Cambridge. The Brattle grounds extended to those of Henry Vassall's widow, also departed, whose house was old even by 1775 standards, having been built before the turn of the century. Across the road stood Colonel John Vassall's mansion, one of the handsomest in town. The colonel had fled to Boston only recently, and before long his confiscated estate would serve as headquarters for the new commander-in-chief of the rebel armies, a Virginian named George Washington, whose appointment was announced by President John Hancock of the Continental Congress this very day—June 16—far to the south in Philadelphia. Next to Vassall's home was that occupied until September of 1774 by Judge Richard Lechmere, the owner of Lechmere's Point, who had been forced out of Cambridge by a mob. Then came Judge Joseph Lee's place, and beyond it, hidden by great trees, the mansions of George Ruggles (occupied now by a distraught Mr. Fair-

One of the stately mansions on Tory Row in Cambridge was the house above, owned by Judge Richard Lechmere, who was run out of town by a mob in 1774. Below is the Wadsworth House, built in 1726 as the residence of Harvard's presidents; here Samuel Langdon was living at the time the building became the headquarters for the rebel army's new commander, George Washington. (*Author's Collection*)

weather and Experience Storrs's men). Where the Watertown Road bent to the left before turning west was the estate of Thomas Oliver, last of the Bay Colony's royal lieutenant governors. Just ten months ago this house had been ringed with an ugly, shouting mob of patriots who presented Oliver with a written document, demanding his signature; and Oliver, fearing for his family's safety as well as his own, had read the paper, seen that it was a formal resignation of his office, and had written on it these words of protest: "My house at Cambridge being surrounded by four thousand people, in compliance with their commands, I sign my name, Thomas Oliver."

But to no avail. Judge, Colonel, Lieutenant Governor—the titles were as meaningless now as the broken world they represented. One after another they had gone, leaving the great houses empty behind them, pushed out by a force they despised and would never understand. In the master's stead, something called the Massachusetts Provincial Congress now deliberated what was to be done about grass growing too tall on the grounds. And a group of men appointed to look into the matter concluded that the Committee of Safety should hire someone to "cut the Grass and secure the Hay in some convenient place, for the benefit of the Colony."

June 16 was almost the longest day of the year, and behind the massed men on Cambridge Common the houses on Tory Row cast lengthening shadows, and the roofs were touched with the last echoes of a lowering sun that promised heat tomorrow. A soft gold light filtered through the towering elms onto the green, and in the stillness the only sound was the whisper of academic robes as the Reverend Langdon moved toward the center of the hushed files and took his place on a little stage. There was a rustle as the men removed their hats. No one ever recorded the prayer Dr. Langdon offered for them that evening, beyond the fact that it was a fervent and eloquent appeal for God's grace; but eighteen-year-old Joseph White, whose home was in Charlestown, remembered how the men formed a circle around the minister, in order to hear his prayer. "After which," White said, "they marched off towards Bunker Hill. I had a lame hand, and they would not let me go."

And so Joseph White saw them off in the gathering dusk of a June evening, heading down the Charlestown Road as the first few stars began to blink against the darkening sky. Stepping off in the lead was Colonel William Prescott, a tall, commanding figure in uniform, with a light, tan smock slung casually over one arm; behind him came two sergeants carrying dark lanterns, hooded so that only a flicker of light shone to the rear, to guide the marching columns.

There is no telling how the men who planned this night's work decided that William Prescott was to lead it, but they could scarcely have chosen better. Like many another local officer, he had fought in the French wars, having served with enough distinction at Louisbourg in '45 to be offered a royal commission when he was only nineteen. He had gone back to farming instead, but in 1774, when the time came for Pepperrell's minute men to elect a colonel, they had turned almost automatically to this big, quiet man whose judgment and courage they respected. There is a clue to their feeling for him in the way Corporal Amos Farnsworth called him "our own Col. Prescott."

The other ranking officer present was also a veteran of the French wars, with one of the most distinguished records of any man in Massachusetts. Colonel Richard Gridley had helped storm Louisbourg in 1745, he was one of the few provincials to go back there in '58, he had fought at Crown Point, and he had seen Wolfe fall on the Plains of Abraham. That service won him a British commission, the grant of a seal and cod fishery, plus three thousand acres in New Hampshire; but he had laid all this and his half-pay on the line to become chief engineer and chief of artillery of the Massachusetts Army on April 26, 1775. Not without recompense, however. In fact the Provincial Congress had shown an extraordinary burst of generosity in its eagerness to get this experienced soldier's services. They wanted him badly enough to pay him £170 a year while he was on active duty and £123 annually thereafter—a contractual arrangement made with no other colonel in the army. But Gridley at sixty-five was no longer the man he had been. There was trouble in his artillery battalion, and if he couldn't see it, some of the authorities were beginning to sense it. "Gridley is grown old," James Warren growled in a letter to John Adams, and "is much governed by a son of his who vainly supposed he had a right to the second place in the regiment." This last was a reference to Scarborough Gridley, currently a major in his father's outfit; but a point even Warren seems to have missed is the fact that another son, Samuel, had recently been made captain—all of which led to much grumbling in the ranks about favoritism. The battalion of artillery had been too hastily organized, it was woefully lacking in powder, ammunition, knowledgeable personnel, and guns themselves, and morale among the raw recruits was at low ebb. Just now there was no love lost on the Gridleys, and the men serving the guns would have traded all their colonel's experience for a younger leader with no sons. The Provincial Congress had caught rumblings of this discontent, for only two days earlier it had noted the absolute necessity of finding "proper officers . . . to command the Train of Artillery," and this very afternoon had asked the Committee of Safety for a list of potential candidates. Unfortunately a solution to this problem lay off in the future, and at the moment the forty-odd gunners in the Train were doing their level best to maneuver their unwieldy, creaking charges along the dusty road to Charlestown.

Ahead of the artillerymen, following the twin dark lanterns that beckoned them on like bobbing will-o'-the-wisps, were three hundred men of Prescott's own regiment, some two hundred troops under Colonel Bridge, and three hundred and fifty or so of Colonel Frye's command, led by Frye's lieutenant colonel, Doctor James Brickett. From the rear came the squeak and rumble of loaded wagons under Captain Thomas Foster's watchful eye.

The road out of Cambridge led due east, and almost as soon as the marchers passed the Harvard buildings on their right they left the little settlement behind and were in open country. From

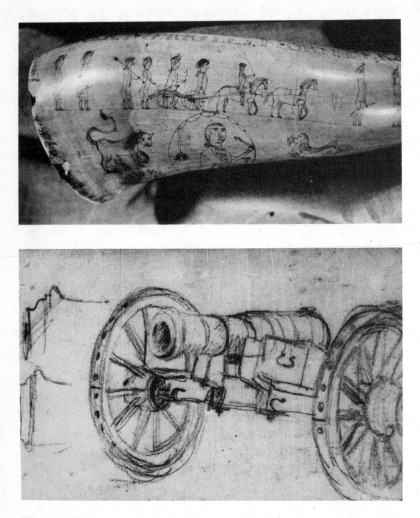

The unwieldy cannons of the Revolutionary period—made of either bronze or iron—were hauled by horses, as shown in the sketch at top. (The drawing, which is one of the rare contemporary depictions of Continental Army uniforms, was etched on a powder horn.) On the battlefield, cannoneers pulled drag ropes to maneuver the guns into position, and the barrel was raised or lowered by means of an elevating screw. Depending on the quality of the cannon and ammunition, and the skill of the gunners, the effective range was between 400 and 1,200 yards. The sketch below is by Charles Willson Peale. (*Collection of Harold L. Peterson; American Philosophical Society Library*)

here on there were few houses—mostly dark clumps of woods, orchards, farmland, with only an occasional dwelling of any sort. Spring had come early this year, and a drought that extended as far north as Exeter, New Hampshire, setting farmers to worrying about their hay crop, meant that the dust lay thick on the Charlestown Road, to be kicked into a choking cloud by some seventeen hundred tramping feet.

About half a mile from town their route skirted a hill and a little red house, off to the left, then leveled off at Pillon Bridge, which crossed Willis Creek. Here Putnam's earthworks still showed raw on either side of the stream, and the road headed northeasterly to avoid the swampy land into which Willis Creek fanned out before joining the wide sweep of water between here and Boston. To the right of the creek the land rose sharply to an abrupt knoll where Phips's Farm stood. In recent years it had become known as Lechmere's, for the Cambridge judge who married former lieutenant governor Spencer Phips's daughter and acquired his property. Beyond was Lechmere's Point, where General Thomas Gage's troops had landed on their way out to Lexington—landed in the drowned lands and stood in water up to their knees until 2 A.M., waiting for provisions they did not need, and cursing the luck that brought them there.

From Willis Creek the flickering lights of Boston could be seen plainly, and the dark shadow of the city looked for all the world like some huge swimming animal. Its bare, protruding back rose high out of the water to the southeast, then sloped off sharply to the head, which was North Boston. Here the slow-swinging masts of the Royal Navy pricked the sky, and off to the left a man standing on Pillon Bridge could see the edge of Charlestown peninsula.

Swinging along behind Colonel Prescott, the marchers crossed another bridge over another branch of perverse Willis Creek, and soon entered the valley that lay between Prospect and Cobble Hills. Here the lane from Ralph Inman's joined the Charlestown Road, and as they drew abreast of it the troops could make out the shadowy figures of other men, waiting quietly in the darkness. There were about two hundred of them—all soldiers from Old Put's Connecticut regiment—and they were commanded by handsome young Captain Thomas Knowlton, a lean, erect six-footer who was very nearly idolized by the men who served under him, and who already had acquired some reputation for leading the first Connecticut company up to Massachusetts.

There is no proof that Israel Putnam himself was here just then, but everything about the man's character leads one to suspect that the tough old Indian fighter was on hand with his men, eager for action, waiting impatiently for Prescott to appear out of the darkness. Putnam had his headquarters at Tory Ralph Inman's elegant house, but he was not in complete possession of it by any means. Even though her husband was in Boston, Mrs. Inman was here, and so were several of her daughters. Their home had been a popular place with British officers in the old days, among whom it was generally known that "Inman kept good cheer, and had pretty daughters." In fact, one of them had married Captain Linzee, who was now commanding the *Falcon* at anchor in the harbor. (Years later, in one of life's gratifying coincidences, a granddaughter of Linzee and the Inman girl married the historian William Hickling Prescott, grandson of Colonel William Prescott, and the swords used in 1775 by the Massachusetts soldier and the English naval officer finally came to rest, crossed on the wall of the historian's library in Boston.) Mrs. Inman was a charming, well-educated, handsome woman who had been married twice before, and who had, rather surprisingly for that day and age, carried on a business of her own between husbands, building up a tidy fortune in the process. Old Put seems to have been much taken with her.

Late that afternoon he told his son Daniel, a volunteer, to stay with her while he went off on urgent business. Daniel was just sixteen at the time, but long afterward he remembered his father telling him to "go to Mrs. Inman's tonight as usual; stay there tomorrow, and if they find it necessary to leave town, you must go with them." From this, Daniel knew that a military movement was under way, and begged his father to be allowed to stay with him. But Put refused gently, saying, "You can do little, my son, where I am going, but there will be enough to take care of me."

So the Connecticut men swung into line behind the Massachusetts companies, and before long the first ranks caught sight of Charlestown Common. To the right of their line of march a little stream wound sluggishly off through the salt marshes toward the open water of the Mill Pond, while the road itself ran through a sparsely settled, desolate stretch of clay pits, moors, and scrub growth. This was then the "common" of Charlestown.

In the middle of this forsaken spot, the files passed beneath the dreadful gibbet where the mummified body of a Negro named Mark had hung in chains since the day in September, 1755, when he had been convicted of poisoning his master. This stark, gruesome scaffold stood on the northerly side of the road, about a quarter-mile from Charlestown Neck; within ten yards of it was the place where Mark's accomplice, Phillis, had been burned at the stake. All the local men knew this site and the dark story that went with it, and a few of them shivered as they marched by in the gloom, possibly reflecting that the two Negroes had been convicted on a charge of treason against His Majesty George II. The thought may have occurred to some of them that the errand they were now engaged on was a far more serious offense against George III.

Before they had gone much farther the men realized for the first time what their destination was. At the narrowest part of Charlestown Neck there was a crossroads. The left-hand road ran past Plowed Hill, on to Ten Hills Farm, Winter Hill, and Medford. But here Colonel Prescott headed to the right, taking the fateful turning that led only to Charlestown peninsula and to Bunker Hill.

IV. Raw Lads and Old Men Half Armed

Beyond the narrow land bridge connecting Charlestown peninsula to the mainland the road bore right, skirting the dark mass of Bunker Hill which rose sharply from the low, marshy Neck. Up there near the crest of the hill, invisible now in the darkness, was a small flèche, or arrow-shaped redan, which the British engineer Montresor had thrown up hastily on the night of April 19 to protect the demoralized, beaten redcoats streaming onto the peninsula after their retreat from Concord. Although it dominated the only land approach to Charlestown, Gage had decided not to risk holding this lonely outpost, and now it lay deserted, an unclaimed monument to the first day of war. About a hundred yards past the Neck, where the road to Montresor's little fort branched off the main route, William Prescott halted his men while he conferred with several officers.

For nearly two centuries historians have quarreled over that meeting and the extraordinary decision taken there; but no one is certain who attended or what was said, and Prescott's council of war remains shrouded in the mists of time and the blackness of a June night, tantalizing and enigmatic. The only existing report of it is in a letter written on July 12, 1775 by Samuel Gray of Roxbury to John Dyer in London. Admitting that his information was secondhand, Gray stated that the engineer, Richard Gridley, and "two generals went on to the hill at night and reconnoitered the ground." There was an argument, Gray understood—one "general" and the engineer favored entrenching on both ends of Bunker Hill (presumably making use of Montresor's fort to cover their retreat, if it should come to that)—but "on the pressing importunity of the other general," this plan was discarded in favor of erecting works farther out on the peninsula. Bunker Hill would not be fortified; instead, a lower eminence southeast of it was chosen, directly across from Boston, and within range of the guns of Copp's Hill and the British fleet.

Certainly Prescott was one of the officers described by Gray, and it is hard to conceive that the other could have been anyone but Israel Putnam. Neither Ward nor Warren nor Heath was present, John Thomas and Greene were over at the Roxbury end of the lines, and old Seth Pomeroy, who had gone home to Northampton for a few days' rest, and heard there of the plan to take Charlestown, was still riding east. Not only does their absence point to Putnam as the third party; it is almost impossible to imagine the belligerent Connecticut officer sitting quietly at Mrs. Inman's while some of his men marched off to twist the lion's tail.

If, as Gray suggests, there was an argument over where to build the redoubt, the discussion must have centered on the topography of Charlestown peninsula. Very nearly an island, this mushroom-shaped body of land was about a mile long from the narrow Neck to its wide base, where it was separated from Boston by a 550-yard expanse of the Charles River. Along the northeast boundary flowed the Mystic, approximately half a mile wide; on the west the Charles backed up into a large bay, the end of which had been made into a mill pond by construction of a stone and piling dam about a quarter of a mile from the Neck. On the Mystic side of the peninsula, running from northwest to southeast, was oval-shaped Bunker Hill, about three hundred yards long and 110 feet high. To the south of it, and connected to it by a lower, sloping ridge, was a height of land not sufficiently distinguished to bear any particular name. Some called it Charlestown Hill; others, considering it an appendage of Bunker Hill, referred to it by that title;

while some of the local people, out of deference to a farmer whose cattle grazed there, called it Breed's. Its steep western flank, covered with orchards and gardens, leveled out near the settlement of Charlestown, whose two hundred and fifty houses had been deserted now for some weeks. On the eastern slope, parallel rail fences slanted down to the water's edge, separating the unkempt pastures of Messrs. Russell, Green, and Breed. None of these farmers had dared put out his animals or cut the hay in this exposed place, and the rank grass was almost waist-high on the heights. Below, meadows tailed off into an area of brick kilns, clay pits, and sloughy ground before rising again to the little mound of Morton's Hill, thirty-five feet high, atop Morton's Point, a swollen protuberance at the junction of the Mystic and Charles rivers.

Anyone looking at the peninsula from the vantage point of Beacon Hill in Boston would have seen it as a series of three nearly treeless hills, each slightly lower than the one to its left, stretching from the Neck to Morton's Point. But whether viewed from Boston or from Bunker Hill, it should have been apparent that the highest one—Bunker—was the only position which commanded an approach from the mainland or from any point on the peninsula itself. The short Neck was not accessible by water from the Charles side because of the milldam; and Montresor's redan, if someone had thought to enlarge it into a redoubt and equip it with cannon, could dominate the Mystic River, all of the roads, and the extent of Bunker Hill. Such a fort would have been beyond the range and elevation of British naval guns, and the cannon on Copp's Hill could have reached it only ineffectually.

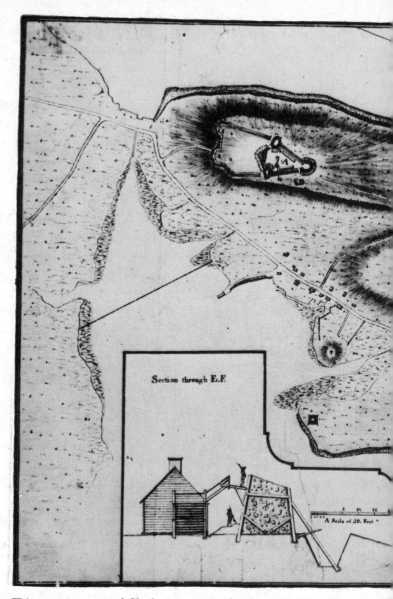

Section through E.F.

A Scale of 20. Feet

This accurate survey of Charlestown peninsula was made six months after the battle by John Montresor, a British military engineer. By then, the redan (A) he had constructed on the night of April 19 had been enlarged into a proper fort, a cross section of which is illustrated in the inset at bottom. The other re

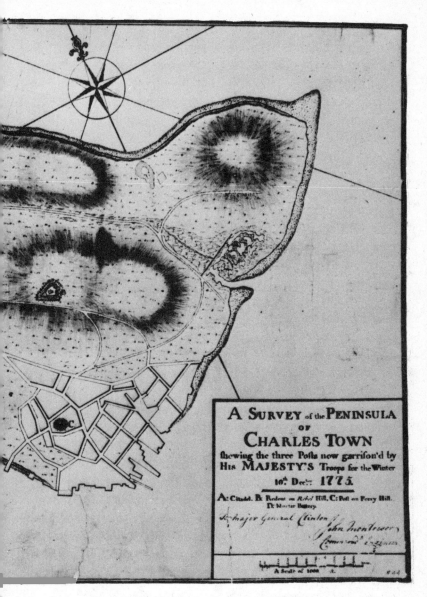

A SURVEY of the PENINSULA OF CHARLES TOWN shewing the three Posts now garrison'd by His MAJESTY'S Troops for the Winter 10th Decr 1775.

A: Citadd. B: Redout on Rebel Hill, C: Post on Ferry Hill. D: Mortar Battery.

By Major General Clinton
John Montresor
Command Engineer

A Scale of 1000 ft.

doubt is, of course, the one the rebels erected atop Breed's Hill. At upper right s Morton's Hill, rimmed by narrow beaches at water's edge. (*Clements Library, University of Michigan*)

Perhaps Prescott misunderstood his instructions, for he later wrote John Adams that he was ordered to march "to Breed's Hill in Charlestown." (The subsequent report of the Committee of Safety contradicts him, stating that Breed's was marked out for entrenchment "by some mistake.") Or perhaps the impatient Old Put, aware as a result of his May 13 outing that Breed's Hill was more exposed than Bunker Hill, closer to Boston, and therefore more of a threat to the city and to British shipping and a goad to British pride, argued strongly for its occupation in the certain knowledge that this would draw the redcoats out at last. Whatever the case, Bunker Hill was *not* fortified, and whether Putnam or Prescott or someone else made the decision to entrench on Breed's matters not one whit. Breed's Hill it would be, there the Americans would have their fight, and whether another location should have been selected was now beyond recall. The participants, their partisans, and several generations of historians could and would argue these matters for years after the thing was done, but all of that was hindsight, something neither Putnam nor Prescott possessed on the night of June 16, 1775.

Once the decision was reached, Prescott turned to Captain Nutting of his regiment and ordered him to take a detail down to Charlestown and keep a sharp eye out for signs of enemy activity. The men in the ranks were restive now, after what must have seemed an interminable wait; the word was passed for complete silence, and the main body began climbing the road that led up Bunker Hill and out to Breed's while Nutting headed down the dusty main route to Charlestown with sixty men, Amos Farnsworth among them. When Nutting's detachment entered the ghostly, abandoned village, sentries were chosen and "sot by the watersides" to patrol the lower town near the ferry. The rest of his men were quartered in the town house, with orders not to shut their eyes.

By this time old Gridley was worried. He didn't think much of the choice of position, and he was even more concerned by the unconscionable amount of time wasted in selecting it. It was getting on toward midnight, and under the best of circumstances the job ahead was a big one: how could a man lay out a proper redoubt on unfamiliar ground in the middle of the night? And how, for that matter, could amateur soldiers erect one in the darkness without alarming British sentries across the water? Daylight was only hours away now, and the engineer's elderly stomach reacted nervously the more he thought about it. As soon as he reached the crest of Breed's Hill he set to work quickly, trying to discern the lay of the land, then marking off as best he could the angular forms so often seen in the plans of eighteenth-century fortifications. When he had finished, Prescott took over, distributing working parties over the terrain, cautioning them to follow the engineer's lines, warning them again to be silent.

There was just enough starlight for the soldiers to see that they were in an open, sloping meadow on top of the hill. Gridley had staked out his fort—a box-shaped affair about eight rods square, or 136 feet on a side—near the back of this plateau, with one corner pointing toward the Neck and one at Boston. As a result, the troops would have a clear field of fire across the length and breadth of the hill on the two sides most susceptible to attack. The strong front of the redoubt, whose center was in the arrow shape of a redan, faced Charlestown and protected the south slope of Breed's; the eastern side commanded most of the sloping meadow and the likeliest approach from the Charles. On the north side Gridley left a narrow entrance opening, but in his anxiety to finish the job he neglected two items which an artilleryman, of all people, should have provided—platforms for guns, and embrasures through which they could be fired.

It was a warm, still, cloudless night, and a few minutes after the pick and shovel work began the clocks in Boston could be heard, tolling the hour of midnight. There was no talking, only the sound of stealthy movement, the shuffle of feet, the slush of spades sliding into dirt as one thousand men began to dig. Whatever other faults they may have had, whatever their lack of training and equipment, these men knew how to use a shovel. Nearly all were farmers, used to the heft of tools, and every account of that night tells of the speed and determination with which they performed their prodigious task. Down below them, virtually motionless in the slow-moving Charles, were the dark outlines of British ships; just offshore were the *Lively* with twenty guns, the *Falcon* sloop with sixteen, the armed transport *Symmetry* with eighteen, and the *Glasgow* with twenty-four. (Until the day just past, the enormous sixty-eight-gun *Somerset* had lain at anchor here, but Admiral Graves, worried lest the rebels set fire to the unwieldy vessel, had had her moved around to anchor off Hancock's Wharf.) Every officer and man knew there would be hell to pay if the watch aboard those warships got wind of what was up, and they worked with a kind of quiet desperation, glancing off toward the east now and again for the first signs of daylight that would mean discovery. Down in Charlestown, Amos Farnsworth heard the muffled sounds of spades picking up the earth, and listened through the long hours of darkness as the men on the hill "careed it on with the utmost viger all night."

These were anxious moments for Prescott, to whom every blow of a pick must have sounded like an explosion, and after the diggers had been at it awhile he sent Captain Hugh Maxwell's company to patrol the Boston side of the peninsula and watch for any signs of British activity. Twice during the night he and Major John Brooks, who had joined the party on this side of the Neck, went down to the river's edge to see for themselves that no alarm had roused the enemy camp. But all was quiet. The only sounds reaching them over the steady slap of the water were the deep boom of Boston's church bells, marking off the half hours, and the reassuring voices of drowsy sentries and the changing watch on the ships, calling "All's well!" into the darkness.

Back Prescott went to the works, goading the men to greater efforts, permitting no one to rest, keeping to himself the gnawing fear that these walls would not be completed by morning and that his raw troops would be exposed to the terrible, shattering fire of British cannon. He had seen big guns at work at Louisbourg, had

The awe-inspiring size and firepower of a British ship of the line like the *Somerset* is suggested by this detail from a contemporary English painting. (*National Maritime Museum*)

seen how mortar shells, rolling along the ground with their fuses burning so that no one could tell when or where they would explode, panicked the bravest of men. At one point he noted with irritation that old Gridley had vanished—"forsook me," was the way Prescott put it—and he may have been reminded of that June day thirty years ago, when the young Lieutenant Colonel Gridley's gunners, throwing shell after shell into the supposedly impregnable fortress of Louisbourg, had forced the Frenchmen to run and dive into the sea to escape the fiery hail of death. However full of patriotism Prescott's farmers might be, they could not stand in the open against trained artillery. The British, it was said, considered digging degrading work for soldiers, and fighting from behind earthworks cowardly and unprofessional; but Prescott agreed with Old Put—a Yankee didn't seem to care about his head, he was afraid of his shins. Cover him up at least halfway and you could depend on him.

The colonel moved about among his men, quietly encouraging them, giving advice, urging them to do a little more than they thought they were capable of, all the time keeping one eye on Boston and the British ships. His soldiers had had no sleep for almost twenty-four hours; they had not eaten since the previous afternoon; and by 3:30 A.M. they were dead-tired, hungry, and running short of water to relieve their dust-choked throats. About this time, the colonel sent word for Maxwell and Nutting to bring their companies back up the hill, and the sleepy sentinels tumbled into the raw fort just before the first faint glow of light streaked the eastern horizon.

Now there was nothing to do but wait. The next move was up to the British, and William Prescott, watching the day begin, could only hope that his men would meet it as well as they had carried out their night's assignment. He was pleased with what they had done so far, but he was also aware that a shock lay in store for them. Now and then a man looked up the road toward Charlestown Neck and cocked an ear, listening for something.

Prescott could see they were expecting relief, and he knew that none was on the way.

Entirely unknown to the Americans, Major General Henry Clinton had been reconnoitering during the night and had either seen or heard the rebels at work. Hurrying back to headquarters, Clinton had urged Gage and Howe to effect "a landing in two divisions at day brake." Howe agreed, and wanted to move against the provincials at once, but Gage "seemed to doubt their intention" and decided to do nothing until daylight revealed the extent of the American preparations. So Clinton went back to his quarters and wrote to a friend, relating his discovery and stating his "strong suspicions" that an attack on Charlestown would precede that on Dorchester Heights. "If we were of active dispositions," he complained, "we should be landed by tomorrow morning at daybrake as it is I fear it must be deferred till two."

Nor was Clinton the only one who had learned of Prescott's activity; the British sentries, according to Howe, "had heard the Rebels at work all night, without making any other report of it, except mentioning it in Conversation in the Morning." And incredibly, nothing was done. The British army in its citadel slumbered on, its sentinels sublimely undisturbed by the sound of an enemy at the gates, its commander heedlessly refusing to stir from his lethargy or interrupt his rest to investigate, to prepare, or to do the one thing that might have inflicted incalculable damage on the provincials—to act.

Fortunately for Prescott's peace of mind he was ignorant of all this, for he was having troubles enough of his own. As the gray dawn crept slowly across the landscape, revealing the outline of hills and harbor, the colonel discovered that someone had made a ghastly mistake. It was, to be sure, an error of omission—something which might not have occurred to anyone working in the dark and in rather considerable haste—but its import was urgently plain. Daybreak showed that the position on Breed's Hill could be outflanked on both sides. The enemy could ferry troops over from Boston, march leisurely along the bank of the Mystic or

From a vantage point on Beacon Hill, a Bostonian had this view of the North End of town and, beyond it across the water, of the village of Charlestown. (*Massachusetts Historical Society*)

through the streets of Charlestown, or both—all beyond effective musket range—and bottle up Prescott and his thousand men without firing a single shot.

Their predicament was equally clear to Peter Brown and his comrades, toiling away on the raw earth walls, who suddenly "saw our danger, being against eight ships of the line and all Boston fortified against us. (The danger we were in made us think there was treachery and that we were brought there to be all slain, and I must and will venture to say that there was treachery, oversight, or presumption in the conduct of our officers.)"

Brown had cause for concern. Aboard the *Lively* a sharp-eyed lookout had spotted the rebel works and passed the word to Captain Thomas Bishop, who was, just then, the unlikeliest man in Boston to let any challenge go unanswered. Bishop, rankling from a recent court-martial for neglect of duty and disobedience to orders, put a spring on his cable, swung the ship around so that her guns would bear, and at 4 A.M., opened fire. The first blast, shattering the dawn stillness, echoed across the water and shook the frame houses of Boston, rousing the British garrison and the townspeople from sleep. In one narrow street after another, doors and windows flew open to frame frightened, questioning faces. Soon messengers were racing in and out of Gage's headquarters; troops poured out of barracks as the drummers beat their anxious tattoo. Off in the camps around Cambridge men wakened with a start, listened, and when they heard a second shot and a third, knew they meant trouble.

Up in the redoubt Prescott's men had stopped their digging to watch a boat, lowered from the *Lively*, skim swiftly across the water toward Boston. Before long a signal went up from Admiral Graves to *Lively*, ordering Bishop to cease fire, and as suddenly as it had been broken, silence returned, uneasy and foreboding.

Prescott ordered his farmers back to work, taking advantage of any respite the British might give him to construct a protective breastwork for his left flank. He laid out an extension of the easterly side of the fort, running it in a straight line nearly 165 feet down the slope of the hill to the swamp. There would not be time to do anything about his right; he would have to rely on the houses of Charlestown and the walls and fences for protection over there. But almost as soon as work on the new breastwork began, the cannonade resumed, this time from several of the British ships. To the green provincials, totally unused to battle, the roar of artillery was terrifying, and although it had almost no effect at first—the guns were too light and could not be elevated sufficiently to reach the target—the incessant thunder of the cannon took its toll on the exhausted men's nerves. Then suddenly one of them was down. It was Asa Pollard of Bridge's regiment, who had been working outside the redoubt, and there was a moment of shocked silence and horror when the others saw he had been decapitated by a cannon ball. No one knew how many would be lost before this day was out, but Pollard's lonely, unspeakable death brought home to the witnesses, as nothing else could, a cold realization of what they faced. There was going to be hell to pay.

A young officer ran over and asked Prescott what to do about the casualty and was stunned when the colonel told him to bury him at once, without prayers. A little crowd of silent, curious men had gathered round the body, and a clergyman stepped forth, offering to perform a burial service. Prescott brusquely ordered them back to work, but in a few minutes they collected again, stubbornly unwilling to let Pollard be consigned to a grave without proper observance. The incident had its effect upon the undisciplined men, working on their fears, and before the parson finished his prayer they began to slip away, one by one, never to return.

Prescott knew he had to keep them busy—not only to finish the redoubt, but to prevent their panicking and disappearing en masse—so to reassure them he mounted the parapet and walked back and forth, ignoring the British shot and calling encouragement to his men. By now the sun was up in a cloudless sky and the workers in the redoubt, caked with dust, were beginning to feel its heat. Many, disregarding orders, had not bothered to bring a day's food and were now weak with hunger; a cannon ball had destroyed their two hogsheads of water, and the only source of supply was off in Charlestown. "We began to be almost beat out," Peter Brown recalled, "being tired by our labor and having no sleep the night before, but little victuals, no drink but rum." And above all there was a gnawing suspicion that treachery was afoot, that they were being left alone to die in a trap.

When Prescott's officers came up and urged that he send to Cambridge for relief, he refused, saying, "The men who have raised these works are the best able to defend them." Because of the heat he had taken off his uniform coat and put on the light linen coat he carried with him the night before, and as he moved in and out of the redoubt, oblivious to danger, bucking up his men and driving them to finish the job through the sheer power of his will, Peter Brown and most of the others decided to stay and see what happened. As long as the colonel remained, they would, and Prescott was not the kind of man who was likely to leave. Years later a veteran of the battle recalled, "I tell ye that if it had not been for Colonel Prescott, there would have been no fight."

Across the water in Boston, waiting at Province House for the three major generals and assorted aides to join him, Thomas Gage may have reflected that now, as in April, his carefully laid plans had gone awry. Somehow the rebels had learned of the move against Dorchester Heights and were anticipating it by forcing the British to attack at a place of their own choosing. Once again Gage had failed to comprehend the temper, the ability, and the resourcefulness of his adversaries (being of a predictable nature himself, he had misjudged completely the rebels' capacity for improvisation). If he had had any hopes of dealing with them from a position of strength, perhaps even of arriving at some peaceful solution, *Lively's* guns slamming their charges across the gray water sounded an end to them. Gage must have known that this was the beginning of a violent ordeal between England and her colonies, but he could hardly have guessed that it would go on for six years, sapping the strength and treasure of Britain, tearing asunder ties of loyalty and language and understanding that had gone into the making of an empire, undoing all the heroism and tenacity and wisdom which England had put into its creation.

It was apparent, as the sleepy major generals arrived, that a few hours' rest had done nothing to restore Henry Clinton's equanimity or to alter his opinion about what must be done. The early-morning council began on a note of friction, with Clinton arguing for immediate embarkation of the troops, to take the rebels in front and rear, before their works could be completed and before additional strength came up from Cambridge. The only possible avenue of retreat or reinforcement lay across the narrow Neck, and although the milldam prevented a British landing on the Charles side of the peninsula, Admiral Graves could bring floating batteries up to rake the Neck continuously and prevent the Americans from crossing in either direction. In fact the *Symmetry*, whose eighteen nine-pounders could overwhelm any cannon the rebels might have, could do the job alone; and if, while Howe led a frontal assault from the point of the peninsula, Clinton and five hundred troops went up the Mystic and seized the unprotected enemy rear, the cork would be in the bottle. As Clinton had perceived, the rebel fort was "incompleat no flanks, neither picketted pallasaded or ditched"—just an isolated outpost fairly crying to be gobbled up from two sides. If his colleagues would not agree to a landing on the Neck, another possibility for encirclement remained: disembark a flanking force on the Charlestown wharves, march through the town and back to the Neck, and the thing was done. But whatever plan they adopted, let it be carried out now—"at day brake," Clinton urged again and again.

As the sun rose, lighting the stage of Charlestown peninsula for the watchful audience in Boston, the high command could see that the rebel works were no more than a raw, dun-colored blotch, erupted like a pimple in the midst of a green landscape. The top of the middle hill was alive with antlike figures, moving restlessly around their heap of earth; cannon balls from the ships streaked hot, angry arcs across the pale sky, making dusty splashes in the lush green pastures where they fell; and as daylight pushed aside the darkness—and with it all uncertainty about what was going on across the Charles River—Gage and Howe and Burgoyne, at least, decided that they could swallow up the rebels with one determined attack. The hill, Howe observed confidently, is "open and of easy assent and in short would be easily carried." No roundabout encirclement, no complicated envelopment was necessary ("My advice was not attended to," Clinton wrote unhappily); they would have a frontal assault in the best tradition of Europe's battlegrounds.

Behind this decision lay a conviction that would influence the British officer corps until the end of the Revolution—that the Americans could not and would not stand and fight. Howe, writing to his brother about the decision to attack, did not even deign to call it fighting—the provincials were to be "removed" from the hill, he said contemptuously. Months after the battle, one officer was reminding an English friend how, during the French and Indian Wars, the Americans ("those of New England in particular") had, by their cowardice, earned the scorn of the British; Lord Rawdon would complain that he wanted to fight a "more reputable enemy" than these "scoundrels, for one only dirties one's fingers by meddling with them"; and another called the Americans the "poorest mean spirited scoundrels that ever surely pretended to the dignity of rebellion." Thoughts such as these persuaded three of the four generals to adopt the quick, bold plan and to discard Clinton's scheme, which accorded the rebels too much respect. (Two other men who were present at the conference may or may not have concurred, but they were to suffer the consequences of the point of view that prevailed: Lieutenant Thomas Page, Howe's aide, received a wound that cost him a leg; and Lieutenant Jorden of the Royal Navy was carried dead off Charlestown peninsula.)

On one point Howe agreed wholeheartedly with Clinton. There should be no delay—just as soon as the troops and boats could be ready, they would shove off. But between that wish and its execution there was to be a considerable gap; under any circumstances, an amphibious assault was a complicated maneuver, and besides, Howe's conception of time was a rather leisurely one. As he saw it, the proper landing place was Morton's Point, nicely removed from the redoubt and from snipers in Charlestown; but since the water was quite shallow there, it meant waiting for high tide —and high tide was not until three that afternoon. The thought seems not to have occurred to him that Charlestown had wharves and other landing places usable at low water, that his redcoats, supported by artillery, could have beaten off the few American skirmishers likely to be in the town, nor did he suggest that they land in shallow water off Morton's Point and wade ashore. "No delay," he said, but since this was to be an expedition, the troops would have to carry a full kit, with blankets and provisions, and bread must be baked and meat cooked before the men could parade. Every hour that slipped away was an hour gained for William Prescott's men, completing their redoubt, extending their lines toward the Mystic River, where Howe planned to attack.

Orders went out from Province House for the British army to prepare, and with them went the order of battle. Ten companies of grenadiers and ten of light infantry, along with the 5th and 38th Regiments, were to march to Long Wharf for embarkation; the rest of the grenadiers and light infantry, with the 43rd and 52nd Regiments, were to shove off from the North Battery. When these two assault waves had departed, the 47th Regiment and the first battalion of Marines were to march to North Battery and await further orders. A skeleton guard was to be left in camp, and all other troops were to be ready to move at a minute's notice. What this meant was that the elite corps, the flower of the army, was being sent against the provincials. In each British regiment there were eight companies of ordinary foot soldiers, a company of grenadiers, and one of light infantry. The latter were chosen for physical ability, and in battle they occupied one of the flanks, a position of honor. The other flank company was the grenadiers, the tallest and strongest men in the regiment, who had originally been used to throw small fused bombs but who, when this weapon was abandoned, were kept on as a picked corps of formidable fighters whose miterlike headpieces made them look even taller and more imposing then they were.

Thus every complete regiment in the British camp was to be represented by its flank companies—fourteen of them in all, split into two corps. In command of the light infantry was Lieutenant Colonel George Clark, of the 43rd Regiment, while Gage's friend James Abercromby was to head the grenadiers. Howe, as senior major general, would have the honor of leading the assault, and his second-in-command was to be Brigadier General Robert Pigot.

On paper, Howe's task force looked to be as nearly ideal as a commander could wish, and in terms of that day it was. But in the final analysis the success of his attack would be up to the individual infantryman, and if ever a man went into action under difficult circumstances, it was the eighteenth-century British soldier. Uniforms, modeled after the admired German style, were as ornamental as could be, and totally impractical. The brilliant scarlet coats, which made such perfect targets, had colored linings, facings, piping, lace, and brass or pewter buttons; waistcoats were either red or white. All men wore knee breeches, so tight that they seemed designed to cut off the circulation, and some regiments had long, buttoned gaiters which came well above the knee. The wide white belt, from which the bayonet hung, was also as tight as possible; a stiff collar and high leather stock restricted the movement of the head; and none of the awkward hats—some of them heavy bearskins—had either visor or brim to shield the eyes from sun or rain. The men's hair was usually worn in a queue or club stiffened with grease and coated with white powder, with tight curls in front of the ears. When fully attired and equipped, the British foot soldier carried a weight computed at approximately

Here, in full regalia, are a British drummer (left) and a grenadier officer. (*Courtesy, Trustees of the British Museum*)

125 pounds, and thus encumbered and restricted, he was expected to march into action and fight efficiently.

The weapon he carried was the smoothbore, Brown Bess musket, a four-and-a-half-foot gun that weighed about ten pounds and fired a three-quarter-inch ball. There was no rear sight on the Brown Bess, since the man who shot it was not expected to be a marksman. Nor did he get any target practice. Because a ball fired horizontally would only travel about 125 yards before it fell harmlessly to the ground, and maximum effective range was between eighty and one hundred yards, fighting had to be at close quarters, and fire-power, not aim, was what counted. This put a premium on volley-firing, with loading and firing executed upon command, which made up in sheer weight and frequency what it lacked in accuracy. Soldiers were taught only to point their weapons in the direction of the enemy, not to aim at them, and a really well-trained company could load and fire about fifteen times in the space of four minutes. To do so involved an extremely complicated operation. The gun was loaded by biting off the end of a paper cartridge containing powder and ball, shaking a little powder into the firing pan, closing the lid, and after resting the butt of the musket on the ground, pouring the remainder of the powder and the ball into the barrel, stuffing a wad of paper into the muzzle, and ramming it home. Then the gun was ready to fire. When the trigger was pulled the firing cock fell, striking flint against steel. The spark lighted the powder in the pan, fire flashed from the touchhole and into the charge, and the ball was projected. But if the flint was worn, if the powder was damp, if the touchhole was fouled—and these things happened with disturbing regularity—there was no explosion.

Yet the British troops, hampered as they were by their diabolically contrived uniforms, had at least two priceless advantages over the Americans: discipline and training. Their weapons were cumbersome, it is true, but they were used to them, and long hours of precision drill had taught them to load and fire almost automatically. For all the flaws of the Brown Bess, it was vastly superior to the average gun in rebel hands, as mixed a bag of firearms as can be imagined. And where the British ranks were largely full of veterans, the men behind those rebel guns were virtually untrained, almost without discipline, totally unused to the sound or sight of battle, and led by officers who were hardly more than enthusiastic amateurs. As the American general Charles Lee put it in his review of the battle, "The Americans were composed in part of raw lads and old men half armed, with no practice or discipline, commanded without order, and God knows by whom."

If Gage and his generals were confident, they had every reason to be. There was much to be done before the troops could embark, but in the meantime they could make things as uncomfortable as possible for the workers in the redoubt. At 8 A.M. the *Lively* cast off her mooring in the river below Breed's Hill, warped down to the Winnisimet ferry route off Morton's Point, which provided a better angle of fire at the redoubt and at the breastwork which Prescott's men were frantically trying to complete, and opened fire again. *Glasgow, Symmetry,* and *Spitfire* were in position abreast the rebel works and beginning to shell them; and at nine o'clock, to Admiral Samuel Graves's intense delight, the big twenty-four-pounders in his Copp's Hill battery began to boom. (One less partisan observer on the Boston side realized that the guns were doing little damage; each time Prescott's men saw the flash from the cannon, he said, "we could plainly see them fall down, and mount again as soon as the Shot was passed, without appearing to be the least disconcerted.") Graves had sent thirty-eight men from *Somerset* to the *Symmetry* to help man the guns, and eleven to reinforce John Linzee aboard the *Falcon.* Linzee was hauling his vessel upriver now by means of a spring on her cable, and by 10 A.M. *Falcon* would be close enough to hit the Americans with grapeshot and small arms. The thunder of cannon was increasing; when it was time for the troops to cross, the navy would provide all the support they needed.

It must have been about nine o'clock, with the council of war finished, orders issued, and subordinates off attending to preparations, when Gage left Province House to view the situation in broad daylight. (It was the one time he left headquarters, apparently; the rest of the day he was there to receive reports from Charlestown and from the lines at Boston Neck.) According to Abijah Willard, who was at his side while he studied the rebel works, Gage handed him the glass and asked if he could identify the tall, commanding figure on the parapet. Willard looked, turned to Gage, and said it was William Prescott, his own brother-in-law.

"Will he fight?" Gage demanded.

"I cannot answer for his men," Willard replied, "but Prescott will fight you to the gates of hell."

Prescott seemed to be preparing for just such an eventuality. By the time his breastwork was finished it ran almost to the swamp, but there was still plenty of ground beyond it for a British flanking movement. As the British gunfire intensified, it was clear that Gage was going to move against him before long; and the positions the ships were taking indicated the probability of a landing on Morton's Point. Prescott called a council of war to consider the situation.

His officers were unanimous in arguing that the men were in no condition to fight. Not only were they exhausted and without food or drink, but there was a dangerous undercurrent of fear and resentment over the fact that no relief had appeared, and desertions were beginning to leave big gaps in the ranks. Prescott was adamant—there would be no relief, he repeated; but he finally consented to send a messenger to Ward, requesting reinforcements and supplies, and shortly after nine Major John Brooks was told to get an artillery horse and ride to Cambridge. Being told to get an artillery horse and talking the artillery out of one were entirely different matters, however. In response to urgent pleas, four guns had been hauled up to the redoubt only recently, under the command of Captains Samuel Gridley and John Callender, and after they had blasted out their embrasures by firing through the walls of the redoubt, seven or eight additional shots convinced the artillerists that they would be better off elsewhere—preferably far

A sense of how the British in Boston were entirely hemmed in by the rebels is evident in these four sketches, which comprise a panoramic view of the American lines encircling the town. Drawn by a lieutenant in the Royal Welch Fusiliers, the panel above shows Dorchester Heights, in the distance beyond a British battery.

The second segment (above) shows Boston Neck at left and Roxbury, visible beyond John Hancock's mansion. The country between Cambridge and Charlestown appears in the third view (lower left). In the fourth panel, (below) to the right of the church steeple, are Bunker's and Breed's hills. (*Author's Collection*)

from the scene of action. As Peter Brown put it, "The captain . . . fired but a few times and then swang his hat round three times to the enemy, then ceased to fire." Two badly aimed balls had passed a hundred yards over John Burgoyne's head in the Copp's Hill battery, to hit a house and a fence in Boston; the others lodged ineffectually in the hillside. The only noticeable effect was to increase the cannonade from the British side, and most of the rebel gunners were thinking about pulling out. So when Brooks requested a horse they turned him down, with the incredible result that Prescott's messenger went for reinforcements on foot.

As Major Brooks strode along the road to Cambridge he met Israel Putnam, who was making his second trip to the peninsula that morning. When the sound of *Lively's* guns awakened him, Put had gone immediately to Ward's headquarters and then ridden out to inspect the redoubt. It was still early morning when he reported back to Ward, urging him to send reinforcements. Reluctantly, the rebel commander had ordered two hundred men from Stark's regiment to join Prescott. By the time Put crossed the Neck again, several floating batteries had worked in closer on the rising tide and were making things hot on the narrow spit of land. (Years later one American remembered his fleeting impression of Putnam at that moment: "Came on a horse," he said. "I expected to see him knocked off.")

Arriving at the redoubt, Putnam advised Prescott to send the entrenching tools back to a safe place while there was still time, but Prescott, who had seen men drifting away whenever they got a chance, disagreed violently. Not one man sent off with tools would return, he retorted; but he was overruled by the general, and soon a large party of eager volunteers began collecting picks and shovels and straggled off toward the rear. Some went only as far as Bunker Hill, and these Putnam put to work throwing up another breastwork; some kept going, across the Neck to the mainland and safety. As Prescott had predicted, none came back to the redoubt.

John Brooks was a twenty-three-year-old major at the time of the battle, long before he had his portrait painted by Gilbert Stuart. Later he fought at Long Island, White Plains, and Saratoga, and after the war served in the Constitutional Convention and became Governor of Massachusetts in 1816. (*Detail of engraving in Author's Collection*)

Putnam's early departure from Cambridge had made his conscientious second-in-command uneasy, and not long after ten o'clock Experience Storrs appeared on Bunker Hill to request orders. He and his chief conferred while the shot "whistled around us," he reported, and he stayed on awhile, fascinated, before returning to get his company ready to relieve the men on the hill. By the time he left, one man had been wounded in addition to the dead Asa Pollard.

It was ten o'clock when John Brooks reached Ward's headquarters in the Hastings house, and he found the commanding general in no mood to listen to his plea for reinforcements. Ward, who was suffering from a severe gall-bladder attack in addition to everything else that was happening to him, resented having been talked into the Charlestown move against his better judgment, and now that the fat was in the fire, he was damned if he would commit the rest of the army until the British made their move. Had anyone considered what would happen to the stores of food and ammunition if the army pulled out of Cambridge and left them unprotected? And who was to stop the British if they merely feinted at Charlestown and made their main thrust across Boston Neck? He had just ordered part of Stark's regiment to Prescott's aid, and until he got more information about what the enemy was doing, that was all he could take the responsibility for sending.

Fortunately for Ward's troubled conscience and for Brooks's peace of mind, the Committee of Safety was in session, and the two men broke in on that meeting with their problem. This was the nearest thing to a command post the Americans had, and the harried civilians were trying desperately to cope with the events set in motion by their decision to fortify Charlestown peninsula. Already that morning they had ordered the selectmen of neighboring towns to send all their powder to Watertown; already they had received a reply from David Cheever, of the Provincial Congress's committee of supplies, dolefully reporting that there were only twenty-seven half barrels in the magazine, thirty-six half barrels just received from Connecticut, and no more available from the towns. A secret dispatch had just arrived from Philadelphia with news that the Continental Congress was sending saltpeter, sulphur, powder, and five thousand barrels of flour for what they called "the continental army," but heartening as this announcement was, it was of no use today. The Committee of Safety had also requested "four of the best riding horses" for the use of express riders, but Cheever had no spare animals either.

At the moment, the Committee was minus its principal figure: Joseph Warren was stretched out on a bed upstairs with a splitting headache. He had worked late into the night, had been up early on congressional business, and the pressure was beginning to tell on him. In his absence, the opinion of Richard Devens prevailed, and Devens agreed wholeheartedly with Brooks that aid must be sent Prescott at once. Ward dispatched a message to John Stark, ordering the rest of his regiment, and Reed's, to march.

While these deliberations were going on, the British were beginning to move at last, answering the question which had plagued poor Artemas Ward all morning. Just after twelve o'clock long files of redcoats began pouring into the cobbled square at the foot of North Battery wharf, where they were spotted immediately by watchful rebels across the river. A rider pounded off toward Cambridge, dashed into the Hastings house with his fateful news, and before one o'clock the general alarm sounded. The bell in Christ Church began tolling ominously, one company drum after another beat out the call to arms, and the sprawling camps came to life as men grabbed muskets and fell in on the double. John Chester of Wethersfield, Connecticut, had just finished dinner when he heard the alarm, and was out on the road when Captain Daniel Putnam, Israel's son, galloped up. Chester hailed him: what was happening? "The regulars are landing at Charlestown," Putnam shouted, and as he kicked his horse and rode off, Chester turned and ran to his tent, picked up his musket and ammunition, and hurried over to the church where his company was quartered. Ordinarily these men were quite proud of their new blue uniforms—they seem to have been one of the few outfits in

Cambridge that were properly turned out—but it suddenly occurred to someone that those blue suits, trimmed in red, were going to be mighty conspicuous. "We were loath to expose ourselves by our dress," Chester said, so they pulled on dingy "frocks and trowsers" over their uniforms and prepared to march.

Although the British were known to be out, there was still no absolutely final assurance that the main strike was aimed at Charlestown. A frantic message went off from the Committee of Safety to John Thomas in Roxbury: "The troops are now landing at Charlestown from Boston You are to judge whether this is designed to deceive or not In haste leave you to Judge of the Nesesaty of your movements." Just what Thomas was to make of this is difficult to say, but he was already preparing for the worst. His scouts on Dorchester Heights must have seen redcoats moving down to the wharves at the same time the men on Charlestown peninsula sighted them, and by one o'clock he had his men stationed at their posts, ready for what might come. In the early afternoon General Israel Putnam, who had a horse but few aides and was therefore doing his own staff work, galloped into Cambridge to speed the departure of the rest of his regiment and find out what was delaying the reinforcements. Yet such was the confusion in the American councils that Put's own second-in-command, Eph Storrs, never reached the scene of battle. Apparently not even Putnam, just arrived from Bunker Hill, was certain where Howe's main attack would fall; for Storrs was told to march his men in the opposite direction from Charlestown, to Fort No. 1, well up the Charles River, where he waited in vain for the enemy to appear.

Possibly because of their uncertainty about British intentions, possibly because of the confusion in camp after the alarm sounded, Ward and the Committee of Safety were slow to commit the Cambridge forces. Nathan Stow, a sergeant in Colonel John Nixon's regiment, recorded in his orderly book that "Col Nixon Col Little Col Mansfield with their Reg'ts 200 Connecticut Troops with two days provision & ammunition march to relieve Col Prescott Col Fry & Col Bridge's Reg'ts Charlestown that they be well dressed before they march from camp and that they be on the parade at 4 o'clock ready to march." Another orderly book from Colonel Little's regiment repeats the four-o'clock marching order. What seems in retrospect like inexcusable caution must, in fairness, be balanced against the odds facing the rebel high command if they put all their eggs in one basket only to discover that they had picked the wrong basket. If the British move against Charlestown were only a feint, the main force could pour across Boston Neck, overrun Thomas, and be well on the way to Cambridge before troops could be recalled from Breed's Hill. Unquestionably, this thought was what prompted Ward to send Storrs to Fort No. 1, where he could backstop Thomas. At one o'clock that afternoon, the only solid information headquarters had was that the redcoats were preparing to embark. But how many were heading for Charlestown? Not until a more definite report came in from Prescott would they know, and Prescott was three and a half miles away and had precious few horses to carry messengers. Some of this indecision must have delayed the departure of John Chester's company, for he could not have set out much before three o'clock.

Fortunately, orders had been dispatched to John Stark when the alarm was raised. Stark and his New Hampshiremen were off in Medford, about four miles from Breed's Hill, and he had already sent off several hundred troops under Colonel Wyman in response to Ward's early-morning summons. When Wyman was preparing to march, Stark discovered that his regiment was not so well equipped as he had thought. The men were so short of ammunition that he lined them up in front of the house which served as an arsenal and distributed one cupful of powder, fifteen balls, and a flint to each—and that was it. Then they had to make up cartridges, which added to the delay and confusion, but as it turned out there were hardly two muskets of the same caliber in any company, so the balls all had to be melted and recast to fit individual guns. Then it was discovered that almost none of the men had cartridge boxes, so they stuffed cartridges into pockets, powder horns, and deerskin pouches, virtually guaranteeing that many would prove unusable.

Stark received word about two o'clock that the remainder of his regiment was needed urgently, and thanks to the advance warning he had had, there was no delay in getting the men under way. But they were almost too late.

Around one thirty a blue signal flag fluttered up the halyard of one of the British warships, and the loaded barges shoved off from North Battery and the Long Wharf. The British attack had begun.

V. A Most Awful, Grand and Melancholy Sight

The sun was blinding white, high in a clear sky. Inside the redoubt on Breed's Hill the dust hung like a motionless curtain, and men inhaled it with every breath they drew; sweat ran down their faces, little rivulets streaking the dirt and stubble of beard.

Across in the town of Boston and on all the surrounding hills, housetops were jammed with onlookers, spellbound by the great act of war unfolding before them, watching their familiar, quiet world erupt in a monstrous cacophony of noise and violence. Now all the warships were firing, their bearing sides exploding in sheets of orange flame followed by clouds of greasy black smoke rolling across the water. As far away as Braintree, where Abigail Adams held the hand of a little boy who would be the sixth president of the United States, windows rattled from the distant concussions, and people who could not see what was happening listened and wondered, as she did, whether "The day—perhaps the decisive day—is come, on which the fate of America depends."

As the loaded barges shoved off from Long Wharf, the British fire intensified, the gunners concentrating on the little rebel stronghold on Breed's Hill. Nine-, twelve-, and twenty-four-pound balls screamed across the water, throwing up spouts of dirt as they slammed into the hillside and the walls of the redoubt. One came so close to Captain Ebenezer Bancroft that it affected the sight in his left eye, leaving him with partial vision for the rest of his life, and moments later another sheared off Lieutenant Spaulding's head, spattering Prescott with his brains. The colonel stood there unconcernedly, calmly brushing away the blood and cleaning off his hands with a bit of fresh dirt.

But for one long, awe-struck moment the worn, dirty, shirt-sleeved farmers, staring over the walls of their earthen fort, had eyes and thought for only one thing. Before them was a sight the like of which no one had seen before, and whether they had an hour or fifty years of life remaining to them, it was something they would remember until they died. Even seasoned British officers, men who had seen the great armies of Europe line up before an attack, admitted they had never witnessed a scene such as this.

Across the third of a mile of water that lay between Charlestown and Boston came the barges—twenty-eight of them, two parallel lines of fourteen boats in single file, loaded to the gunwales with scarlet-coated British soldiers. Here was all the pageantry and color and drama of war in the eighteenth-century manner, the face of battle that caught at men's hearts and made them see it as beautiful and majestic and terrible all at once. The long white oars swept back and forth across the blue water in carefully ordered cadence, bringing the barges closer, ever closer, to the waiting rebels. In each of the two leading boats were six bright brass field-pieces; behind them came the flower of the British army, nearly fifty men to a barge, massed at attention. The glistening steel of their guns and bayonets made a thousand points of light, the sun glinted from polished brass and gleaming white, and the riot of blue and red and gold and white was reflected again and again in the shimmering water.

On and on the barges came, like lines of ancient galleys, sweeping ever nearer until men's faces were distinguishable beneath their hats; one by one the boats ground ashore, spewing troops onto the narrow beach at Morton's Point, big men, heavily loaded with muskets, blankets, and haversacks, who leaped out and jogged up the hill to form in long, disciplined lines. And as soon as they had unloaded their human cargo the barges turned again toward Boston and began their rhythmic crossing, this time to pick up some 450 additional foot soldiers, blue- and red-coated men of the Royal Regiment of Artillery, and the commanding officer of the assault force, Major General William Howe.

In all, 1550 infantrymen landed in the first two waves—plenty of troops for the assignment as originally conceived—and thanks to the pounding guns of the fleet and the Copp's Hill battery, there was no opposition. But Howe perceived, while he was en route across the Charles, that the situation had changed drastically, and soon after arriving he sent a message back to Gage asking for reinforcements at once. Beyond the redoubt, along the top of Bunker Hill, Howe could see a huge, milling throng of colonials which he took to be reserves; and at just about the time he landed he saw several bodies of men make their way through that crowd, hurry down the eastern slope of the hill, and take position on the flat shelf above the Mystic River. This put an end to his hopes for an unopposed flanking movement around the American left, and forced him to send for his reserve. But in the meantime he unaccountably revealed his intentions by ordering George Clark, commanding the light infantry, to take an advanced position along the water's edge. "I was sent immediately forward with four companies of the corps of light infantry within about 400 yards of the works of the enemy, where we lay covered under the bank of the water and other banks extending to our left," Clark said. And here they lay on their arms until the attack began. Forming the other troops who had landed, Howe pushed three lines up to the top of Morton's Hill, and there the men unslung their haversacks and calmly ate dinner while the general waited for support to arrive. Once again he was giving the rebels precious time to consolidate their defenses.

As soon as Prescott saw that the entire British force would land at Morton's Point, he ordered two fieldpieces to "go and oppose them." Considering the number of guns available to him, and what they would face, it was a pitiful gesture, and Prescott knew

An original sketch of the burning of Charlestown & battle of Bunker Hill. J.

By all odds the best contemporary impression of the battle is this water color by an English officer, who was an eyewitness. As the *Glasgow* (left) and the *Symmetry* fire on the rebel works, the village of Charlestown is almost entirely enveloped in flame and smoke, and the barges carrying the British regiments

across the water from Boston are nearing the beaches. The rebel redoubt is visible on the hill to the left of the fiery church in Charlestown. (*Emmett Collection, Manuscripts and Archives Division, The New York Public Library*)

it, but he had very few alternatives left now. He turned to young Captain Knowlton and told him to take his Connecticut men along in support of the artillery. Before long the detachment disappeared from sight beyond a clump of trees below Breed's Hill, and when they did not reappear where Prescott expected to see them, he could only assume that they had "marched a different course, and I believe those sent to their support followed, I suppose to Bunker Hill."

He was mistaken in this, but only partially. Captains Samuel Gridley and John Callender had their men seize dragropes and haul the four guns out of the redoubt in near panic, and indeed they made straightaway for Bunker Hill, claiming to all who questioned them that they were out of ammunition. But just as they were about to beat their teams into a gallop for the final dash to safety across Charlestown Neck, Putnam halted them, skeptical about their excuse, and throwing open the lids of their side boxes, found them full of cannon balls. Put ordered them back to the redoubt, but as soon as he departed the officers and men ran, abandoning their guns. (Old Gridley's other son, Scarborough, the major, had never even crossed the Neck to go out on the hill, but stayed on the mainland firing a few ineffectual shots at the British ships with his three-pounders.)

Thomas Knowlton, however, did what Prescott ordered him to do, and although he may have misunderstood the colonel's instructions as to the exact spot he was expected to defend, he occupied the first defensible position beyond the swamp, forming a line which ran almost parallel to the extended breastwork and about two hundred yards behind it—a line bounded on one side by a road leading up Bunker Hill and on the other by the bank of the Mystic River. As Lieutenant Dana, who was with Knowlton, described their position, they dug in "behind a fence half of stone and two rayles of wood. Here nature had formed something of a breast-work, or else there had been a ditch many years agone. They grounded arms, and went to a neighboring parallel fence, and brought rayles and made a slight fortification against musquetball." The result of their efforts was thus a double fence, with hay stuffed between the two lines of rails; and since the fence at the rear was on top of a low stone wall, with a ditch behind it, the position was stronger than it might seem. (One Englishman stated later that the completed breastwork was ten feet thick.) There was still a gap between the rail fence and the breastwork, however, and although the swamp in front of it would hinder Howe's advance, someone—Knowlton, possibly, or reinforcements who came up later—had the presence of mind to construct here three little flèches or V-shaped trenches, each one behind and slightly above the other.

For all his determination to hold his extended position, William Prescott had no staff, no communications that went beyond the sound of his own voice, and no settled plan other than a will to resist. Untaught, confused, tired officers, knowing next to nothing of what they were expected to do, moved restlessly among equally tired soldiers, assuming little authority and providing no real leadership. The men in the ranks were even more baffled by the train of events than the officers, but they kept at their work, those behind the breastwork still shoveling away, Knowlton's men tearing up the tall grass and stuffing it between rails of the fence, cramming stones, sticks, and anything they could lay hands on into the cracks in a pitiful, ostrichlike effort to seal themselves off from the foe—a foe which was just six hundred yards distant now, calmly finishing off its midday dinner and lighting a last pipe before attacking.

By this time the one serious hole in the rebel lines—the open area between the end of the rail fence and the Mystic—was being filled in. The men Howe had seen running down the hill as he disembarked were Stark's and Reed's commands, who arrived at the crucial spot at precisely the right moment. Fortunately for the provincials, the British barges had to make two round trips before Howe appeared on the scene, and this extra margin of time allowed John Stark to drive his men from Medford to Charlestown peninsula and get them into line alongside the Mystic River at the right instant to foil Howe's plans. Stark had had his troubles getting there, however. When he reached the Neck, it was crowded with men from two regiments who were afraid to cross in the face of fire from British ships in the river. The *Symmetry*, with eighteen nine-pounders, lay off Charlestown, and two floating batteries or barges, each carrying a twelve-pounder, had hauled in close to the milldam, and these three vessels were raking the Neck, preventing fainter hearts than Stark from crossing. As one eyewitness described the scene, "the low ground over which they were to pass was so continually raked by a constant fire from the ships and floating batteries, with every kind of shot, that it rendered it impossible to bring a proper number of men over." This was a spot where courage and leadership counted, and John Stark possessed both. Without a moment's hesitation, he started for Bunker Hill, ordering his men to follow; and when one of his officers suggested nervously that they quicken their pace, Stark fixed him with a withering eye and said, "Dearborn, one fresh man in action is worth ten fatigued ones," and walked on as before.

Putnam was in command on Bunker Hill, but Stark was not about to take orders from any Connecticut officer, nor did he need anyone to tell him what to do. He saw immediately the unprotected gap on the American left, pushed his men through the confused crowd on the hill, and led them at a trot down to the rail fence, where he joined Knowlton. Howe and the second contingent of redcoats were disembarking as they came down the slope, and Stark halted his men just long enough at the rail fence to deliver "a short but animated address," followed by three cheers, before having them extend the lines to the bank of the Mystic. Apparently some of the grass in these fields had been cut, for Henry Dearborn recalled how it lay in windrows and cocks, and the men gathered it up, stuffing it between fence rails as Knowlton had done in his sector, and repairing the fence as best they could. Their defense was scarcely ball-proof, but at least it gave the appearance of a breastwork and lent the men behind it some sense of security. Adding to that feeling was the presence

John Stark of New
Hampshire, shown here in
a contemporary silhouette,
had been a woodsman and
Indian fighter before the
Revolution, and during
the war was the kind of
tough, uncompromising
leader about whom
legends naturally arise.
Forty-seven years old at
the time of Breed's Hill,
he lived to the age of
ninety-three.

Thomas Knowlton's
promising military career,
which began at Breed's
Hill, was cut short when
he was killed leading his
Connecticut rangers at
Harlem Heights the
following September.
(*Anne S. K. Brown
Military Collection,
Brown University Library*)

of Major Andrew McClary, a giant nearly six and a half feet tall, who was everywhere, bolstering their courage, giving encouragement and advice, seeing that all was in readiness. McClary was one of the most popular officers in the New Hampshire camp and was already something of a hero as a result of planning and leading a raid on the Castle at Portsmouth in December of 1774, five months before Lexington, when many of the muskets now carried by the New Hampshire regiments had been seized.

When Stark went over to the riverbank, where the fence ended, and saw that the steep bank fell off about eight or nine feet to a narrow beach, he realized at once that the British could march in complete safety along the water's edge, just below the little cliff. He hailed "his boys" and had them bring stones to make a wall right down to the river, and behind it he posted a triple row of defenders.

The American line was now as complete as it was ever going to be, and a British soldier scanning it from the vantage point of Morton's Hill would have seen four distinct elements from left to right: the redoubt, the breastwork, the rail fence, and the stone wall on the beach. (Between the end of the breastwork and the beginning of the fence was the gap in which the three flèches had been built.) When the battle began, the redoubt and breastwork were manned by the remains of Prescott's Regiment and parts of Brewer's, Bridge's, Nixon's, Woodbridge's, Little's, and Doolittle's Massachusetts Regiments (the last commanded by Major Willard Moore); the fence by Knowlton's Connecticut troops, Reed's New Hampshiremen, and portions of Stark's Regiment; the stone wall on the beach by Stark and the rest of his command. The extreme American right consisted of two unfortified positions: a little cartway along a fence, between the redoubt and Charlestown, where a company of Little's Regiment and a few other troops, among them Nutting's company, had been posted; the main street of Charlestown, at the bottom of Breed's Hill, where three companies from Doolittle's, Reed's, and Woodbridge's Regiments were stationed.

Unlike John Stark, who knew where to go and what to do when he got there, most rebel officers did not, or were not so inclined. Colonel Scammon of the Massachusetts Army was subsequently tried for "backwardness in the execution of his duty" (a nice way of saying cowardice), one witness testifying that as soon as the regiment got near Bunker Hill, where the shot was flying thick and fast, the colonel ordered a general retreat. Yet from other evidence given at the trial it appears that Scammon's trouble was as much confusion as cowardice, and in this respect he was no different than many another officer. Behind the lines the situation was chaotic. Of nine Massachusetts regiments ordered out from Cambridge at the time of the alarm, only five were even partially represented on the field when the British attacked. Whole regiments and fragments of regiments went astray, wandering hither and yon because their commanders either misunderstood or disobeyed orders, or because the orders were uncertain or garbled to begin with. Some halted on the wrong side of the Neck, some went no further than Bunker Hill, some headed in the wrong direction altogether. As one informant wrote Sam Adams after the battle, "To be plain it appears to me there never was more confusion and less command. No one appeard to have any but Col. Prescott whose bravery can never be enough acknowledged and applauded.—General Putnam was employd in collecting the men but there were not officers to lead them on." What orders Ward may have issued no one knows; but in addition to Scammon's regiment, parts of Brewer's, Gerrish's, Little's, and Nixon's, at least, were under arms and marching about with only the foggiest notion of what they were supposed to accomplish. Poor old Eph Storrs, who had marched his men in vain in the opposite direction from Charlestown, up to Fort No. 1, tried just as futilely to get them back to Bunker Hill, but the battle was over by the time he arrived. One man who did get his orders straight that day was Sam Trevett, who salvaged what little reputation the artillery had left by bringing two guns from Cambridge in time to join Knowlton and Stark behind the rail fence. The evidence indicates that

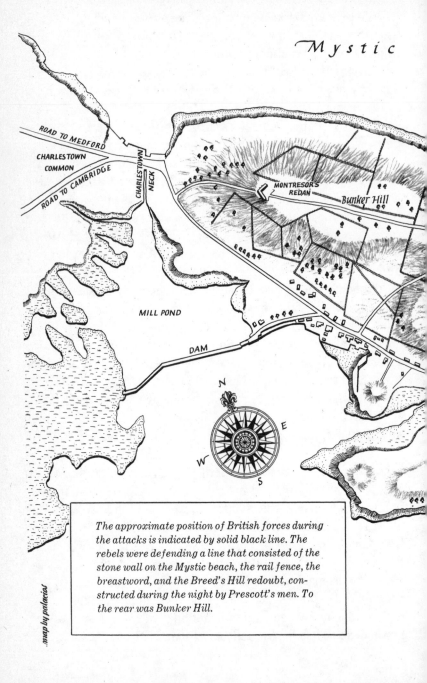

Mystic

ROAD TO MEDFORD

CHARLESTOWN COMMON

ROAD TO CAMBRIDGE

CHARLESTOWN NECK

MONTRESOR'S REDAN

Bunker Hill

MILL POND

DAM

N
E
W
S

map by palacios

The approximate position of British forces during the attacks is indicated by solid black line. The rebels were defending a line that consisted of the stone wall on the Mystic beach, the rail fence, the breastword, and the Breed's Hill redoubt, constructed during the night by Prescott's men. To the rear was Bunker Hill.

yards 0   100   500

River

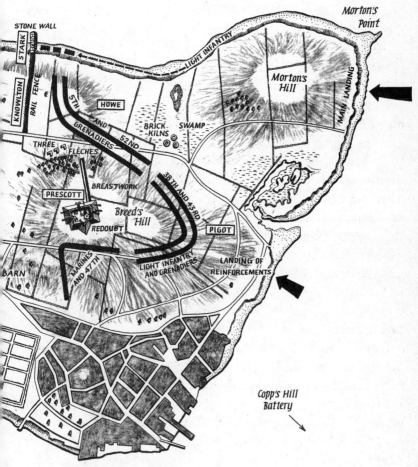

Morton's Point

STONE WALL

STARK

LIGHT INFANTRY

Morton's Hill

MAIN LANDING

KNOWLTON

RAIL FENCE

5TH AND GRENADIERS 52ND

HOWE

BRICK KILNS

SWAMP

THREE FLÉCHES

BREASTWORK

38TH AND 43RD

PRESCOTT

Breed's Hill

REDOUBT

PIGOT

BARN

MARINES AND 47TH

LIGHT INFANTRY AND GRENADIERS

LANDING OF REINFORCEMENTS

CHARLESTOWN

Copp's Hill Battery

Charles River

these guns were ably served that day. Ensign Studholme Brown-rigg of the 38th Regiment, saying that the cannon were "very advantageously planted behind a fence on a flat to the right of the rear of the redoubt," was impressed by the exceptionally heavy fire repeated "with the greatest vigour."

It is difficult to imagine anyone who could have been spared less easily by the Provincial Congress and Committee of Safety than Joseph Warren, but Warren operated on the theory that major generals were supposed to fight, and since he was a newly commissioned one, minutes after the alarm sounded in Cambridge he was heading toward Charlestown with young Dr. Townsend, one of his medical students. Along the way someone must have recognized him and given him a horse, for two of his friends subsequently reported that Warren had overtaken them on horse-back, exchanged greetings, and disappeared down the Charles-town Road. He reached the Neck between two and three o'clock when the British cannonade was at its height, and made his way up the northwest side of Bunker Hill, where he found another of his students, William Eustis, on duty as a surgeon. James Brickett, who had led the ailing James Frye's regiment onto the hill the night before, was there also; he had been wounded slightly, and had left the redoubt in order to serve on Bunker Hill as a physi-cian. When he learned that Warren was planning to fight, he gave him his musket.

Putnam caught sight of Warren and came over to ask for orders, but the doctor refused, saying he had come as a volunteer. (Even in all the din and confusion, the contrast between these two must have occasioned a smile from the soldiers: Warren the man of intellect, tall and handsome in his best clothes; Old Put the man of action, his shirt sleeves rolled up and a battered hat on his head.) After asking where he could be of most use, Warren went out to the redoubt, where Prescott also offered to relinquish his command. Again Warren refused, saying, "I have no command here; I have not received my commission"; and before taking his place in the line, he added a graceful word about how he would consider it a privilege to fight under Prescott.

Another volunteer who apparently showed up about this time was Seth Pomeroy, a veteran of the Indian wars, who had gone home to Northampton for a few days' rest and hurried back when he heard that Charlestown was threatened. He had started riding east at noon the day before, and a story is told of his arrival at the Neck on a borrowed horse; he watched the balls flying across the narrow strip of land, then handed the reins to a bystander, saying it was "too valuable an animal to be shot," and walked out to Bunker Hill. Pomeroy was seventy years old and a recently elected general of the Massachusetts Army, but like Warren, he had not received his commission, and turned aside Putnam's offer of command. Supposedly he went down the hill to join John Stark's men at the rail fence, and, loading the gun he had made himself and carried thirty years earlier at the siege of Louisbourg, awaited the British attack.

While waiting for his reserve, William Howe saw the last sizable gap in the rebel line filling up, saw what looked like a breastwork being erected on the American left, and concluded that some armed boats, sent up the Mystic to a point behind the rail fence, could drive the farmers out of their lines easily; so he ordered that useful pair of floating batteries over by the milldam to suspend action there and come around to the Mystic side. An hour or so earlier the plan would have worked, but the tides were with the Americans this day, and once the boats left their anchorage they could not work their way up either river again. While this abortive maneuver was in progress, Howe turned his attention to his own left wing, fearful that the rebels in Charlestown might turn his flank or at least cause trouble during the attack. Snipers were beginning to annoy the British even at long range, so Howe posted a regiment on the left to protect his advance on that side and, turning to Admiral Graves, asked if the fleet could assist in routing the provincials from the town. Graves asked eagerly if Howe wanted the place burned, and when the general agreed, signaled the ships to fire red-hot balls, which had been prepared for just such an eventuality, into the town. The Copp's Hill battery was instructed to shoot carcasses, or balls containing combustibles, and before long a landing party came ashore at the eastern end of town and put the buildings to the torch. ". . . the town was immediately set in flames," Henry Hulton wrote, and, "we saw the fire and the sword, all the horrors of war raging."

And now Howe's reserve reached him; between Morton's Point and Charlestown landed the grenadier and light infantry companies which had been left behind at the North Battery. (The boats carrying them were under the command of Midshipman Cuthbert Collingwood, who would one day succeed the dying Admiral Horatio Nelson at Trafalgar.) Along with them came the 1st Marines and the 47th Regiment, giving the English general some twenty-two hundred rank and file, plus his artillery. As soon as they were in position he formed his men into two wings, with Pigot commanding the left and himself the right.

The plan of attack was a simple one. Howe had sized up the American left as the weak point, for it was logical to assume that men who had taken a position only an hour or so earlier would have had far less opportunity to fortify than those who had been working all night in the redoubt. Therefore, the British right wing would strike the hammer blow, with the elite light-infantry companies advancing in columns along the narrow beach to overrun the low stone wall and sweep in behind the defenders at the rail fence; while the big grenadiers, supported by the 5th and 52nd Regiments, advanced in two lines against the fence. The flank companies—light infantry and grenadiers—not only had the advantage of physically stronger men and better training, they also averaged about thirty-two men each, to twenty-six for the regular battalion companies. Although the paper strength of a regiment was 360, almost none achieved that number, but averaged closer to three hundred effectives.

Although Howe had taken most of the picked men from the flank companies for what was to be the decisive attack, Pigot nevertheless had three companies each of light infantry and grenadiers, plus the 38th, the 43rd, and 47th Regiments, and the 1st Marines. Both wings were approximately equal, Howe having thirty-seven companies and Pigot thirty-eight, and Howe planned to roll up the American left and charge in on the redoubt from behind while Pigot moved around the fringe of Breed's Hill, skirting the houses of Charlestown, and struck the redoubt from that side. The British general saw no reason for the attackers to stop and fire: the assault would be made with the bayonet alone—cold steel was the proper antidote for rebellion.

Just before the signal was given for the advance, Howe apparently addressed his men in the eighteenth-century manner. (Both Warren and Stark supposedly did the same.) He knew they would behave like Englishmen and good soldiers, he said, and he would not ask one of them "to go a step further than where I go myself at your head"—a promise he kept.

About three o'clock the long lines of British infantry stepped off, their advance heralded by a sharp cannonade from two twelve-pounders on Morton's Point, while out in front one of the grenadier companies pushed forward the little sixes for closer work. Almost at once these light guns were in difficulty; there was trouble getting them through the soft clay and swampy ground at the foot of Morton's Hill, and the gunners discovered to their dismay that the side boxes were filled with twelve- instead of six-pound balls. The men blamed Colonel Samuel Cleaveland, the chief of artillery, for this; one officer wrote that "The wretched blunder of the over-sized balls sprung from the dotage of an officer of rank in that Corps, who spends his time in dallying with the schoolmaster's [John Lovell's] daughters."

But Howe had no time for recriminations now; he sent immediately for the proper balls, ordering the substitution of grapeshot until they arrived, but the range was too much for grape and the guns were temporarily worthless. However, the ships' cannon, those on Copp's Hill, and the twelve-pounders on Morton's Hill concentrated their fire on the rebel works, and with this support the redcoats pushed forward. The Americans noticed that it was "a very slow march."

Off to the right along the narrow strip of beach, the light infantry led the way, with a company of the famous Welch Fusiliers, the 23rd Infantry, out in front. Four abreast, eleven companies marched in precise columns, their bright uniforms sparkling in the sun, bayonets gleaming, the men's eyes trained on the low stone wall in the distance.

To their left came the long, double battle line, stretching nearly halfway across the peninsula. This was a parade march, with ten companies side by side—some three hundred scarlet-coated men— marching forward on the broad front, followed by another wave of ten companies in step behind them, and these two lines were duplicated farther to the left, as Pigot's wing began its advance. The day was fiercely hot, and the British soldiers, steaming in red woolen uniforms, were loaded with three days' provisions, blankets, cartouche boxes, ammunition, and muskets—about the same weight as if they carried a good-sized deer on their backs. The unmown grass through which most of the battle line had to maneuver was thick and high, reaching almost to the waist in places, and concealing—as anyone who has walked through an uncut New England meadow knows—countless rocks and potholes. There were ten or twelve stone walls and fences to clamber over, a brick kiln, swamps, and sticky clay; and for Pigot's troops the going was all uphill. To those straining for a glimpse of the action from a Boston rooftop, it was like a scene from a picture book—a scarlet and white ribbon of toy soldiers, contrasting coats and breeches bright above the green grass, helmets and bayonets flashing in the blazing sun, the ribbon undulating and curling as the tiny figures sought to keep their ranks straight. Portions of the lines stopped at times, slowed by fences (Burgoyne said they "met with a thousand impediments from strong fences," and Howe complained that these obstructions broke the perfection of his line); again they halted to let the fieldpieces come up and fire. To the onlookers in Boston this snaillike progress made the suspense almost unbearable, and the waiting Americans would remember vividly that "deliberate march," that approach "with a slow step."

At the western end of the peninsula the village of Charlestown was in flames, "a most awful, Grand and Melancholy Sight," one young loyalist said. To John Burgoyne, watching from the battery on Copp's Hill, it was "one of the greatest scenes of war that can be conceived: if we look to the height, Howe's corps, ascending the hill in the face of intrenchments, and in a very disadvantageous ground, was much engaged; to the left the enemy pouring in fresh troops by thousands, over the land; and in the arm of the sea our ships and floating batteries cannonading them; straight before us a large and noble town in one great blaze—the church-steeples, being timber, were great pyramids of fire above the rest; behind us, the church-steeples and heights of our own camp covered with spectators of the rest of our army which was engaged; the hills round the country covered with spectators; the enemy all in anxious suspense; the roar of cannon, mortars and musketry; the crash of churches, ships upon the stocks, and whole streets falling together, to fill the ear; the storm of the redoubts, with the objects above described, to fill the eye; and the reflection that, perhaps, a defeat was a final loss to the British Empire in America, to fill the mind—made the whole picture, and a complication of horrour and importance, beyond any thing that ever came to my lot to be witness to."

Behind their earthworks and flimsy fences the rebels watched and waited; men faint with hunger and fatigue, dirty farmers in floppy felt hats and homespuns, fingering their muskets nervously, feeling instinctively for spare cartridges, anxiety and disbelief welling up in their dry throats as the finest infantry in the world moved closer and closer, threatening to engulf them. Peter Brown had the sensation that "they advanced towards us in order to swallow us up." Just behind the firing line, officers crouched low and moved swiftly back and forth, passing the word to shoot low, to wait for the order to fire, to pick out the officers and aim for the crossing of the belts, to wait until they could see the whites of

BOSTON

What this primitive painting may lack in accuracy of detail it makes up in spirit and in the general tenor of the battle. While the neat, orderly ranks of redcoats climb the slope of Breed's Hill, ships fire on the rebel works and shells

from the Copp's Hill battery arch over the Charles River. (*National Gallery of Art, Washington, D.C., Gift of Edgar William and Bernice Chrysler Garbisch*)

their eyes. And the red tide moved slowly nearer, near enough now so the defenders could distinguish faces beneath the tall pointed helmets, make out rows of shining buttons and belt buckles. Now and again there was a strange moment of silence—the big guns had stopped firing, for fear of hitting their own men—broken only by the steady dull thump of marching feet, the swish of long grass as two thousand men pushed through it, the crackle of flames and the occasional splintering crash of a building in Charlestown.

Over along the beach Howe's light infantry moved forward rapidly across the level, unobstructed sand, and the long, lancelike column was almost close enough to charge. Still there was silence behind the rebel barricade, no sign of movement. The British were only two hundred feet away, then one hundred, now fifty, when a row of dull musket barrels leveled along the stone wall, a nasal New England voice twanged, and the wall disappeared in a sheet of flame and oily black smoke. The blast of fire tore apart the leading ranks of Fusiliers, and as the rows behind closed up they were shattered by the violent hail of bullets. Officers fell, men spun around and dropped headlong into the shallow water, and the column stopped, recoiled, then came on again, the King's Own Regiment shoving through the broken Fusiliers, clambering over the dead and wounded only to be met with that withering fire from the wall. Officers' voices shouted hoarsely through the din, ordering the men forward, but with each advance the men in the lead simply melted away, falling grotesquely and piling up the awful carnage on the narrow beach until there was nothing to do but turn back. And turning back, the men began to run, terror-stricken, pelting along the wet sand toward safety. Behind them the defenders peered through thick smoke that lay like a greasy blanket around the stone wall, saw their flight, saw the fallen "as thick as sheep in a fold," the dead floating crazily on the ebbing tide, the shallow water lapping red against the sand.

The flank attack on which Howe's hopes rested was shattered. Reverend Peter Thacher, watching from the Chelsea side, saw the light infantry retreat "in very great disorder down to the point where they landed, & there some of them even into their boats; at this time their officers were observed by spectators on the opposite shore to . . . use the most passionate gestures & even to push forward ye men with their swords." There could be no retreat; even though the flank attack had failed, Howe could still rely on his long line of grenadiers and regulars and a direct frontal blow. These men, advancing steadily on the level above and out of sight of the beach, had been delayed by the long grass, the rough terrain, and the fences, and just as they were readying for the charge heard the great roll of musketry off to their right and the screams of wounded men. There was one last fence to cross before they could attack, and they had just clambered over it and were forming for the charge when a few defenders behind the rail fence opened on them.

Lieutenant Knowlton had given orders not to fire until the enemy came within fifteen rods, and then not until the word was given. But Lieutenant Dana told his friend John Chester that he had been the first to shoot, "and that he did it singly, and with a view to draw the enemy's fire, and he obtained his end fully, without any damage to our party. Our men then returned the fire, well-directed, and to very good effect, and so disconcerted the enemy that they partly brok[e and re]treated. Many of our men were for pursuing, [but by] the prudence of the officers they were prevented lea[ving s]o advantageous a post." It is hard to believe that Dana alone forced the redcoats to fire, but whatever the cause, apparently they halted to do so and were struck at that moment by a blast from the rail fence that shattered their lines. By some miracle, Howe was not hit, but all around him officers and aides were down, and his tough grenadiers fell by threes and fours, leaving gaping holes in that once-perfect line. They loaded again and fired, but their aim was hurried and the bullets went over the Americans' heads, while the standing, redcoated figures made perfect targets for the defenders, sighting their pieces along the fence rails. The line of regulars, coming up behind the grenadiers, was torn apart by the murderous volleys, and at last both lines turned and ran out of range, too badly mauled to continue.

Off on the British left, Pigot's lines had advanced slowly in what was intended only as a feint or delaying action, while Howe's forces should punch through on the right. In spite of the raging fire in the streets of Charlestown, rebel skirmishers there harassed Pigot so effectively that his men were unable to mount a real attack on the redoubt, and when he saw what had happened to Howe he called them back.

Along the entire British line the attack had failed, and behind their bulwarks ragged defenders jumped with joy at the sight of those redcoated backs dashing for cover. Captain Benjamin Mann, of Reed's Regiment, said "a portion of the company twice passed the fence huzzaing, supposing, at the time, that we had driven the enemy." In every section of the rebel defenses, the troops were jubilant with the realization that they had repulsed a frontal attack by the famous regulars. Ninety-six British dead lay on the beach alone, and all over the field were prone bodies, scattered pieces of equipment, the wounded crying piteously, some trying to drag themselves back to their lines. And it had all been done so easily, at so little cost to the Americans. Only Prescott and Stark and a few others knew that the battle was far from won, and they walked back and forth along their lines, praising the men, encouraging them, reminding them that there would be more work to do. By now Prescott had only one hundred and fifty men left in the redoubt; another two hundred or so were behind the breastwork, and there were between four and five hundred along the American left, posted behind the rail fence and the stone wall—a force, in all, of no more than seven hundred or a thousand. Peering out of the redoubt, Peter Brown estimated that there were only seven hundred "of us left not deserted"—a bitter reference to those who had slipped out of the lines since last night. Up on Bunker Hill there were hundreds of men, probably as many or more than there were at the front, but few of them had any intention of moving into a more exposed position. Putnam had a good many at work with picks and shovels, preparing a second line of defense up there on the hill, but he was far too busy rallying men, sending for help, riding back and forth between the hill and the front lines, trying to create some kind of order out of chaos, to see that the work progressed as it should. Besides, the milling stragglers were too interested in what was going on below to accomplish much of anything, with the result that most did nothing. Reinforcements from the Cambridge camps had arrived at the Neck, but few were willing to risk a crossing, despite the fact that the *Symmetry* was now the only vessel firing. Putnam may have done everything he could to get men down to the redoubt and the rail fence, but only a handful ever came.

Within a quarter of an hour Howe had reformed his broken ranks, but this time he decided not to assault that murderous stone wall on the beach. He regrouped what was left of his light infantry and put them into line with the grenadiers on the right; these flank companies would storm the rail fence, supported as before by the 52nd and the 5th Regiments. This time, however, Pigot was expected to carry the redoubt on his own, without waiting for a flanking movement from the right.

Again the scarlet lines, thinner now, but with the foot soldiers still carrying full packs, stepped off, and as in the first attack there was no fire from the rebels until the foe was within a hundred feet. Then came that devastating explosion of musketry, then another and another, the Americans firing and loading as fast as they could. "As we approached," a British officer said, "an incessant stream of fire poured from the rebel lines; it seemed a continued sheet of fire for near thirty minutes." Howe's right was being raked now by Samuel Trevett's cannon, which ripped into the advancing grenadiers. Meanwhile the same British officer reported that "Our Light-infantry were served up in Companies against the grass fence, without being able to penetrate—indeed, how could we penetrate? Most of our Grenadiers and Light-infantry, the moment of presenting themselves lost three-fourths, and many nine-tenths, of their men. Some had only eight or nine men a company left; some only three, four, and five. On the left, Pigot was staggered and actually retreated. Observe, our men were not driven back; they actually retreated by orders." Once again Howe saw his men thrashing through the long grass and climbing over fences in the face of the American volleys, saw his grenadiers and light infantry try to fire, then crowd together in a confused mass only to have the oncoming second line plow into them from behind. As he confessed later, "The Light Infantry at the same time being repulsed, there was *a Moment that I never felt before.*" (Prescott remembered seeing Howe standing almost alone, surrounded entirely by dead or wounded.) It was inconceivable; the vaunted British infantry could not get close enough to drive home a charge with the cold steel, but were mowed down as if by a giant scythe as they struggled to advance. It was too much to endure, and suddenly the decimated ranks turned and ran again.

Among the fallen was Colonel James Abercromby, the commander of the grenadiers. Nine months earlier he had been safe in England, writing his good friend Thomas Gage, sympathizing with his predicament and wishing him "a happy and glorious retreat from [his] sea of trouble." Then, late in April, Abercromby had arrived in Boston with reinforcements, to become immersed in that same sea of troubles, and on a reconnaissance up the Charles he and his party were fired on from the shore. ("I dont hear that he has been as fond of reconnoitring since," Lieutenant John Barker of the King's Own wrote acidly.) Apparently Abercromby had called the provincials some highly unflattering names on that occasion, for now, as the men in the redoubt recognized him and saw him fall, they jeered, "Colonel Abercromby, are the Yankees cowards now?" And with their taunts ringing in his ears the British officer was carried from the field, to die a week later of his wounds.

From the housetops and steeples of Boston loyalist and patriot alike had watched breathlessly while that ribbon of scarlet and white ascended the hill a second time. There were wives and sweethearts, sons and daughters of men on both sides, whose eyes were glued to the slow upward movement of the line, and their hearts caught in their throats as they wondered, in spite of themselves, which man was theirs. As they looked there was an orange flash like "a continual sheet of lightning" along the string of earthworks, and even before the sound (one observer described it as "an uninterrupted peal of thunder") reached them from across the water, the ribbon of toy soldiers was struck and shivered as in a high wind, then crumbled into ruin. Where there had been a solid row of figures now there was only a jagged line; on the ground was a narrow carpet of red, many of whose parts were still and silent, with here and there a twisting, writhing movement. Now and then an arm waved back and forth, helpless and appealing, single figures half rose from the heap of bodies and sank back again as the living pushed on toward the breastworks, were hit again, and then surged back toward the water's edge, trampling dead and wounded in their terrible haste.

In his own straightforward way, Colonel William Prescott tells what happened in the redoubt: "The enemy advanced and fired very hotly on the fort, and meeting with a warm reception, there was a very smart firing on both sides. After a considerable time, finding our ammunition was almost spent, I commanded a cessation till the enemy advanced within thirty yards, when we gave them such a hot fire that they were obliged to retire nearly one hundred and fifty yards before they could rally." To Prescott's right the village of Charlestown was almost totally destroyed, but the defenders he had stationed there were still fighting valiantly from behind what cover they could find. Some were in a barn not far from the redoubt, others had moved out of the flaming town to take positions back of stone walls, trees, and brush, and they had repulsed Pigot's attempt to outflank Prescott's little fort.

In the frightful confusion of disaster, the British wounded were taken aboard the waiting boats and ferried across to Boston; the hillside was strewn with the dead and the dying, and from every section rose the pitiful moans and cries of the wounded. There are reports that some of Howe's officers begged him not to attack again; he was faced with the choice of abandoning the attempt altogether or of trying another frontal assault, for the tides would not permit him to land in the Americans' rear even if he wanted to do so. He had seen what a direct attack cost, but he decided to try at least one more; and to execute it he needed more men. So while his battered units reformed along the banks of the Charles, Howe sent a message to Clinton requesting reinforcements. Gage had made Clinton responsible for supporting Howe with troops as he needed them, and Clinton had already sent the field commander reserves in time for his first attack; now he dispatched the 63rd Regiment and the 2nd Marines. But further inactivity was more than Clinton could stand; he and Burgoyne had been at the Copp's Hill battery from the beginning, watching the flow of events on the opposite shore, and when he saw the complete collapse of Pigot's left and the wounded gathering leaderless on the shore, he acted. Telling Burgoyne to explain to Gage why he had left without orders, he commandeered a boat and was rowed toward Charlestown. As they landed north of the town, two men in his boat were wounded, proving that there were still some rebels in the stricken village, but Clinton ignored the opposition and "collected all the guards and such wounded men as could follow which to their honour were many and advanced in column with as much parade as possible to impress the enemy." With Henry Clinton in the lead, this heroic little company of invalids made its way back to the battlefield to rejoin Pigot and fight once more.

In the rebel works there had been another scene of elation when the redcoats retreated for the second time, and during the long interval occasioned by Howe's regrouping and wait for reinforcements, the Americans began to doubt if he would attack again. Then, with renewed signs of British activity, the defenders looked to their ammunition and suddenly realized they were virtually out of powder. Some men had used all theirs, others had but a few shots left, for in the hectic moments when the British lines loomed ever closer they had fired not in volleys, but as fast as they could reload and discharge their weapons—often three or four shots a minute—and now the powder supply was almost exhausted. Men shared what they had with comrades to right and left, and Prescott apparently broke open an unused cartridge or two that had been left behind by the artillery and distributed that powder to the men. But there was not enough for what had to be done.

To the rear the scene was chaotic. Troops were milling around beyond the Neck, afraid to run the gauntlet of cannon fire, while hundreds more were wandering about leaderless atop Bunker Hill. Old Put was doing his best to get units into action, and on the safe side of the hill he came across one outfit whose commander, Colonel Samuel Gerrish, "unwieldy from excessive corpulence," lay prostrate on the ground, pleading exhaustion. According to one of Gerrish's men, the moment they came in sight of the enemy "a tremor seiz'd" the fat colonel and "he began to bellow, 'Retreat! retreat! or you'l all be cutt off!' which so confus'd & scar'd our men, that they retreated most precipitately." Putnam ordered Gerrish to collect his wits and his soldiers and lead them to the lines, even threatening some of them and slapping them with the flat of his sword, but he could do nothing. The only detachment from this outfit to see action was one led by the adjutant, a Dane named Christian Febiger, who rallied a handful of men and took them into the fight.

John Chester, captain of the Wethersfield, Connecticut company which had decided to cover its bright blue and red uniforms with drab clothes before marching out of Cambridge, arrived at the Neck in time to witness the confused scene: "When we arrived there was not a company with us in any kind of order, although, when we first set out, perhaps three regiments were by our side, and near us; but here they were scattered some behind rocks and hay-cocks, and thirty men, perhaps, behind an apple-tree, frequently twenty men round a wounded man, retreating, when not more than three or four could touch him to advantage. Others were retreating, seemingly without any excuse, and some said they had left the fort with leave of the officers, because they had been all night and day on fatigue, without sleep, victuals, or drink; and some said they had no officers to head them, which, indeed, seemed to be the case." Chester saw one entire company deserting, led by its officers. He shouted to the company commander, asking why he retreated, but was ignored, upon which Chester halted his own men, ordered them to cock their muskets, and informed the other officer that he would open fire unless he took his men back to the lines. The deserters immediately about-faced and headed for action.

But if Chester was calmly confident, some of the soldiers with him were not. Samuel Webb, who was at his side as they marched off Bunker Hill toward the front lines, made no apologies for his nervousness: "Good God, how the balls flew,—I freely acknowledge I never had such a tremor. I confess, when I was descending into the Valley from off Bunker's Hill . . . I had no more tho't of ever rising the Hill again than I had of ascending to Heaven as Elijah did, Soul & Body together."

Fortunately, many Americans went down to the battlefield, singly and by groups, up to the last possible moment. One of them was Joseph Hodgkins, an Ipswich shoemaker, who later wrote his wife that he had been "Exposed to a very hot fire of Cannon and small arms." Hodgkins knew how lucky he was to be "Presarved"—a ball took a big piece out of his coat just below the arm, and he had buckshot holes in his coat and jacket. Colonel Thomas Gardner's regiment, which had been stationed in the road leading to Lechmere's Point until early afternoon, went into line just after the second British attack; so did part of Ward's own regiment, which was not ordered to Charlestown until late in the day; and two Connecticut companies, under James Clark and William Coit, arrived in time to participate in the last few moments of the fight.

During and after the engagement there was criticism of Ward, on the grounds that he had not been aggressive enough, that he had not moved from headquarters. James Warren, full of indignation that Ward "never left his house," wanted him replaced immediately with a general "of spirit and abilities." But surely even the waspish Warren must have known that someone had to run the army and try to see things whole from the Cambridge command post. That was the center, the base of supplies and operations, and it was Artemas Ward's responsibility to see that it was not overrun by a quick surprise thrust via Roxbury. John Thomas was there and had made his preparations, felling trees across many of the streets and stationing men where they would do the most good, but even so some regiments could find no real protection. Spencer's, for example, marched to the top of Roxbury hill and spent the night there, while Larned's troops withdrew to the "burying ground, which was the alarm post, where we laid in ambush with two fieldpieces placed to give it to them unawares, should the regulars come." But the regulars were far too busy to do anything in that sector beyond shelling the Roxbury lines.

On Breed's Hill the grisly task of bringing off the dead and wounded had begun. In comparison to British losses, those of the Americans were slight, but a number of officers and men were down. Colonel Brewer, whose men had taken a position between the breastwork and the rail fence, was hurt, and so was John Nixon, who was carried off the field with a serious wound. Major Willard Moore, who had taken command of Ephraim Doolittle's regiment in the absence of its colonel and lieutenant colonel, had been wounded in the thigh, and as his men were carrying him up Bunker Hill he was hit again. He pleaded with someone to bring him water but there was none to be had, and he lay there in agony, telling his men to look after themselves. A sergeant saw two boys standing nearby and told them to run and get some rum. "Major Moore is badly wounded," he said, "go as quick as possible." One of the youngsters was Robert Steele of Dedham, a drummer in Doolittle's regiment who had beat his comrades into line that morning to "Yankee Doodle"; the lad with him was Benjamin Ballard. A glance at the flames of Charlestown told them there was no hope of finding anything in that quarter, so they hurried off toward the Neck. The *Symmetry* was still firing, and as they raced across the little isthmus they heard the balls fly overhead. On the other side they located a store which appeared to be deserted, so Steele stamped on the floor and called out, asking if anyone was there. When a man's voice answered from the cellar, Steele said they wanted rum. No reply. After a moment Steele called again, asking the man why he stayed in the cellar. "To keep out of the way of the shot," came the honest answer, and then, "If you want anything in the store, take what you please."

So Steele took a two-quart earthen pitcher and filled it with rum, Ben Ballard drew a pail of water, and they set off for the front lines again, passing through throngs of skulkers on the safe side of the Neck and atop Bunker Hill, arriving at the entrenchment just as the British prepared to advance for the third time. "Our rum and water went very quick," Robert Steele noted.

Dozens of British officers had been killed or maimed, and the hillside was covered with dead and wounded who were too close to the rebel defenses for anyone to rescue. Major Spendlove, who had served forty years in the 43rd Regiment, received a mortal wound during the second charge, and his command was taken over by John Gunning, who had applied that very morning for a vacant majority in another regiment. Among the light infantry, which had borne some of the heaviest fighting, Captain Edward Drewe of the 35th was hit in the shoulder, thigh, and foot; Lieutenant Massey was shot through the thigh; Bard, the third officer of the same outfit, was badly hurt; and the noncoms were virtually wiped out. Captain Lyon of the 35th, whose pregnant wife had watched the course of the fighting from the Boston shore, was loaded into a boat and taken back to be nursed by the grief-stricken woman; but, like Drewe and Bard, he died of his wounds. By the end of the day, this light company of the 35th Regiment was without a single officer, sergeant, or corporal, and the command fell to the senior private, who led the five remaining men. All told, the grenadiers and light infantry lost nearly seventy per cent of their strength.

Howe, preparing for the third assault, was substantially without aides or staff, so many had fallen in the first two charges. One aide, Thomas Hyde Page, was hit in the ankle and later lost the leg;

Lieutenant Jorden, a naval aide, was dead with a bullet through his head. Even Howe's batman, Evans, who had followed him doggedly all over the field with refreshments, had had a wine bottle shot out of his hands, and was nursing a badly bruised arm. However, the British commander now had four hundred fresh troops of the 2nd Marines and the 63rd Regiment for support, and more significantly, he had decided to vary his tactics. At last he allowed the men to remove their packs and leave behind all superfluous equipment. This time his troops were to march most of the way in column before deploying for the final bayonet charge, and he shifted the weight of his line to the left, sending what remained of the grenadiers and the 52nd against the breastwork instead of the rail fence, leaving only a few troops to make a demonstration against the latter works. To support the assault he brought up his artillery, stationing the guns where they could rake the American lines with grape, and as the cannon moved forward the third British attack got under way, the long columns slanting up the hillside into a lowering afternoon sun.

Ahead of them the rank grass was snarled and trampled, the green strands streaked red with blood and patches of scarlet cloth, and the entire rim of the slope was pockmarked with depressions where fallen men lay, most of them still and silent, a few thrashing in agony, begging a comrade for help. Many of the marchers wore bandages or a rough sling, and as the drums beat they headed up the hill through the low-lying smoke, faces set, their hearts pounding, dreading the resumption of that withering blast from the rebel lines. An Ipswich man remembered that "they looked too handsome to be fired at; but we had to do it," and another American told how the British "advanced in open order, the men often twelve feet apart in the front, but very close after one another in extraordinary deep or long files. As fast as the front man was shot down, the next stepped forward into his place; but our men dropt them so fast, they were a long time coming up. It was surprising how they would step over their dead bodies, as though they had been logs of wood." There was no need to wait for a

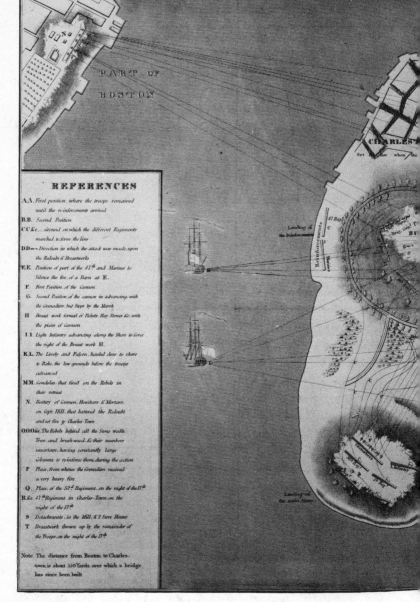

British Lieutenant Henry de Berniere had an infantryman's eye for terrain, but his map of Charlestown peninsula has Breed's Hill labeled as Bunker's. His excellent plan indicates the British landings, the attack along the beach, the brick kilns, swamp, and position of the three flèches. The breastwork above the arrow

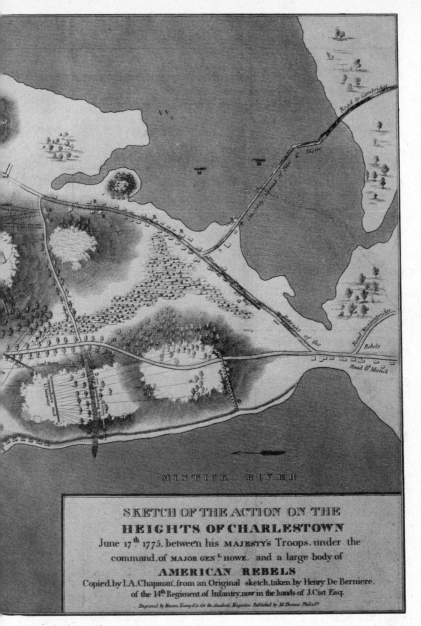

MISTICK RIVER

SKETCH OF THE ACTION ON THE
HEIGHTS OF CHARLESTOWN
June 17th 1775, between his MAJESTY'S Troops, under the
command, of MAJOR GENL HOWE, and a large body of
AMERICAN REBELS
Copied by I.A.Chapman, from an Original sketch, taken by Henry De Berniere,
of the 14th Regiment of Infantry, now in the hands of J.Cist Esq.
Engraved by Messrs. Young &Co. for the Analectic Magazine. Published by M.Thomas Philad.a

(which shows the direction of the current in the river) is on the site of Montresor's redan, which the British rebuilt after the battle. (*Emmett Collection, Manuscripts and Archives Division, The New York Public Library*)

chance to fire, one rebel said; all you had to do was load and there would be a mark at hand, as near as you pleased.

But running out of targets was scarcely the problem. Behind the rampart, men with powder-blackened faces bit the end off their last cartridge, rammed it home, pulled the trigger, and then looked around for something else to shoot. Some were firing nails or little scraps of metal picked up off the ground, others grabbed handfuls of rocks and began hurling them at the oncoming enemy, desperately trying to prevent that terrible gleaming forest of bayonets from coming any closer.

Captain George Harris—the same man who, a few weeks ago, had looked out across the Charles and admired the poetic serenity of the countryside—now led the grenadiers of the 5th Regiment up the slope, scaled a little rise between the breastwork and the redoubt, was pushed back, and on the third attempt a ball grazed the top of his head. As he fell backward he was caught by his lieutenant, Lord Rawdon, who called four soldiers to help him to safety. Three of the men were hit as they took him back down the hillside and Harris told them irritably, "For God's sake, let me die in peace." Somehow they got him out of gunshot to safety, and Harris's servant, who had been searching frantically for him, came running up just in time to get his master into the last boat then available for the wounded. Although it was jammed, they took Harris aboard, faint and shivering from shock, and shortly after he arrived in Boston a surgeon performed a trepanning operation on him which the stolid Englishman watched by means of mirrors.

Atop Breed's Hill the fighting raged on toward its fiery climax. Despite the barrage from the British fieldpieces, no breach had been made in the American defenses. Then suddenly, Lord Rawdon said, "our men grew impatient, and all crying 'Push on, push on,' advanced with infinite spirit to attack the work with their small arms. As soon as the rebels perceived this, they rose up and poured in so heavy a fire upon us that the oldest officers say they never saw a sharper action. They kept up this fire until we were within ten yards of them; nay, they even knocked down my captain [Harris], close beside me, after we had got into the ditch of the entrenchment. . . . There are few instances of regular troops defending a redoubt till the enemy were in the very ditch of it, [yet] I can assure you that I myself saw several pop their heads up and fire even after some of our men were upon the berm. . . . I received no hurt of any kind, but a ball passed through a close cap which I had."

Lying on the outside of the redoubt, under the protection of its wall, Rawdon called out to young Ensign Hunter of the 52nd, to show him how narrowly he had missed death. Another officer, Major Williams, was badly wounded, and Rawdon asked Hunter to go and find a surgeon to tend him; but Hunter, who had just seen Harris's rescuers shot as they carried him off, "had sense enough to know that I was much safer close under the works than I could be at a few yards from it, as the enemy could not depress their arms sufficiently to do any execution to those that were close under, and to have gone to the rear to look for a surgeon would have been almost certain death."

Samuel Webb took his place in the American line just as the fighting reached its peak and, looking around at his dead and wounded countrymen, had "no other feelings but that of Revenge." It was a good thing he had the stomach for fighting: five or six more Americans dropped within five feet of where he stood, and a musket ball grazed his hat. Webb saw Gershom Smith of his company go down. Edward Brown, who was at Smith's side, fired his own gun, then reached for Smith's and shot it. At that moment bayonets loomed over the breastwork and the regulars began pouring in; Brown leaped for an enemy, seized his musket, and killed him with it on the spot.

At the far left of Pigot's line, which had swung around the west side of the redoubt in order to flank it, the British marines ran into the same shattering fire that had characterized the entire American defense. As they fell into confusion, most of the marines began to fire at the works instead of charging, and Adjutant Waller had all he could do to keep two companies in formation. Major John Pitcairn, who had commanded the British at Lexington in April, was attempting to rally his men; they heard him shout that the enemy had abandoned the fort, heard a boy call from behind the wall, "We are not all gone!" And at that moment, men said later, a Negro named Salem Prince shot Pitcairn through the head. He fell into the arms of his son; close by him a captain and a subaltern were down, and Waller realized that "had we stopped there much longer, the enemy would have picked us all off. I saw this, and begged Colonel Nesbitt of the 47th to form on our left, in order that we might advance with our bayonets to the parapet. I ran from right to left, and stopped our men from firing; while this was doing, and when we had got in tolerable order, we rushed on, leaped the ditch, and climbed the parapet, under a most sore and heavy fire."

There was a moment at the last when the British staggered once again—a moment when the battle's outcome hung in the balance—then they recovered and came on with a rush. Prescott said later that one more round of ammunition might have pushed them back then and there, but there was not one more round. The last American volley sputtered out "like an old candle" and with a great animal roar that was heard in Boston the redcoats surged forward. Bayonets glinted in the smoky gloom, the mitered hats of the big grenadiers loomed over the breastwork. Angry, sweating redcoats, the breath sobbing in their throats, stormed up the dirt walls of the redoubt as the marines poured in from the right. All the pent-up anger and misery and frustration of that ghastly afternoon was in their charge, and there was no stopping them. They had murder in their eyes and they lashed out, stabbing and slashing with the bayonet, not bothering to fire, cursing, yelling, pressing the assault home with the terrible brutal fury of which man is sometimes capable. Almost none of the Americans had bayonets—nothing but clubbed muskets or fists or rocks—yet they fought, one regular said, "more like Devils than Men" in this hand-to-hand melee. Even so, Prescott saw there was no chance

One of the sketches made by John Trumbull for his painting of the battle (page 174) shows a Connecticut officer and, behind him, his Negro servant, Salem Prince, who was said to have killed British Major John Pitcairn. (*The Historical Society of Pennsylvania*)

and ordered his men to retreat, to get out as best they could. Peter Brown was "not suffered to be toutched, altho' I was in the fort when the Enemy came in, and jumped over the walls, and ran half a mile where Balls flew like Hailstones, and Canons roared like Thunder." Captain Ebenezer Bancroft had just taken the ramrod from his firelock when a British officer leaped at him; he fired, killing the man, then rushed for the entrance to the redoubt, holding his gun "broadwise before my face" to keep from being clubbed. A rifle butt smashed down on his shoulder, and as he ran toward Bunker Hill, weak with fatigue, sightless in one eye, he realized that the forefinger of his left hand was gone. Coffee Whittemore, a Negro, had a hole in his hat from a musket ball, and in the final moments of the fight he seized a sword from a fallen British officer and carried it off in triumph (to the disgust of his friends, he sold it a few days later).

Amos Farnsworth was another who stayed in the redoubt until the enemy broke through, and when the retreat began he raced out about ten or fifteen rods past the outlet, where he "receved a wound in my rite arm, the bawl gowing through a little below my elbow breaking the little shel bone. Another bawl struck my back, taking a piece of skin about as big as a penny. But I got to Cambridge that night." Colonel Ebenezer Bridge had his head and neck laid open by a British sword. His second-in-command, Moses Parker, was groveling in the dirt, one knee fractured by a ball; but it was every man for himself in these frantic closing moments of the fight, and Parker was left behind, to be taken prisoner and to die after a British surgeon amputated his leg. Captain Walker of that regiment suffered the same fate.

The redoubt that had preserved Prescott's men all day nearly became a deathtrap for them now. There was only one narrow exit at the rear of the fort, and the black smoke and dust were so thick the men had to feel their way along the walls to find it. Yet this weird gloom kept the uneven struggle from becoming a massacre; the British could not tell friend from foe and dared not fire into the mass of men crowded around the passage. It was a nightmare of confusion and chaos, with the shadowy figures of wildly shouting, moving men, half-panicked as they surged and fought their way toward the only exit, half-mad with rage as they beat off the thrust of death from behind. Prescott refused to run; striding toward the opening with sword raised, he parried the swipes of bayonets, and although his coat and waistcoat were pierced he was not injured.

When he and the other Americans emerged from the fort they found themselves between two approaching bodies of the enemy which had enveloped the redoubt from opposite sides, and while neither of these could fire for fear of hitting their own men, other British were coming up from behind, scaling the rear wall of the redoubt, shooting into the retreating rebels. Prescott's adjutant went down, and Captains Maxwell, Dow, and Farwell were wounded. Late that night the wounded Reuben Dow discovered that eight men of his Hollis company were dead—one-fifth of the casualties in Prescott's regiment.

Somewhere, in the last wild rush, Joseph Warren disappeared in the murk of battle. The man Lord Rawdon called "the greatest incendiary in all America," who had once said he would like to die fighting the British in blood up to his knees, got his wish. No one saw him fall, but he was hit in the head by a ball and must have been killed instantly. "He died in his best cloaths," a British officer wrote, "every body remembers his fine silk-fringed waistcoat."

All resistance in the redoubt and the breastwork collapsed at last, but fortunately for those who were fleeing, the rail fence held firm and the defenders there were able to cover their comrades' retreat before withdrawing themselves in good order. A handful of fresh men led by William Coit and John Chester kept up a "brisk fire" from behind a stone wall along the way, and some thirty of Stark's men helped Samuel Trevett bring off one of his field-pieces—the only one the rebels managed to save. They succeeded in hauling it to the summit of Bunker Hill before a British company sighted the prize and stormed after them, and there was a

John Trumbull's heroic *Battle of Bunker's Hill* illustrates the climactic moment, with Warren dying in the left foreground while the mortally wounded Major Pitcairn (right center) is carried from the field. Although he saw the battle from four miles away, Trumbull scarcely qualifies as an eyewitness to this scene, which was painted in 1786 in Benjamin West's London studio.

Eleven years later he still had the canvas with him and it saved his skin: stranded in Paris during the French Revolution, he showed it to the Ministry of Police to prove he was a good revolutionary, and got a passport to leave. (*Collection of Howland S. Warren*)

rough little encounter, with several American losses, before Trevett and the New Hampshiremen drove off the attackers and dragged the gun down to the Neck. The whole American left, acting as a rear guard, fell back stubbornly, carrying their wounded with them, taking cover wherever they found it, and returning the British fire like professional troops. The story is told of how Seth Pomeroy, the old Indian fighter, was with them, carrying his ancient musket, its stock shattered, as he backed off, still facing the enemy.

The last rebels to leave were those with the most to fight for— the Charlestown company of Thomas Gardner's regiment, who had hurried into line at the rail fence just before the third British attack. They had lost their colonel (Gardner was mortally wounded while trying to lead reinforcements to the redoubt, and was carried off the field on a litter of rails by his son and some other men); they had watched, helpless, while their village and their homes went up in flames; and if ever a company was fighting mad, it was this one. But there was nothing much that anyone could do now, beyond saving his own skin.

Fortunately for the Americans, the British had very nearly reached the end of their string. They had climbed Breed's Hill three times that afternoon and the grisly slopes were littered with their dead; twice victory had eluded them, and when it came at last it was because discipline and courage overcame fear and exhaustion and defeat. By all rights these men had been beaten; now they were utterly worn out by their efforts, their losses were staggering, their morale was nearly gone, and if they paused to draw breath and failed to pursue the still contentious Americans, it was no wonder. Some of the best of them were gone. Abercromby was dying; so was Major Pitcairn of the marines, who had been carried back to Boston by his son. Someone who saw the younger man, covered with blood, wandering dazedly through the streets of the town, was about to help him when he was informed that the blood was from the father's wound. Gage sent a doctor immediately to Pitcairn, but the marine knew he was dying and refused to let the physician waste his time. To young Jeremy

Lister fell the task of telling Lieutenant Kelley's wife of her husband's mortal wound and of standing by helplessly while she "for some time sat motionless with two small Children close by her."

Henry Clinton arrived at the scene of victory at the moment when Howe, seeing as if for the first time the number of British dead on the field, was beginning to realize its cost. Not one of the general's aides was left; all were either killed or wounded. The pride of the army, the flank companies, had been cut to ribbons, and the toll of officers and men in all regiments was appalling. When Clinton saw him, Howe was far from a victorious general; he was exhausted, his white gaiters streaked with blood from the long grass on the hill, and he had the look of a man who has stared death and disaster in the face.

Howe admitted privately to Clinton that his left "was totally gone" just before the final onslaught, and Clinton was so disturbed by all he saw and heard during these few moments that he committed his impressions to cipher: "All was in Confusion, officers told me that they could not command their men and I never saw so great a want of order."

But if Howe, undone by the battle, wanted energy, Clinton did not. He saw at once that the rebels must be driven off the peninsula while they were still disorganized, and after stationing a detachment of a hundred men in Prescott's abandoned redoubt, he took all the able-bodied troops that were available, caught up with Pigot, who had already moved after the Americans, and headed up the road to Bunker Hill. Off to his right, Stark and Knowlton and Gardner were still making their way deliberately and obstinately toward the rear, their men putting up "a running fight," Lord Rawdon wrote admiringly, "from one fence, or wall, to another." Burgoyne, too, complimented the rebels on their retreat. It was, he said, "no flight: it was even covered with bravery and military skill." (They were so successful in bringing off their wounded that the British took only thirty-one prisoners, most of them mortally injured.) Despite the sudden collapse of their defenses and the precipitous retreat from the redoubt, the provincials simply refused to give up. A few diehards were even firing from the remains of houses around Charlestown (Clinton was annoyed from that direction while he proceeded down the middle of the peninsula), but the end was in sight. Clinton, expecting the rebels to make a stand at Montresor's little fort on the back side of Bunker Hill, was amazed to find it deserted; he posted a force there, sent skirmishers out to man the stone walls between this point and the Neck, and satisfying himself that the enemy was being vigorously pressed, returned to Boston.

As in the redoubt, the Americans paid dearly for having left themselves but one narrow avenue of retreat. To make an orderly withdrawal under fire from a losing field was too much to expect under the best of circumstances, but when more than a thousand frantic, disorganized troops, heading for the safety of the mainland, were suddenly compressed into a solid mass to funnel across the Neck, which was only about thirty-five yards wide at its narrowest point, the result was chaos. Progress was impeded by the wounded and by the debris of battle, British musket fire was closing in from the rear, and to make matters far worse the entire Neck was being raked by the guns of the *Glasgow*. One thought was uppermost in the mind of everyone, and that was to reach the other side as quickly as possible. Desperately they surged forward, pushing and shoving, stumbling and falling over wounded men and pieces of men blown apart by the merciless British cannon, shouting in anger and terror and frustration as they fought to get out of this trap. Thirty-six hours ago they had last rested, they had been a full day without food or water, and for men totally unused to war and unprepared, they had seen it all— continuous pounding from enemy cannon, frontal assaults by veteran infantry, the shattering climax of a bayonet charge and hand-to-hand combat. Already driven beyond the limits of human endurance, they were forced to call forth some final reserve of energy, and incredibly they did so, to make this frenzied dash across the confining causeway. Once the solid artery of retreat hit the wider reaches of the mainland it broke up into little groups that scattered across the moors and clay pits of Charlestown Common, moving inland toward a sinking sun. Utterly spent, some of the provincials did not even bother to look back; their only thought was of camp and rest and a security that had seemed unattainable minutes before. And as they disappeared, straggling off along the dusty roads toward Cambridge and Medford, the battle for Bunker Hill was over, except for one last incident.

It must have been after five thirty when the *Somerset* log reported that the "firing slackened," that Major Andrew McClary, of Stark's regiment, reached the mainland. Looking back, he saw Clinton's detachment moving onto the crest of Bunker Hill, and just to make certain that they had no plans to push on toward the mainland, he recrossed the Neck, went close enough to the British lines to decide that no further attack was intended, and finally headed back to rejoin his command. Walking alone in the gathering dusk, he had almost reached safety when a last cannon ball from the *Glasgow* tore him to pieces. As a historian wrote long afterward, "No smaller weapon seemed worthy to destroy the gigantic hero."

Back in Boston, the impatient Clinton had turned his thoughts to a counterstroke, to be delivered immediately. Such was "the Panick" in the rebel ranks, he thought, that a thousand men could easily sweep up their entire defenses. But the Americans, to their everlasting credit, were already at work digging again, fortifying Winter Hill on the mainland side of Charlestown Neck, where, as Lieutenant Colonel Experience Storrs recorded in his diary, "we immediately went to entrenching; flung up by morning an entrenchment 100 feet square. Done principally by our regiment under Putnam's directions, had but little sleep the night."

Henry Clinton should have known better. No one wrote a better epitaph on the battle than he did that evening, nor gave a more convincing reason for not resuming it: "A dear bought victory, another such would have ruined us."

VI. I Wish This Cursed Place Was Burned

Lengthening shadows turned to dusk and dusk to night. Along the riverbanks, frogs began their drowsy evening chorus. Off in the direction of Roxbury, British cannon boomed sporadically, breaking the soft peace of summer darkness; clouds drifting over the Charles picked up the eerie glow of flames still licking the embers of Charlestown, brightened as they passed overhead, faded, and disappeared into the black sky. Across the trampled slopes of Breed's Hill, down among the brick kilns, and along the gravel beach, wounded men still writhed, moaned, and screamed in agony. On both sides of the river the night was pierced with bobbing, moving lights. Sweating surgeons picked their way across the battlefield, hurrying toward the sound of a human voice, giving directions to litter bearers, seeing to men for whom there was still hope, shaking their heads over the mortally injured. Hour after hour the barges ground to a halt on the beaches, took aboard their grisly cargo and shoved off for Boston, pointing toward the waiting circle of lanterns, where they would unload and return.

Through the hours of darkness carts and wagons of every description pulled up at Long Wharf—coaches, chariots, chaises, even handbarrows, sent by loyalists to haul the desperately wounded men—and lurched off on the agonizing journey to hospital or home, wherever a hurt soldier might be tended. Doctors made do with what few drugs they could muster. Often a carpenter's saw was the handiest tool for an amputation, and the same sponge was used to clean a score of ugly wounds. There was no anesthetic; just a draught of rum and a bullet clenched between the teeth to see a poor wretch through the agony of an operation. The sight of the wounded and the dying, "with the lamentations of the women and children over their husbands and fathers, pierced one to the soul," Ann Hulton wrote. "We were now every moment hearing of some officer, or other of our friends and acquaintance,' who had fallen in our defence, and in supporting the honor of our country." People stood in their doorways all night, silently watching while the wounded went by, running out now and then to comfort a man or provide one with a drink of water. The Englishman John Clarke saw several carriages pass, entirely filled with dead or dying officers; Peter Oliver wrote of the "Shocking Sight and Sound" of those dreadful hours; another eyewitness called it "the most melancholy scene ever beheld in this part of the world." Wounded were taken to the almshouse, to the workhouse, to an old factory opposite the granary, which served now as a hospital. This building and the entire yard around it were crowded with casualties, many begging to be put out of their misery, others waiting in tight-lipped silence for a surgeon to get to them. One doctor named Grant, who with four assistants was up for two nights treating the wounded, had to amputate both legs of many men. The reason, he wrote in a shocked letter, was that the "Provincials had either exhausted their ball, or they were determined that every wound should prove fatal; their muskets were charged with old nails and angular pieces of iron; and from most of our men being wounded in the legs, we are inclined to believe it was their design, not wishing to kill the men, but leave them as burdens on us, to exhaust our provisions and engage our attention, as well as to intimidate the rest of the soldiery." Highly colored versions of this story were soon circulating, infuriating the British and loyalists. According to one correspondent, "In Cutting out the Bullets from our Wounded it was found that they were all very ragged and had occasioned infinite Pain, there can be no doubt but they were purposely made so, and there is another Circumstance well worth enquiry, which is that a white crusted matter is said by the Surgeons to have adhered to all those Balls, which is supposed to have been some poisonous mixture, for an uncommon rancorous suppuration has followed in almost every Case." And a merchant writing to his brother in Scotland said flatly that the balls "were all found to be poisoned"—proof of the "hellish disposition of the accursed rebels."

Orders went out from headquarters; each corps was to send two "carefull sober Women" to the hospitals, "the wounded being in the greatest want of assistance." Isaac Lothrop, a member of the Provincial Congress in Watertown, heard that "All the surgeons in the army, with what they could get in Boston," were insufficient to care for the influx. For twenty-four hours, he said, they were busy taking them off the battlefield, and many died in the streets on the way to a hospital. Typical of many letters which must have been written in the days after the battle was one from John Randon to his wife and children in England: "I have received two balls, one in my groin and the other near the breast. I am now so weak with the loss of blood, that I can hardly dictate these few lines, as the last tribute of my unchangeable love to you. The Surgeons inform me that three hours will be the utmost I can survive."

Early the next morning one Boston merchant went over to the battlefield. It was, he admitted, "the first thing of the sort that I ever saw, and I pray to God I may never have the opportunity of seeing the like again." Burial details were just beginning a task that took two days to complete, and when the officer in charge turned in his report to Howe it showed that they had interred ten sergeants, seven corporals, and 142 privates (some whose regiments were "not distinguishable being stript of uniforms"). The British privates and ninety-two provincials were buried "in holes," unmarked graves presumably being quite suitable for these lower levels of humanity. And all the time they worked, the more im-

is water color depicts British soldiers walking over the Breed's Hill battle-
und. Some weeks afterward, the field was quiet, with no evidence beyond
e broken fences, scarred trees, and grass-covered remains of the rebel redoubt
t right center) that a bloody encounter had taken place here. (*Emmett
llection, Manuscripts and Archives Division, The New York Public Library*)

mediate business of the army had continued; atop Bunker Hill picks and shovels crunched into the dirt through the night of the seventeenth and on into Sunday—eventually Howe's men would have a proper fort there, ditched and palisaded, with its forward edge within musket range of the Neck.

On what she referred to as the "day after that dreadful one," Margaret Gage revealed the state of her emotions to a friend. The general's American wife, torn by conflicting loyalties, was reminded of the touching lines from Shakespeare's *King John*, in which Blanche of Spain says:

"The Sun's o'ercast with blood; fair day, adieu!
  Which is the side that I must go withal?
  I am with both; each army hath a hand
  And in their rage,—I having hold of both,—
  They whirl asunder, and dismember me.
  Husband, I cannot pray that thou mayst win,
  Uncle, I needs must pray that thou mayst lose.
  Father, I may not wish the fortune thine.
  Grandam, I will not wish thy wishes thrive.
  Whoever wins, on that side shall I lose,
  Assured loss, before the match is played."

Margaret's impassive husband waited until June 25 before writing his official report on the battle—eight days during which the death toll swelled. The casualties were staggering: of some 2300 rank and file who carried the burden of the attacks, 1054—or nearly fifty per cent—had fallen (226 were killed and 828 wounded). Among the flank companies in particular the statistics were appalling. Those of the King's Own and the Royal Welch Fusiliers each had thirty-nine men when they set off along the Mystic beach; after the battle all but four of the first company had been killed or wounded and only three of the Fusiliers were unscathed. The percentage of officer casualties was even higher; according to a reliable estimate that reached American headquarters, twenty-seven had died and sixty-three were wounded. (A Connecticut officer explained this to a friend, saying, "you will naturally be amazed at so large a number of officers being killed, I have only to observe that a choice party of our best shots under cover were appointed to fire at none but the Reddest coats.") Yet Gage in his report treated the affair matter-of-factly, stating that much as he regretted the number of casualties and the loss of so many good officers, victory had been essential. What surprised him, he admitted, was the spirit of the rebels—they were not the "despicable Rabble" they were supposed to be. They made a good stand behind cover, and built their trenches and fortifications well; the conquest of this country would not be easy.

Then, to his old friend Lord Barrington, Gage unburdened himself in a letter that revealed his anger, his perplexity, and his heartsickness. The "Rage and Enthousiasm" of the rebels were such that the government must proceed in earnest or give up entirely. "The loss we have Sustained," he reported confidentially, "is greater than we can bear." And then, in a moment of pure anguish, his real feelings burst out: "*I wish this Cursed place was burned!*"

Others in the British army had begun to acquire a grudging respect for their opponents: "Damn the Rebels—that they would not flinch," officers were heard to say. George Clark, who had commanded the light companies in the fateful assault along the Mystic beach, admitted that the Americans "behaved far beyond any idea I could ever have formed of them." He was bitter about the cost of the attack; the day had been "a great smash by such miscreants." Another British officer was most impressed by the Americans' use of terrain. Writing to a friend in England, he stated that "The ground on the peninsula is the strongest I can conceive for the kind of defence the rebels made, which is exactly like that of the Indians, viz. small inclosures with narrow lanes, bounded by stone fences, small heights which command the passes, proper trees to fire from, and very rough and marshy ground for troops to get over. The rebels defended this ground well, and inch by inch."

There were discussions and arguments amongst Gage and his major generals as to their next move: Gage thought it was futile to try and hold Boston, Howe believed that was all they *could* do, Clinton proposed another offensive. In fact on Sunday, the day after the battle, the ever-eager Clinton was prepared to strike at Dorchester. It must be assumed that no one else had the stomach for it just then, but Clinton, like a dog worrying a bone, persuaded Gage to let him plan an attack on the following Saturday. It was called off at the last moment, when troops were actually in the boats, ready to shove off. Had they seized Dorchester while the Americans were so unprepared, the siege of Boston might have ended differently; but Clinton's proposal was abandoned, and Gage did no more than strengthen his defenses on Bunker Hill, at Boston Neck, and in the town itself.

On every side loomed the dark shape of disaster. Penned up like so many cattle, the beleaguered army suffered increasingly as the siege continued. One man who left the city early in July said there were between ten and thirty funerals a day—so many that Gage finally put a stop to the mournful tolling of the church bells. Fresh fruits and vegetables were virtually unobtainable and it was not long before the soldiers were suffering from scurvy. Even fish, that staple of Boston diets, was at a premium, so few were the boats or fishermen left to bring it in; there was no fodder for the horses; fresh meat, the scarcest item of all, had to be reserved for the wounded. An enterprising camp follower named Winifred McCowen who stole the town bull and had him slaughtered had the misfortune to be caught; she was sentenced to be tied to a cart and receive one hundred lashes on the bare back, to be delivered "in different portions in the most public parts of the town and Camp." (Nor was that all: she also got three months' imprisonment.) Sickness, the long casualty lists, the humiliation of the army's position and the growing improbability of doing anything about it—all undermined the morale of the troops. Desertions increased daily, and there was a thriving black market in passes from the city. Yet there was little news from the mainland: "We hear nothing from the country," one man wrote; the battle "has put an entire stop to the communication we had before."

What they did not know the British might have surmised. In the camps around Cambridge and Medford the Americans were sorting out the pieces, adding up their own toll of slain and wounded, but because of the army's lack of organization it was some time before anyone could be certain of the facts. No one could state with any accuracy how many provincials took part in the battle (figures ranged from a wild British guess of fourteen or fifteen thousand down to one American writer's estimate of five hundred). The actual number seems to have been about thirty-five hundred, with casualties distributed among nineteen regiments. After his arrival in camp, George Washington wrote to his brother on July 27 and put the American losses at 138 killed, 36 missing, and 276 wounded—a total of 450—and this is as close to the truth as one is likely to come. On the evening of the battle the following entry was made in Ward's orderly book (the only reference to the engagement it contains): "June 17. The battle of Charlestown was fought this day. Killed, one hundred and fifteen; wounded, three hundred and five; captured, thirty. Total, four hundred and fifty." His total, although based on fragmentary returns, jibed with Washington's, and the disparity between the other figures must be laid to the fact that many of those Ward listed as wounded subsequently died.

In addition to the 450 men, the provincials had lost five of six fieldpieces plus a substantial quantity of entrenching tools, abandoned in the wild flight from the battlefield. Enormous amounts of powder had been expended, reducing Ward's supply to a dangerous inadequacy. In September an American informer sent word to British headquarters that there was "not one half lb: of powder left that night the bunker hill was taken and had you pursued, the Camp must have been broken up—this they confess." Equally serious, the rebel general could now count on only one regiment of five hundred men. Some outfits had less than half that number, others were without guns. What concerned all Americans, military and civilian alike, was what the British might do now. "It is expected they will come out over the Neck tonight," Abigail Adams wrote her husband on the eighteenth, "and a dreadful battle must ensue. Almighty God, cover the heads of our countrymen, and be a shield to our dear friends!" Samuel Haws, whose company had gone to its alarm post in Roxbury on the afternoon of the battle, noted in his diary that they had marched at daybreak on Sunday to "prosket [Prospect] Hill expecting to come to an ingagement." During the afternoon some of the men had gone down the hill toward the Neck, hoping to find some flour, "and the troops fired at them and wounded David Trisdale in the shoulder and another in the Leg." That same morning, according to Lieutenant Barker of the King's Own, "all the Houses beyond the Neck were burnt to prevent the Rebels lurking there." The British were still in earnest.

Of all losses suffered by the rebels, the one that affected men most deeply was that of Joseph Warren. His ability and energy, his great charm, and his devotion to the cause had endeared him to everyone, and without him the whole organism of command seemed virtually headless. ("We want him in the Senate; we want him in his profession; we want him in the field," Abigail Adams wrote.) Yet no one really knew what had happened to him; all that could be said with certainty was that he had disappeared during the battle. As late as Monday, two days after the engagement, some doubts about his fate lingered; the Provincial Congress, meeting that day, set the hour of 3 P.M. for the election of a president to replace Warren, who was "supposed to be killed in the late battle at Bunker's Hill." By Tuesday, people seemed to have lost hope. Abigail Adams expressed the wish that she "could contradict the report of the Dr.'s death; but it is a lamentable truth, and the tears of multitudes pay tribute to his memory." Soon stories began making the rounds about his last words—"I am a dead man, fight on, my brave fellows, for the salvation of your country" (a difficult statement for a man shot through the head to have made). Dozens of soldiers claimed to have seen him fall; it was said that Howe, who had slept on a pile of moldering hay the night of the battle, was awakened and told that Joseph Warren had been identified among the dead; that Warren had been buried and dug up and buried again; that John Burgoyne had come over from Boston to see the body; and so on.

What had become of Warren was related bluntly by Captain Walter Sloane Laurie, who was in charge of an English burial detail. He found the body, he said, "and stuffed the scoundrell with another Rebel into one hole and there he and his seditious principles may remain." If these were plain, unfeeling words, they were those of a man who had commanded the British detachment at the North Bridge in Concord, who had been badly pushed around on that occasion, and who was now in the best possible position to see exactly what his comrades had suffered at the hands of men such as Warren. Laurie was in no mood for the niceties. Someone learned that the other rebel—Warren's companion in death—was "a person with a frock on," and this was one of the few clues available months later, when Warren's two younger brothers, with a sexton and some friends—among them Paul Revere—rowed over to Charlestown from Boston to search for the hero's body. They found two men who had been buried together, one in a farmer's frock, and Paul Revere, that extraordinary jack-of-all-trades, settled the matter of Warren's identification. Just before the battle of Lexington he had installed two false teeth for his old friend, and now, almost exactly a year after he and Warren had stood watching the movements of British troops and decided that messengers must ride at once to warn the countryside, Revere examined the corpse of a man shot through the head, identified the two artificial teeth in the skull, and recognized as his own the silver wire with which they were fastened.

One unforeseen result of Warren's death was the unmasking of an American spy. Some Britisher—possibly Laurie—inspecting the

Few artisans of the day were as versatile as Paul Revere—master silversmith, goldsmith, engraver, inventor, dentist, the first man to roll copper in the United States, militiaman, and express rider for Boston's Sons of Liberty. This portrait of Revere at his workbench was painted by John Singleton Copley. (*Courtesy, Museum of Fine Arts, Boston*)

contents of the dead man's pockets, discovered some letters from James Lovell, letters written to him from Boston giving the number and disposition of English troops there, along with other information of considerable interest to the rebels. Before long someone remembered the business of the wrong-sized cannon balls that had made Howe's artillery useless in the early stages of the battle; they recalled that the clerk of artillery stores—the man responsible for sending the balls—was Benjamin Lovell, James's brother; and they were reminded that Samuel Cleaveland, the British colonel of artillery, had been spending most of his idle hours in the company of James Lovell's sisters. It began to look as if this family had played a rather large role in the day's villainies. All of them, that is, but the old man: John Lovell, who had been Master of the Boston Latin School from 1734 until April 19, 1775 (he dismissed his last class with the cryptic words, "War's begun —school's done"), was loyal to his King and he was an intimate of General Thomas Gage's. What had happened to him was symptomatic of the times; and the story of the Lovells was the story of what was occurring up and down the eastern seaboard in 1775, with children turning against their parents, brother against brother, indicating that the war was going to be a bitter civil conflict as well as a revolt against the Crown. To Lovell Senior it was obvious that he would support his King; to Lovell Junior it was just as plain that he would not, and the ties of family were going to have to suffer as a consequence. As far back as 1771 James Lovell had been known as an "ultra Whig," and that year was chosen to deliver the first oration in Old South Church on the subject of the Boston Massacre (the "Bloody Tragedy of the 5th of March 1770," the Sons of Liberty called it). When John Lovell got the news he went to his son and begged him not to go through with it for fear of his life. "Is that the case?" young Lovell had replied. "Then my mind is decided—my resolution is fixed—I will attempt it at every hazard."

For his devotion to the cause of rebellion, James Lovell landed in Boston Gaol two weeks after the battle, where he remained until the British evacuated the town the following March. He was considered valuable enough to exchange, so they took him to Halifax where his father, by then a refugee, visited him in prison. The old man died brokenhearted two years later; James was taken to London, exchanged, and returned to America, where he eventually became a Congressman, Receiver of Continental Taxes, and Collector of the Port of Boston.

Lovell was not the only civilian picked up at this time: a man described by a friend as "poor, harmless Shrimpton Hunt" was jailed after someone heard him express the hope that the rebels would win; another fellow was confined for hailing his sister and asking her (rather cheerfully, in all likelihood) to come and watch a British funeral procession; and a man named Carpenter who swam over to Dorchester and back under cover of darkness was caught, tried, sentenced to hang, and then let off. Peter Edes, the printer's son, spent 107 days in jail (sixty-three of them on bread and water) for possession of a concealed musket.

Two-thirds of the rebel soldiers captured at Bunker Hill died; for most of those taken had been too seriously wounded to escape, which meant that the likelihood of their survival was slim. Even though Gage meant for them to be humanely treated (and Burgoyne urged that the prisoners be released and sent home), the character of their jailors made certain that they would not. Civilian and military captives alike were often brutally treated by the sheriff, Joshua Loring, Jr., whose wife was now Howe's mistress, and by William Cunningham, a big, stout bully who was in charge of the jail. One of the civilian prisoners wrote in his diary that the wounded had "no wood to burn for many days together to warm their drink, and dying men drink theirs cold. Some of the limbs which have been taken off, it is said, were in a state of putrifaction, and not one survived amputation." The civilians were confined in miserably close quarters, and two British noncoms who brought them water were imprisoned by the provost for this minor act of mercy. Fortunately, most of the Americans who survived were finally freed before the British left Boston, but not until they had learned much about the inside of an army prison.

One event that seems to have shocked the partisans on both sides almost as much as the battle itself was the burning of Charlestown. This seemingly wanton act filled every property owner with horror and foreboding. One American called the British "savages"; another was furious at the way "The British Troops, to their eternal disgrace, shame, and barbarity, set Charlestown on fire with torches." The Reverend Andrew Eliot of Boston's New North Church, who had seen the battle from the opposite shore, described the scene to a friend in England: "Amidst the carnage of Saturday," he wrote, "Charlestown was set on fire; and I suppose every dwelling-house and every public building is consumed, till you have passed the passage to the mills, and are come to the houses where Woods, the Baker, dwelt. You may easily judge what distress we were in to see and hear Englishmen destroying one another, and a Town with which we have been so intimately connected, all in flames." Personal possessions, as well as houses, went up in the conflagration, for the evacuation had been made hurriedly. Dr. Mather, who departed Charlestown in haste a day or so before the battle, hoping to send a wagon back for his belongings, had left all of his papers at a friend's house, but "his whole furniture, with his library, plate &c" were consumed in the fire. When John Adams heard this from his wife, he spoke from the heart as a historian in replying that "The loss of Mr. Mather's library, which was a collection of books and manuscripts made by himself, his father, his grandfather, and great-grandfather, and was really very curious and valuable, is irreparable." And a statement prepared by the Provincial Congress for transmission to England voiced the official outrage of America in terms a professional propagandist might envy: "The Town of Charlestown, the buildings of which were in general large and elegant, and which contained effects belonging to the unhappy sufferers in Boston to a very great amount, was entirely destroyed; and its chimneys and cellars now present a prospect to the Americans, exciting an indignation

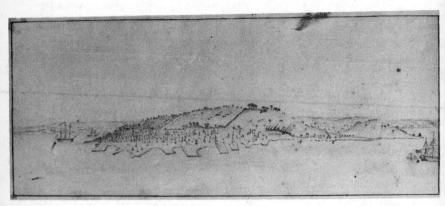

A drawing found in Clinton's papers shows the results of the deliberate British destruction of Charlestown—an act that infuriated colonists. "It was a pretty town!" one Bostonian wrote, "but now there is not one house left standing! It is nothing but a heap of ruins!" Below is an American propaganda leaflet, aimed at tempting redcoats into deserting by contrasting conditions at British-held Bunker Hill with those at the rebels' Prospect Hill. (*Clements Library, University of Michigan; Massachusetts Historical Society*)

PROSPECT HILL.	BUNKER's HILL.
I. Seven Dollars a Month.	I. Three Pence a Day.
II. Fresh Provisions, and in Plenty.	II. Rotten Salt Pork.
III. Health.	III. The Scurvy.
IV. Freedom, Ease, Affluence and a good Farm.	IV. Slavery, Beggary and Want.

in their bosoms which nothing can appease but the sacrifice of those miscreants who have introduced desolation and havock into these once happy abodes of liberty, peace, and plenty."

For a time it began to look as if there might be further Charlestowns, further bloody battles, with both armies preparing for the worst. "We have no communication with those on the other side of the water," Andrew Eliot wrote on the twenty-second, "but can perceive they are fortifying at Chelsea, Malden, Winter-hill, the hills in Roxbury, Dorchester, and *where not?* Every inch of ground will be disputed. Can no way be found to accommodate these unhappy differences? The God of heaven preserve us!" And speaking as one who had seen enough of the troubles men make for themselves, the minister looked to another quarter for help: "It is an inexhaustible source of comfort that the government of the world is just where it is."

If the relentless Henry Clinton had had his way, there would have been another fight immediately; and his zeal was matched on the American side by Prescott, who had returned to Cambridge after the battle, made his report to Ward, and offered to retake the hill that very night if the commanding general would give him three regiments of fresh men, well equipped with ammunition and bayonets. Wisely, Ward refused to permit Prescott to re-enter the trap from which he had just escaped, and with the frustration of these two offensive plans, a period of relative calm descended on Boston and Cambridge, allowing the two armies to lick their wounds and ponder the future. The same difficulties that had beset Ward before the battle plagued him increasingly now: shortages of arms and equipment and money, the steady attrition of men. Appeals went out to the New England colonies for more troops, and from some quarters the response was gratifying. That summer, for example, nearly half of the able-bodied men and boys from Mason, New Hampshire, were in the army. When it was learned that four fresh British regiments were arriving, strenuous efforts were made to fill the complement of existing American units as rapidly as possible. Some regiments called up in haste from outlying towns in Massachusetts were called back just as fast by their anxious townspeople, and all the while men were deserting, simply disappearing from camp and heading for home, tired, disgusted, or unable to remain away from their families and occupations any longer. Frantically, Ward searched for powder, with no immediate success, and partly because of this, partly as a result of his men's experience in battle, he asked the Congress for a supply of spears. These, he said, "might have saved the intrenchment" in the late action, and Congress acted quickly, ordering 1500 "good spears" to be bought or rented at once. About July 1 they began arriving, and soon the rebel breastworks bristled with menacing, long-handled pikes stuck into the ground.

Groups of soldiers went from town to town, from house to house, asking for blankets and clothing. Many of the men were almost naked, having lost or left their clothes and bedding on Breed's Hill, and the agent of the Committee of Supplies reported sorrowfully that no stockings, shirts, shoes, or blankets remained in his store. Blankets were needed not only to keep the men warm but to keep their powder dry in case of rain. "If our men must be in the rain without covering and we should be attacked Immediately after ye rain is over pray what are we to Expect?" Ward asked, and ruefully supplied his own answer: "Destruction."

But despite all the glaring shortages, despite the beating they had supposedly taken, the Americans acted like men who were ready to fight again any time the British cared to resume. As the Reverend Andrew Eliot had observed, they seemed to be fortifying everywhere, and Joseph Trumbull, writing from Cambridge to his friend Colonel Dyer, described the rebel lines as running from the Charles River to the Mystic. In addition to Putnam's fort on Prospect Hill, which anchored the American center, there were at least five redoubts, giving them, as Trumbull colorfully put it, "a compleat line of Circumnallations" between the two rivers. The main American and British works, on Prospect and Bunker Hills, respectively, were within cannon shot of each other, and Trumbull confidently expected that Cobble Hill, which lay between the two, would be hotly contested before long. At Roxbury, Trumbull reported, the rebel entrenchments were so strong that "every man in Boston & at Bunkers & Breed's Hills must fall, before they could force a passage that way into the country." But there was no action in the offing, the siege dragged on, and as Peter Oliver wrote, the two armies "kept squibbing at each other, but to little Purpose; at one Time a Horse would be knocked in the Head, and at another Time a Man would be killed, or lose a Leg or an Arm; it seemed to be rather in Jest than in Earnest; at some Times, a shell would play in the Air like a Sky Rocket . . . and there burst without Damage; and now and then, another would fall in the Town, and there burst, to the Terror or breaking of a few Panes of Glass: and during the whole Blockade, little else was done but keeping both Armies out of the Way of Idleness."

And all the while Ward sought to keep his army together and Gage puzzled over what to do with his, the news of the battle began to spread. On Saturday evening, June 17, the first ripples of intelligence had gone out to the world beyond, and with every passing day post-riders and ships carried the word farther. In an age of high-speed, professionally operated communications systems, it is all too easy to forget how reliant the eighteenth century was on reports from ordinary citizens, passed on by word of mouth or by letter. Newspapers of the day contained paragraphs headed "Intelligence from New York," or "From a Correspondent in London," usually the contents of a letter passed along to the editor, and as like as not containing rumors picked up at second hand.

On the day of the battle, people in villages and farmsteads near Boston heard the sound of firing, stopped what they were doing, and began to ask for news. "When I say that ten thousand reports are passing, vague and uncertain as the wind, I believe I speak the truth," Abigail Adams wrote from Braintree soon afterward. Off in Scituate, Paul Litchfield made this laconic entry in his diary on June 17: "Something warm. an almost continual firing heard all day supposed to be near Boston. a large Smoke arose & a fire seen in the evening. Went to ye Neck in ye afternoon." (For a man curious enough to have gone to the Neck, who may have seen the final climactic moments of the struggle, his is easily the most tantalizing and least satisfying report of the day.) Benjamin Guild, who taught school in Wrentham and preached at a Dedham church on Sunday, first learned of the battle on the night of the seventeenth, when "Just as it began to grow dark we discover'd a fire to the South" which "seem'd to rage very high till 9 or 10 when it seem'd to cease. We concluded it was Charleston." The next morning he learned that "Charlston was all in Ashes & that our men was driven from Bunkers Hill with considerable loss." That noon he expected further news, but none came. A messenger rode up in the afternoon with an urgent demand for powder, but not until the conclusion of Guild's evening sermon was there any satisfactory information concerning the battle.

Those early tidings emanating from around Boston all bore the solemn implication Benjamin Guild received—that the Americans had been driven from Bunker Hill with heavy losses. In the eighteenth century the army that held the ground after a battle was thought to have won the day, so from the very first the tendency was to think of this as a defeat for the rebels.

The immediate and inevitable reaction was to lay the blame on various officers of the army. In a letter to John Adams, James Warren flatly accused Ward of cowardice, and then ventured a further opinion: "Had our brave men, posted on Ground injudiciously at first taken, had a [Charles] Lee or a Washington, instead of a general destitute of all military ability and spirit, to command them, it is my opinion the day would have terminated with as much glory to America as the 19th of April. This is our great misfortune, and it is remediless from any other quarter than yours. We dare not supersede him here." An American who was spying for the British said that if the army had its way, Ward would have been cashiered, "for he never so much as gave one Written order that day." Fortunately for Ward, wiser heads prevailed. Three days after the battle, the Connecticut assembly generously voted that its colony's troops remain subject to command of the Massachusetts general. And Samuel Adams, writing from Philadelphia on the twenty-eighth, urged James Warren to "take Care lest Suspicions be carried to a dangerous Length. Our Army have behavd valiantly. There may have been an Error; but that Error may have proceeded not from a Want of Spirit but a Want of Judgment."

There had been ineptness and insubordination, cowardice and bad planning, however, and the critics were legion. Samuel Gray, a civilian, could see that things had gone wrong at the top: "The reason why our men on fatigue all night were not relieved, or attempted to be relieved, I cannot assign; had they been supported in a proper manner, there can't remain a question but that the enemy must have been totally defeated." Captain John Chester had his own ideas on the subject. He observed that the men in the redoubt had behaved like soldiers once they became accustomed to the noise of the cannon; the fault was with those who came up late or who did not come forward at all. Terrified by the fearful racket of the guns, they "did not march up with that true courage their cause ought to have inspired them with," Chester said; if only the rebels had had five hundred more men, used to the sound of battle, they could have pulled the thing off. Doctor Jeremy Belknap, who walked over the ground sometime after the engagement, appraising it with a historian's eye, concluded that this had been "a most hazardous and imprudent affair on both sides." The Americans should never have occupied such an advanced position unless they had an adequate escape route; the British were foolhardy to make a frontal assault when they could so easily have taken the rebels in the rear.

It was perfectly natural for men ashamed and dismayed by what they thought of as a defeat to try and fix the cause of it somewhere; and it was just as natural that they should single out for blame those who had lost their heads or turned tail in battle. Three days after the engagement the Provincial Congress appointed a committee to look into a report that there had been treachery among some of the officers. The corpulent Samuel Gerrish and James Scammon were subsequently court-martialed for their behavior, and the former was cashiered for keeping out of range of the fight; John Callender and Scarborough Gridley were tried and dismissed from the service (Callender, it should be noted, rejoined the army in 1776 as a volunteer, and fought with such signal bravery at the battle of Long Island that Washington removed his sentence from the orderly book and restored his commission). While no evidence of treachery was brought forth, a number of officers were criticized for cowardice or for panicking, and caustic remarks were circulated about those hundreds of private soldiers who had remained on Bunker Hill, hanging back while their comrades did the fighting. But it was inexperience, not cowardice, that cost the Americans the battle. Of course there was confusion and indecision at headquarters, but if Ward had had a staff, or regimental officers equal to the situation, the men and ammunition he ordered to Breed's Hill—had they all reached there on time and been committed to battle—should have sufficed. And for every cowardly officer, many amply demonstrated their courage. The most obvious example was General Joseph Warren, who was killed while fighting in the redoubt. Two colonels, Gardner and Parker, were mortally wounded; and at least four others—Bridge, Nixon, Jonathan Brewer, and Gridley—were hit; while Stark, Prescott, Putnam, Little, and other ranking officers were under fire almost continuously.

On a day which had seen so much valor, the tragedy was the lack of over-all American leadership, for the problem was not the lack of fighters but the lack of genuine commanders. Knowlton's and Stark's men, for instance, who were only lightly engaged during the final British assault, might have charged Howe's right wing from the side and rear just when the redcoats were storming the redoubt; but there was no one in over-all command to order such a move, no one to coordinate the efforts of the two American wings, so that they might have been waging entirely separate battles. To the rear, on Bunker Hill, were hundreds of fresh men who could have turned the tide by falling on the exhausted British at the last minute; but without leaders or coherent orders they remained idle and useless, only six hundred yards from Prescott's beleaguered redoubt. Fortunately for the army and for the future of the rebellion, the problem of command was about to be settled for good.

Not until June 22 did a courier reach Philadelphia, bringing vague word of a bloody clash to the north. Just as George Washington was making his final preparations for departure from the city to take command of the newly named Continental Army around Boston, a long letter from Governor Jonathan Trumbull of Connecticut was delivered to the Congress, containing this brief passage at the end: ". . . we have just received the important (but very imperfect) news of a vigorous attack on our Army, on Friday night or Saturday morning last, in consequence of their attempting to take possession of the important posts at Bunker's Hill in Charlestown. Our forces have been obliged to retreat, but on the whole suppose they have suffered far less than their enemies." (The governor or his informant was shrewd enough to realize that the British might have lost more than they had won.) On the twenty-fourth two expresses reached Philadelphia, one carrying a fairly full account of the battle as observed from Winter Hill by Captain Elijah Hide of Lebanon. And on June 25, when Washington arrived at Colonel Lispenard's in New York, a rider galloped up with an urgent message from the Provincial Congress of Massachusetts to the Continental Congress. Even though it was not addressed to him, members of the New York Congress who were with Washington persuaded him to open the dispatch on the grounds that the information it contained must be of vital concern. It was a paper bearing the signature of James Warren, the new president of the Massachusetts Congress, and it described the battle in some detail. Washington scanned it quickly, his attention drawn to the casualty figures: "Americans killed and missing was unknown but supposed by some to be about sixty or seventy, and by some considerably above that number," while the British were said to have lost as many as one thousand men. The new commander-in-chief of the Continental Army had had some experience with casualty lists, and knew the natural tendency to minimize one's own while magnifying those of the enemy; but if the facts were half so favorable as this report indicated, the Americans might beat the British regulars after all. He could not have foreseen the long years of hardship and struggle that lay ahead, the difficulties of keeping an army in the field, the desperate poverty of men and supplies in the midst of plenty.

It was a long time before the public in general regarded the battle as anything but a defeat, rashly planned and poorly executed. As the historian Richard Frothingham wrote, "No one, for years, came forward to claim the honor of having directed it; no notice was taken of its returning anniversary." But victory or no, the provincial leaders wanted England to get the news of the affair, and get their version of it. They had achieved something of a propaganda victory after Lexington and Concord and the aim was to do so once more—making it clear to the people of England that the government troops had acted aggressively again, capitalizing on the divided public opinion in the home country, and strengthening the hand of those who supported colonial ambitions either through sympathy or political opportunism. On July 6, 1775, the Massachusetts Committee of Safety registered its concern over "the advantages our enemies will derive from General Gage's misrepresentations of the battle of Charlestown, unless counteracted by the truth of that day's transactions being fairly and honestly represented to our friends and others in Great Britain," and the upshot of this was the appointment of a committee of three clergymen, charged with preparation of an impartial account. Written largely by the Reverend Peter Thacher, who had seen something of the battle from a house on the Malden side of the Mystic River, near the Penny Ferry, the report was a fairly straightforward summary based on reports by various witnesses, including Colonel Prescott. But just in case any reader missed the significance of the facts, someone on the Committee of Safety added that reference to "miscreants who have introduced desolation and havock into these once happy abodes of liberty, peace and plenty," and worked in an aside about "Ministerial assassins" and "rapacious despots."

The rebels were not so fortunate with their message as they had been after Lexington and Concord. Beginning on July 20, rumors of a battle near Boston were circulating in London, and on the twenty-fifth of the month they were confirmed officially by the publication of Gage's own description of the fight. It provoked immediate and heated arguments, of course—Tory and Whig taking stances that might have been expected—but generally, people were shocked and deeply troubled by the news, and military men were aghast at the losses suffered by the British army. "I see the American War full of horrors," one of them wrote to Clinton. And on the heels of the published news came the first wave of letters from friends and relatives in Boston, most of them striking the same theme. "A few such victories would Ruin the Army," poor Abercromby wrote from his deathbed to Lord Loudoun, and that was the refrain that ran through much of the correspondence. One officer in Boston said he could not see that a single advantage had resulted from the attack. "We have, indeed, learned one melancholy truth," he added, "which is, that the Americans, if they were equally well commanded, are full as good soldiers as ours; and as it is, are very little inferior to us, even in discipline and steadiness of countenance." From another came a somber warning: ". . . all you have yet sent by way of troops to this Continent are but a mouthful. If you send more to add to us, we may make them a dinner; and you may continue to supply them with a supper, and then it will be a good night." Still another pointed an accusing finger at those in command: "We are all wrong at the head," he cried, and went on to make a more serious charge. "Such ill conduct at the first out-set argues a gross ignorance of the most common rules of the profession, and gives us, for the future, anxious forebodings. I have lost some of those I most valued. This madness or ignorance nothing can excuse. The brave men's lives were wantonly thrown away. Our conductor as much murdered them as if he had cut their throats himself, on Boston Common." And, almost inevitably, there was a bitter echo of Burgoyne's now-famous remark: "We have got a little elbowroom," an officer wrote, "but I think we have paid too dearly for it."

If the Americans were unsure of the results, it did not take the British long to perceive that Gage had won no triumph. One critic suggested to Lord North that if there were eight more such "victories" no one would be left to report them. All the English had to see were letters such as these, the casualty lists, the shiploads of widows and orphans and wounded returning home, and they began to wonder if suppression of the revolt did not entail "the most ruinous consequences." Aboard the *Charming Nancy* when she docked at Plymouth early in September were Margaret Gage and 170 sick and wounded officers and men—"some without legs, and others without arms; and their cloaths hanging on them like a loose morning gown, so much were they fallen away by sickness and want of proper nourishment. There were moreover near sixty women and children on board; the widows and children of the men who were slain. Some of these too exhibited a most shocking spectacle; and even the vessel itself, though very large, was almost intolerable, from the stench arising from the sick and wounded, for many of them were hardly cured yet." A few men began to wonder if the government would dare to pursue its policies. During the summer of 1775 the itinerant Methodist preacher, John Wesley, talked to a great many common folk as he traveled about the English countryside, and what he saw and heard disturbed him deeply. Thousands were unemployed, people were going hungry, business was bad, the widows and orphans of soldiers killed in Boston were sorely in need of help, ships were laid up, trade was slow—and all these things were the direct result of the trouble in America. They indicated, Wesley thought, that the people of England would neither endorse nor support the program of George III.

But if there was one thing the King was not worrying about,

it was public opinion as represented by the people Wesley saw. He had the backing of the segment of the country that mattered; what preyed upon his troubled mind was the dark specter of Great Britain breaking up, and he was more determined than ever to teach the colonists a lesson. His first act was to issue a proclamation "for Suppressing Rebellion and Sedition," binding all officers and subjects to aid him in putting down the revolt; then he refused to acknowledge or answer the so-called "olive branch" petition from the Continental Congress, the colonists' final effort at settling matters amicably. And it was quickly evident that this hard line had the support of the Tory majority. Writing to Lord Dartmouth just after he heard the news of Bunker Hill, Sir James Adolphus Oughton stated flatly that "Treating with Rebels, while they have Arms in their Hands, would demonstrate a Weakness in Government which no Victory could compensate for." If the rebels were sincere, Oughton said, they could lay down their arms and ask forgiveness. Otherwise, England's might should be directed at once to bringing them to terms; "The sooner they are made to Taste Distress the sooner will that happy Effect be produced, and the Effusion of Blood be put a stop to."

The point of no return had been reached. Not ten years earlier, George Mason of Virginia had been able to write: "We claim nothing but the liberty and privileges of Englishmen, in the same degree, as if we had still continued among our brethren in Great Britain." But George III effectively put an end to all such claims; he and his ministers and their policies had driven a wedge between England and her colonies, creating a unity in the latter which would have been unthinkable at the time Mason wrote, and the news of his proclamation and his rejection of the "olive branch" meant that the battle lines had been drawn, that there would be no turning back. Some Americans welcomed the change in political temperature, realizing that it would stiffen the spines of patriots and bring a good many of the uncommitted into camp. Prior to the battle, it was generally conceded that the temper of northern and southern colonies was entirely different, and not for some time did the British perceive that public opinion had undergone a chemical change. On June 24 Richard Reeve ventured an opinion to Sir George Howard: the northerners, he said, would not listen to the British government's case if it was presented by an angel from heaven. "You can have no conception of the People if you imagine that fair reason and argument will take hold upon them—they have been too far gone long ago." Force was the answer, and if it was impossible to spare more troops from England, the government would have to resort to mercenaries or "share America with some foreign power & subdue the rest, for subdue them you must at any rate (these Northern Colonies I mean) or for ever relinquish your authority over them." What Reeve and most men like him failed to realize was that a profound change had taken place in America after June 17. No longer was it going to be possible to deal separately with the northern and southern colonies. As Samuel Ward, a Rhode Island member of the Continental Congress, put it, "Thank God, the happy day which I have long wished for has at length arrived; the southern colonies . . . no longer look back to Great Britain; they are convinced that they have been pursuing a phantom, and that their safety is a vigorous determined defense." One southerner who had been suspicious of the New Englanders came up to Ward and greeted him as "Brother Rebel," saying that he would be willing now to "declare ourselves independent."

Curiously, despite all the evidence that there were large numbers of loyalists in the colonies who were ready and eager to fight for the Crown, the government must have considered them, along with Americans generally, cowards or of little use militarily, for no intelligent effort was made to capture this substantial reservoir of manpower and put it to use where it could do the most good. Nothing was done to win over Americans of uncertain loyalties, to aid those who had stood fast in support of the Crown, or to enlist their support. They were simply ignored, and even though there were subsequent attempts during the war to rally American loyalists to the flag, it was at best an off-again, on-again policy, and the fact that the government forsook these people from the very beginning was to cost Britain dearly.

Ironically, governmental neglect of this potential source of military strength came at a time when there was deep concern over the weakness of the army. Recruiting was not going well, as John Pownal wrote to Henry Clinton: "Unless it rains men in red coats I know not where we are to get all we shall want." Lord North decided that the rebellion must be considered like any other "foreign war," and so, to fill the ranks, the Crown began negotiating for the hire of German mercenaries—those hapless serfs of Hesse-Cassel, Waldeck, Brunswick, and Anspach-Bayreuth whose princes rented them out for any military adventure so long as the blood money was paid. Few of George III's acts incurred such wrath in the colonies as this one, and in England the Opposition took up the cry against the mercenaries; but even on such an unpopular issue the ministerial majority was overwhelming. England had settled for war, not reconciliation, and the rebels were to be crushed; the war party had the bit in its teeth, and long-range plans were being made for military expeditions to the Carolinas and to Canada. But first, there was a piece of unfinished business.

Thomas Gage's report on Bunker Hill had aroused public feeling in England, and along with the mourning for the brave men who had died there was a rising tide of indignation and anger that this thing had been permitted to happen. The public and the government wanted a scapegoat and the first person they thought of was Gage himself. Here he was calling again for more troops, implying that the government had been responsible for the failures in America; it was obvious that the man whom George III called "the mild General" had to go. Three days after the news of Bunker Hill reached London the decision was made to dismiss Gage and replace him with William Howe. On September 26 Gage learned his fate and two weeks later received his last salute as commander-in-chief of His Majesty's forces in North America. Almost no one saw him off when he sailed from Boston on October 11, after two decades of devoted service in the colonies. For nearly half of those years he had been the most powerful British official on the continent; he was an honorable man and a thoroughly courageous one, and he had given all he had to his task. It was supremely ironic that his career in this country should have begun and ended with the two greatest disasters of British arms in North America —Braddock's defeat and the battle for Bunker Hill. Between those two isolated contests the whole temper of the English colonies had changed forever, and forces far beyond Thomas Gage's capacity to control had swept across the land like a whirlwind, catching him up, helpless, in the process, and leaving behind the wreckage of his career.

Even before Gage's departure, according to Lieutenant John Barker, the word was out that "England is determined to go through with this Affair for which reinforcements are to be here soon." Supposedly five thousand oxen, fourteen thousand sheep, and a huge quantity of hogs were to be shipped to Boston, along with mountains of vegetables, coal, and ten thousand butts of beer. Apart from the fact that no such shipment ever arrived in Boston, the implication was plain—in England they were preparing for a long war. And Gage's successor, buoyed by reports of supplies and reinforcements, decided that nothing would be lost by waiting until spring to settle accounts with the besieging rebels. Once that was accomplished, Howe reasoned, he could move his forces leisurely down to New York, where conditions would be more favorable. But once again a British commander reckoned without the rebels' industry—this time in the huge, bluff personage of a man named Henry Knox, who left Cambridge late in November bound for Fort Ticonderoga, his mission to bring back the cannon that lay within those walls. Washington regarded the need for these guns as so great that "no Trouble or Expence must be spared to obtain them," and he gave the assignment to the ambitious Knox, a former Boston bookseller who, shortly before the attack on Bunker Hill, had slipped out of town as stealthily as a 280-pounder can. In the dead of winter, Knox brought forty-three cannon and sixteen mortars from Lake Champlain to Lake George, then to

Henry Knox, who was made commander of artillery late in 1775, had no experience of military matters beyond what he had read in his Boston bookstore, but he proved an able choice and became one of Washington's most trusted officers. In this portrait, the artist Gilbert Stuart concealed the hand Knox had maimed in a hunting accident and kept swathed in a handkerchief. (*Courtesy, Museum of Fine Arts, Boston*)

Albany and across the Hudson, over the Berkshires ("mountains," the city-born Knox said, "from which we might almost have seen all the Kingdoms of the earth"), on to Springfield, and at last to Framingham, where he held his "noble train of artillery" ready for delivery to the commander-in-chief. The arrival of those cannon sealed the fate of Boston and its garrison.

It is not often that men profit from past experience, but now the Americans did so. George Washington decided to seize Dorchester Heights, resurrecting the old plan which the British attack had forced the rebels to abandon. To achieve this objective, as at Breed's Hill, the Americans would have to erect fortifications in the darkness of a single night before the British cannon opened on them. The problem was even more difficult because the ground was frozen now, but a great many lessons had been learned. There was an abundance of men, tools, supplies, ammunition, and weapons; the staff work had been done properly, and everything was in readiness. Soldiers were put to work making fascines, or bundles of sticks, which would be held together by wooden frames, or "chandeliers," to be erected as prefabricated breastworks and covered with dirt. On the night of March 2, to divert the redcoats' attention, Washington's new artillery began to cannonade Boston, and the bombardment continued for the next two nights. Meanwhile, on March 4 all the militiamen from the surrounding towns were called up, Washington's theory being that a Massachusetts man would fight harder on the fifth—Boston Massacre day—than on any other day of the year, and these troops were given the assignment of defending the lines while the Continental Army was otherwise engaged. After dark, a working party of some twelve hundred men under John Thomas headed up the hill while Knox's guns poured shot into Boston and British gunners returned the fire, effectively sealing their own ears to any sounds from Dorchester Heights. Great quantities of hay were piled along the route to screen the carts, laden with equipment, which would be traveling back and forth. Under the supervision of Knox and Colonel Richard Gridley, fascines and chandeliers were put in place, trees were felled to provide abatis, and incredibly, by ten o'clock that night two forts strong enough to withstand small-arms fire and grapeshot were nearly completed.

Then there was another curious repetition of the night of June 16: a British lieutenant colonel reported to Brigadier General Francis Smith that "the rebels were at work on Dorchester Heights," but Smith did nothing, and no report reached Howe. By 3 A.M., three thousand fresh American troops arrived on the hill, plus five companies of riflemen, and the work on the redoubts continued until daylight. Only then did the British indicate that they were aware of the activity by opening fire from the ships and shore batteries, but ominously, all the balls fell short of the target.

The British were dumbfounded. Someone overheard Howe saying that "The rebels have done more in one night than my whole army could have done in months," and he told Clinton "they could not have employed less than 12 or 14,000 Men that Night." Another officer, astonished at the sight, said the forts had been built "with an expedition equal to that of the genii belonging to Aladdin's wonderful lamp." These two forts, mounted with cannon, fully manned, surrounded by abatis, and out of range of the British artillery, were impregnable except by a frontal assault; and the guns in these works commanded the British fleet anchorage, the shipping channels, Castle William, and the town of Boston itself.

Faced with disaster, Howe decided to drive the Americans out, and prepared his forces for the attack. They were to assault with unloaded guns (not pausing to fire as they had at Breed's Hill), depending solely on the bayonet. One American who watched the redcoats embark for the Castle, their jumping-off point, noticed that "they looked in general pale and dejected, and said to one another that it would be another Bunkers Hill affair or worse." It stood to reason it would be far worse. The Americans had chosen a more defensible position; they were well supplied with artillery; they had good protection, both natural and man-made; there was plenty of ammunition; skilled riflemen were on hand to pick off attackers at long range, and pikemen were available for hand-to-hand combat, while the men in the fort were fresh and had ample support standing by. They also had George Washington, who was on the scene ready to direct the fight, and he had prepared for virtually every eventuality. In addition to other precautions, he had arranged for signals to be made from Dorchester to Roxbury to Cambridge the moment Howe's attack began, at which a fleet of boats loaded with troops and floating batteries would cross the Back Bay and attack Boston.

Howe did not move that day; presumably he was waiting for nightfall and a favoring tide. But night came, and with it what one Bostonian termed "A Hurrycane"—an extraordinary windstorm that would have kept Howe's force from shoving off even if he had wanted to go through with his plan. But there is reason to believe that Howe had no intention of doing so, that he saw the folly of a frontal attack under these circumstances, and only made preparations for one in order to preserve the honor of his troops. At 8 P.M. on March 5, after hearing the arguments of all his officers against the planned attack, he countermanded his orders. The day before, the British and the loyalists had been serene and secure in Boston; now only one choice remained to the British commander—to evacuate the town.

Early on the morning of March 6, 1776, the sad, dirty job of packing began, only this was no ordinary moving day—time was running out, and a kind of frantic haste prevailed. Infantrymen considered themselves lucky that they had only their own gear to worry about; quartermasters, engineers, and artillerymen were everywhere at once, rounding up all the stores and equipment they thought they could save. Colonel Samuel Cleaveland, as inefficient as ever, managed to drop three of his great mortars into Boston harbor, and left a fourth behind in the mud. The army, preoccupied by duties large and small but glad to be doing something at last, prepared to board the hated transports for an unknown destination, while on the fringes of the commotion—part of it yet irrevocably separate—were the loyalists. As Washington wrote,

"No Electric Shock, no sudden Clap of thunder, in a word the last trump could not have struck them with greater consternation" than Howe's order to evacuate the town. There were more than a thousand of them who were going—people of all ages from every class and walk of life, from lieutenant governor and customs official to clergyman and farmer, merchant and mechanic—united in their conservatism and their unbearable sense of loss, thrown together in their desperation to be saved. On one boat went Benjamin Hallowell, the customs commissioner whose house had been ransacked the night Thomas Hutchinson's mansion was put to the torch, who had suffered every manner of indignity and abuse, including a stoning, at the hands of Liberty Boys; now he put to sea in a cabin with thirty-six others—"men, women, and children; parents, masters, and mistresses, obliged to pig together on the floor, there being no berths." Some, more foresighted or fortunate than others, managed to bring off the most valuable of their possessions; a few even got some household goods aboard the vessels. On the eleventh, however, Howe ordered all furniture and "other useless luggage" that could not be shipped to be thrown overboard, and there were stories of such belongings floating around the wharves or drifting ashore on distant beaches.

All too often, dazed and hurried and scared, the loyalists snatched up from their homes what they could quickly lay hands upon, and came away with the most pathetic and useless of remnants. These were people who believed in an ordered, carefully stratified society where a man knew and appreciated his station— a society that did not change. What had happened to them shattered not just their world but the entire order of things, to the point that they did not even know their destination now, only that they were going, leaving behind the nightmare and the terrible, crushing experience. Many were old and sick and could only follow where someone else led; God knew where they would land. There were those who went to Halifax—"a cursed, cold, wintry place"—to try and hew a farm out of a harsh, unyielding soil; like it or no, pioneering would be their lot from now on, and it was all many could do to survive. Others went to England to rely on the compassion and charity of relatives, friends, or the government; but there they found they were strangers except to one another, and so met, in London or in Bath, huddling together for security in the manner of refugees since time began, talking of the past, their hearts and minds forever looking back on what had been and what might have been. Many learned that they had been proscribed by the rebels, outlawed like common criminals and forbidden to return to Massachusetts; others heard that their property had been confiscated; and with all hope gone they simply lived on for lack of anything better to do. Still they requested that they might be buried in New England. Home was where they wanted to be.

The last day of the British occupation of Boston was March 17 —St. Patrick's Day of 1776. That morning a marine lieutenant named Adair was ordered to distribute crow's feet—four-pointed irons which lay on the ground with one point up—out beyond the town gate along the no-man's land of Boston Neck. "Being an Irishman," an English officer observed, "he began scattering the crowfeet about from the gate towards the enemy, and of course, had to walk over them on his return, which detained him so long that he was nearly taken prisoner." About eight o'clock another Irishman, Brigadier General John Sullivan of New Hampshire, was making his rounds when he sighted boats moving across the river and ships getting under way out in the harbor. That might mean a British attack on Dorchester Heights or it could be what everyone was waiting for—the evacuation. Hurrying up Plowed Hill, Sullivan reached the summit and looked through his glass; from here he could see redcoats scrambling out of boats and up the sides of the ships, which certainly indicated that they were preparing to depart. But if so, Sullivan wondered, why were sentries still occupying the fort on Bunker Hill? He trained his glass on them again and as he watched, it suddenly dawned on him that they were not moving; they were dummies. Quickly he and two other officers strode out over Charlestown Neck and up Bunker

Hill to the stronghold that had replaced Montresor's little redan. As Sullivan had surmised, it was manned with dummy sentinels, and to the Americans' amusement they were dressed in uniform, with horseshoes for gorgets and paper ruffles for lace. One of the scarecrow soldiers bore a sign on his chest that read "Welcome Brother Jonathan." Sullivan and his companions headed down to Prescott's old redoubt on Breed's Hill, found it deserted too, and proceeded to the water's edge where they hailed the ferry operator. He rowed up and told them the British had abandoned the town.

The Whigs who remained in Boston had watched with something akin to disbelief while the rear guard piled into longboats and shoved off, leaving the town free of redcoats for the first time in seven years. The moment they were safely out in the harbor a pack of little boys burst out of doors, ran screaming and yelling down Orange Street toward the town gates, and pelted across Boston Neck toward Roxbury, somehow darting in and out between Lieutenant Adair's booby traps. Shouting with glee, the youngsters rushed up to the rebel outposts and breathlessly delivered the news that Boston was free at last. Selectmen, slower by far than the boys, finally arrived in Roxbury and confirmed the story to Artemas Ward, who immediately ordered Colonel Ebenezer Learned to select five hundred men with smallpox scars who could enter the town with no fear of contracting the disease (the pox had flared up in November and December, and there were still cases around). About eleven o'clock Learned unbarred the gates on the main road into Boston and the men marched in, dodging crow's feet as best they could. Some of Putnam's men followed shortly afterward by boat, and Old Put began rounding up all public property and the guns and impedimenta left behind by the British. Most of the heavy iron cannon had been spiked, but so carelessly that more than half could be used again. Virtually all of the British medical stores were intact, and on the wharves were three thousand blankets and a variety of other equipment.

More baffling than these signs of negligence was the fact that the British had not yet headed to sea. In fact, they were still ominously near; between the Castle and Boston Light a long line of ships rode at anchor—"a formidable sight," one rebel officer noted. While Washington watched and waited to see what the enemy would do, he turned part of his attention to the liberated town to see how much damage had been done. Down by the wharves a number of stores had been looted; British officers had removed the pews from several churches and turned the buildings into riding schools; and several old frame structures had been condemned and torn down for firewood. But Boston, "although it has suffered greatly, is not in so bad a state as I expected to find it," Washington wrote. He was impressed by the British defenses; they were "amazingly strong . . . almost impregnable, every avenue fortified," and when he went out onto Bunker Hill and looked at the redoubt he decided that "Twenty thousand men could not carry it against 1000" had it been well defended.

Two nights after the British left Boston they demolished the defenses at Castle William and blew up all the buildings there that could not be burned. Meanwhile the Americans waited, their doubts and their worries growing. The twenty-second of March came, and the twenty-third, two days when the wind was favorable for the fleet to put to sea, and still the enemy lingered. Washington put men to digging a defensive position atop Fort Hill, which commanded the harbor and from which he could "render the landing of troops exceedingly difficult, if not impracticable." And at the same time the American regiments were preparing to march, for Washington was convinced that Howe would strike at New York, and the moment the British sailed he had to move overland at once to meet them. On March 24 Washington decided that Howe must be preparing a major blow: "As these favorable winds do not waft the fleet from Nantasket," he wrote to Ward, "my suspicions are more and more aroused." He suggested that Ward prepare fire rafts to send against the fleet in case of an attack. "I cannot but suspect they are waiting for some opportunity to give us a Stroke, at a moment when they conceive us to be off guard," the commander-in-chief wrote to another of his corre-

General Howe issued this notice prior to the evacuation of Boston to prevent useful articles from falling into the hands of the rebels when they reoccupied the town. Before the British departed from the harbor for good, they destroyed Castle William, on the rocky promontory illustrated below. (*Culver Pictures; Map Division, The New York Public Library*)

BY HIS EXCELLENCY

WILLIAM HOWE,

MAJOR GENERAL, &c. &c. &c.

AS Linnen and Woolen Goods are Articles much wanted by the Rebels, and would aid and assist them in their Rebellion, the Commander in Chief expects that all good subjects will use their utmost Endeavors to have all such Articles convey'd from this Place: Any who have not Opportunity to convey their Goods under their own Care, may deliver them on Board the Minerva at Hubbard's Wharf, to *Crean Brush*, Esq; mark'd with their Names, who will give a Certificate of the Delivery, and will oblige himself to return them to the Owners, all unavoidable Accidents accepted.

If after this Notice any Person secretes or keeps in his Possession such Articles, he will be treated as a Favourer of Rebels.

Boston, March 10th, 1776.

spondents. Thoroughly exasperated, he decided that the British "have the best knack at puzzling people I ever met with in my life." Discipline was tightened in all units of the army and Sullivan's men had orders to be ready at a moment's warning.

Men in the ranks knew they would be marching soon. On the day the British abandoned Boston Lieutenant Joseph Hodgkins wrote to his wife Sarah in Ipswich, asking her to send him an extra pair of "Briches." And three days later, realizing that she was worried about him, wrote again to reassure her and to explain why he had to depart: "I am willing to sarve my Contery in the Best way & mannar that I am Capeble of and as our Enemy are gone from us I Expect we must follow them," he said. But just in case she thought he wanted to go, he added, "I would not Be understood that I should Chuse to March But as I am ingaged in this glories Cause I am will to go whare I am Called."

For all Washington's anxiety, Howe was merely waiting, taking his own good time until the vessels were fit for sea; water was taken aboard and the transports received a month's supply of food. On March 27, with the tides running higher than normal, a fresh wind out of the northwest flecked the waters of Massachusetts Bay with whitecaps, and at eleven o'clock the flagship *Fowey* hoisted a signal, the decks of every vessel in the fleet sprang alive with activity, and by three that afternoon more than one hundred ships were making sail, heading down Nantasket Roads and standing out to sea. Aboard the armada—bound not for New York but for Halifax—were nearly nine thousand officers and men, plus twelve hundred women and children attached to the army, and eleven hundred loyalists. It was the army's last glimpse of Massachusetts and for most Tories it was their final sight of home.

The siege of Boston was over at last. More than nine months had passed since the battle for Bunker Hill, but the meaning of that day had only begun to be visible. For one thing, the rebels had seen the value of those temporary works thrown up in the fleeting hours of a June night. Their opponents might consider digging somehow cowardly or degrading and no part of a soldier's training, but Boston owed its deliverance to the spades and pick-axes used on Charlestown peninsula and Dorchester Heights. Another effect might have been observed late in the fall of 1776, when officers of the Fort Ticonderoga garrison received new general battle orders. They were to be "deliberate and cool in suffering men to fire, never allowing them to throw away their shot in a random, unsoldierlike manner." Higher authority had observed that "One close, well directed fire, at the distance of eight or ten rods, will do more toward defeating the Enemy, than all the scatter'd random shot fired in a whole day." The lesson of Breed's Hill had sunk home.

Something else, something entirely intangible and perhaps not even recognizable at the time, had occurred on June 17, 1775. Men who were not fighters by trade or inclination had stood side by side behind their earthworks and their fences and had waited calmly while some of the most formidable fighters in the world advanced against them in ordered ranks. They had not run from artillery fire, they had stood up to the wild terror of a bayonet charge, and they had broken only when their ammunition gave out and they could fight no more. A few months earlier the odds against the success of any American military effort would have been overwhelming; the regular army was an object of dread, not to be tested. Now Americans had met it face to face, and like a figment of darkness suddenly exposed to the light, it could be seen for what it was—an army that commanded great respect, but one composed of men no taller or stronger than any others. By demonstrating that some rather ordinary American farmers had stood against this formidable enemy, the battle of June 17 proved, as nothing else could, that others might accomplish the same thing. Had they failed, it is just conceivable that the rebellion might have sputtered out.

Beyond anything else, Bunker Hill meant that a war would be fought to secure the liberties of Americans. As John Adams was to observe many years later, the Revolution took place first in the minds and hearts of the people; but it required six years of fighting to make independence an accomplished fact. Through some blessing, the majority of those who had manned the redoubt and the fences on Charlestown peninsula knew why they were there and what they were fighting for. Many of them never carried a musket again, for one reason or another; but to their eternal credit, enough stayed on to become a nucleus of veterans who were with the army until the very end. These were not the summer soldiers Tom Paine complained of; they were the men who made the long marches to New York and Quebec, to Saratoga, the Cowpens, and Yorktown, who froze and starved at Morristown and Valley Forge. The war they fought was a hard, bloody, tragic business, and it was a war they came very close to losing.

At Bunker Hill, men from Massachusetts found themselves side by side with those of Connecticut and New Hampshire, and in the course of six bitter years of warfare these soldiers and others gradually perceived that they were involved in something that went far beyond the interests of their separate colonies. As they fought on, a nation was born, and many years later, when all but a handful of his comrades in arms had gone, one of the last surviving veterans of that war remembered how, "when peace was declared, we burnt thirteen candles in every hut, one for each State."

GEORGIO WASHINGTON SVPREMO DVCI EXERCITVVM ADSERTORI LIBERTATIS

COMITIA AMERICANA

On March 25, 1776, the Continental Congress received word of the British evacuation of Boston and commissioned a gold medal to be struck in Paris and presented to Washington. The obverse bears a likeness of the general and the reverse shows the town of Boston, the British ships under sail, and Washington and his officers in their moment of final triumph. (*Author's Collection*)

HOSTIBUS PRIMO FUGATIS

BOSTONIUM RECUPERATUM
XVII. MARTII
MDCCLXXVI.

A NOTE ON SOURCES

Considering the number of people who saw the battle for Bunker Hill, either as participants or as eyewitnesses, it is remarkable that so few useful contemporary accounts survive. Of those that remain only a handful are American, a fact which leads one to wonder whether more Englishmen knew how to write, or whether the letters they wrote were treasured because they had crossed the Atlantic Ocean, thus acquiring a higher value than the correspondence of an American who might have returned home within a few days or weeks after his letter arrived. No matter; the fact is that the British hold the honors so far as eyewitness evidence is concerned.

In addition to such reports, a number of second-hand versions of the battle remain—that is, letters written by someone who did not see the fight but who talked or corresponded with one who did. Some are valuable additions to the literature, since they replace an original letter which has been lost, or add in some way to our knowledge of contemporary thinking on the subject.

On the American side, virtually no official information exists beyond the report made by the Committee of Safety shortly after the battle. Designed for transmittal to Great Britain, this document was prepared for the Committee by three clergymen—the Reverend Dr. Cooper, the Reverend Mr. Gardner, and the Reverend Mr. Peter Thacher—and the writing seems to have fallen largely upon Thacher, a twenty-four-year-old pastor from Malden who could claim, at least, to have seen snatches of the fighting from a rather poor vantage point on the opposite side of the Mystic River. Ward's orderly book contains only the most laconic entry—a marginal note stating that a battle was fought on June 17, and listing the casualties—while none of the other orderly books adds much to our knowledge of events.

A few descriptions of the battle appeared in subsequent years; then in 1818 the floodgates of controversy opened with publication by General Henry Dearborn of an article attacking Putnam's behavior and questioning his courage. As Harold Murdock described it, Dearborn's account "abounds in absurd misstatements and amazing flights of imagination. He marshalled good men and true to utter words in his support, and General Putnam's son also rallied a reputable host to oppose their muddy recollections to the vagaries of Dearborn's friends." Depositions by the score were taken by both sides; ancient veterans, suddenly possessed of the most amazing memory for the most minute details of a battle that took place forty-three years earlier, were trotted out in defense of one claimant or the other. Not content to leave matters alone, the directors of the Bunker Hill Monument Association decided to collect further depositions from forty-odd "survivors" of the battle who attended the fiftieth-anniversary celebration in 1825. Nearly a generation later, when these documents were turned over to the Massachusetts Historical Society, George Ellis reported on them to his fellow members as follows: "Their contents were most extraordinary; many of the testimonies extravagant, boastful, inconsistent and utterly untrue; mixtures of old men's broken memories and fond imaginings with the love of the marvellous. Some of those who gave in affidavits about the battle could not have been in it, nor even in its neighborhood. They had got so used to telling the story for the wonderment of village listeners as grandfathers' tales, and as petted representatives of 'the spirit of '76,' that they did not distinguish between what they had seen and done and what they had read, heard, or dreamed." Quietly, the

1825 depositions were allowed to disappear, and although some had already been published by Samuel Swett, the verdict of the Historical Society served warning on future students.

The narrative of this book is based wherever possible on contemporary evidence. I have tried to draw conclusions from the testimony of men who were there, to see things through their eyes and in their terms. Only in rare instances have I drawn from later material, and then only when a vivid recollection met the test of plausibility and did not affect substantive conclusions. Such material is carefully labeled when used; an example is the Ipswich soldier's memory of how the British "looked too handsome to be fired at; but we had to do it" (page 130).

A number of popular stories connected with the battle were rejected because they could not be documented; others because they seemed to lack the ring of truth. One that failed on both counts is the legend of Putnam running along the breastwork and knocking up the leveled muskets of Americans in order to keep them from shooting his friend, Major Small. On the other hand, certain matters which have been accepted by generations of historians had to be *proved*. A good example is the weather on June 17, 1775—seemingly a minor detail, yet one that had a direct bearing on the course of the battle. Virtually all histories of the engagement state flatly that it was a clear, hot day (French mentions "the hot sun beating down"; Frothingham speaks of a "burning sun"); but nowhere in these studies is there any support for this conclusion. Not until Stephen Riley of the Massachusetts Historical Society sent me some excerpts from Paul Litchfield's diary for 1775 did I have any satisfactory proof that it was a hot day: Litchfield stated feelingly that it was "Something warm." Confirmation that the night of June 16 and the following day were fair and clear comes from the logs of the *Glasgow*, *Lively*, and *Somerset*.

Two other problems confront the student of the battle: false evidence and contradictory evidence. Fortunately, much of the false or misleading material has been exposed as a result of excellent detective work by such writers as Allen French and Harold Murdock. French, for example, showed that the first book published on Bunker Hill (a volume on which a great many later writers had naturally relied) was full of errors. This work, *An Impartial and Authentic Narrative of the Battle Fought on the 17th of June, 1775 Between His Britannic Majesty's Troops and the American Provincial Army, on Bunker's Hill, near Charles Town, in New-England* (they believed in complete titles in those days), was written in 1775 by John Clarke, First Lieutenant of Marines, and it purported to be an eyewitness account. But Clarke, as Allen French was able to demonstrate, was a drunk who was being shipped back to England to be cashiered after thirty-six years of service, and what he knew of Bunker Hill he had picked up second-hand, embellished freely, and written down in colorful fashion in order to turn a fast shilling or two. (French's article on Clarke's Narrative appears in *Publications of the Colonial Society of Massachusetts*, Vol XXXII, Transactions, 1933–1937, pp. 362–373). Murdock took apart the story of the Reverend John Martin, who was long cited as an authority on the battle. This urbane, amusing essay appears in *Bunker Hill, Notes and Queries on a Famous Battle.*

On the subject of contradictory evidence, Bernhard Knollenberg has drawn an apt parallel with the law, and with "the conflict in testimony among witnesses seemingly desirous of telling the truth." Even with the best of intentions, eyewitnesses produce different accounts of the same event, and where this happened I tried to select the version that seemed most logical in the light of other available facts.

Every man, Bacon said, is a debtor to his profession, and in addition to the contemporaneous materials used, I have consulted many critical studies. Again and again I found myself coming back to Allen French's *The First Year of the American Revolution*, a superb book which is, in my opinion, indispensable to the study of Bunker Hill (and indeed to the twelve-month period that began with the siege of Boston). This is a profound work of scholarship, at the same time well written and full of wisdom, understanding, and rare insight into the minds and mood of that bygone generation. A debt of gratitude is also due Mr. French's many predecessors, especially Peter Force, that almost forgotten collector and publisher of the *American Archives*. Force's industry, dedication, and scholarship were responsible for the preservation of hundreds of Revolutionary documents. When I first approached those enormous volumes my heart sank at the thought of how much had to be read; but it is almost impossible to spend any time with the *American Archives* and avoid the spell of those old letters, the Committee of Safety and Provincial Congress and Continental Congress minutes, the newspaper reports that bring history suddenly to life. Before long the problem is not how one will finish reading the *American Archives*, but if one will find time for anything else.

By all odds the best of the earlier studies of Bunker Hill is Richard Frothingham's invaluable *Siege of Boston*. This work and Henry B. Dawson's *Historical Magazine* for June, 1868 are also extremely important for the number of original documents reprinted, although Dawson's personal commentary is overly biased. Harold Murdock's *Bunker Hill, Notes and Queries on a Famous Battle* is as entertaining as it is challenging. A collection of essays on separate aspects of the subject rather than a narrative account of the battle, this is the product of an original and stimulating mind. On page 234 I mention my obligation to Bernhard Knollenberg for letting me read his paper—"Bunker Hill Reviewed: A Study in Conflict of Historical Evidence." This is an extremely useful examination of some ten or twelve important questions concerning the battle. Mr. Knollenberg gives his conclusions after a careful weighing of the available contemporary evidence.

Several excellent short accounts of the battle appear in Ward's *The War of the Revolution*, in Bruce Lancaster's *From Lexington to Liberty*, and in *The American Heritage Book of the Revolution*. Some of the important contemporary accounts are printed in *The Spirit of 'Seventy Six* by Commager and Morris, and in *Rebels* and Redcoats, by Scheer and Rankin. Justin Winsor's *Narrative and Critical History of America*, Volume VI, contains an excellent guide to the early literature and sources on the subject, and French's *First Year* supplements it nicely. A good critical essay on the battle is Charles Francis Adams' "The Battle of Bunker Hill from a Strategic Point of View."

ACKNOWLEDGMENTS

Not until the time comes to make a list of all those who have assisted him does the writer of a book of this kind realize the full extent of his indebtedness. My first thanks go to my wife Barbara, for her unfailing encouragement and for frank comments and questions regarding the manuscript, which have been continuously helpful. Since the research and writing of this book could be done only when I had some spare time, it consumed more nights, weekends, and vacations than I care to admit; for their patience and understanding, my grateful thanks to Barbara and to Liza and Tom Ketchum.

I am deeply indebted to Francis Ronalds, Superintendent of the Morristown National Historical Park. Drawing on his knowledge of the Revolution, he assembled for me a suggested list of sources on Bunker Hill which saved countless hours of labor, and he has sent me copies of numerous letters and documents from the Morristown collection.

Bernhard Knollenberg kindly let me read in manuscript a paper on Bunker Hill which he had prepared for the Massachusetts Historical Society. This essay was most helpful in clarifying certain disputed aspects of the battle.

The manuscript was read by Bruce Catton, Oliver Jensen, and Bernhard Knollenberg, to each of whom go my wholehearted thanks. It goes without saying that none of these gentlemen bears any responsibility for opinions expressed in the book or for any factual errors which may be found therein.

Stephen Riley, Director of the Massachusetts Historical Society, answered numerous requests and came to my aid on many occasions. I am also grateful to Malcolm Freiberg and others of the staff of that remarkable institution for their assistance.

Howard Peckham, Director of the William L. Clements Library at the University of Michigan, helped me to locate some of the most useful material in the Gage and Clinton Papers in the Library Collections.

Bruce Lancaster, John Bakeless, and Miss Esther Forbes all took time out from busy writing schedules to answer questions and give me the benefit of their wide experience.

I am indebted to Allan Nevins, who gave me valuable counsel and loaned me certain books which I had been unable to locate; and to James Parton, who generously gave me a copy of a centennial newspaper which I had not seen.

Professor Richard Morris of Columbia University was helpful in many ways, including searching his files for references to contemporary material on the battle. On several occasions Edward O. Mills wrote to suggest sources of information that I might otherwise not have seen. Arthur Tourtellot was most cooperative in calling my attention to possible sources of material.

For the enthusiasm and interest which first encouraged me to go ahead with this project, I want to acknowledge my thanks to Harry Shaw. I also wish to express my gratitude to Miss Louisa Thorn for her generous assistance. For his suggestions I am much obliged to Irwin Glusker. My thanks are also due Miss Nina Page for her help.

I have relied heavily upon the following institutions for information and aid, and I am most appreciative of the cooperation shown me by the various staffs: the Massachusetts Historical Society, the Boston Public Library, the New York Public Library, the Library of Congress, and the William L. Clements Library. For permission to use the facilities of the Frederick Lewis Allen

Memorial Room of the New York Public Library, I want to thank Gilbert Cam.

The fullest cooperation was received from British institutions, and I have to thank V. Lindray-MacDougall of the Manuscript Department, National Maritime Museum, Greenwich; R. F. Hunnisett of the Public Record Office, London; and E. J. Davis, Archivist of the County of Buckingham, Aylesbury. For permission to quote from certain papers, I acknowledge with thanks the generosity of Major-General Sir Richard G. H. Howard-Vyse, K. C. M. G.

Mrs. Olive S. D'Arcy Hart carried out an extensive search for information in the Public Record Office in London, and I am greatly in her debt for the judgment and energy she brought to the task.

It should be noted that the above acknowledgments appeared in the original edition of this work. In addition to those already listed, I wish to express my appreciation to Mrs. Lilyan Glusker for her assistance in obtaining most of the illustrations that appear in the present edition.

NOTES

The chapter notes that follow appear in narrative style since their purpose is not so much to document my sources as to comment on them, and to add information that I have found interesting, useful, entertaining, or of possible help to others.

Chapter I

Information on the voyage of the *Cerberus* comes from the ship's log for this period (see the general note on the ships' logs, with the Notes for Chapter V below). In a day of almost instantaneous communications, it requires some effort to realize that news of the fighting at Lexington and Concord on April 19 did not reach England until May 28. The *Cerberus* sailed from England on April 21, and on May 8 spoke a brig from Baltimore; but that vessel must have left Baltimore by April 23, at least three days before Israel Bissell, the postrider who carried the news south, arrived there. It is possible, of course, that those on board the *Cerberus* received the news when a Salem fishing schooner was encountered on May 23, but in all probability the first report of any consequence came with the meeting of the *Otter* on the morning of May 25. Frothingham, in his *Siege of Boston*, p. 114, quotes a contemporary newspaper to the effect that the news was received from "a packet" coming out of Boston Harbor. The only such meeting recorded in the *Cerberus* log is the one with the *Otter*.

In the same note, Frothingham relates the story of Burgoyne's "elbowroom" remark. It is quite apparent that the phrase enjoyed a wide currency at the time; Gentleman Johnny struck a responsive chord, since a high percentage of letters written from Boston at this time make use of the expression. In satires of the period Burgoyne was always known as "Elbow Room," and there was an ironic aftermath to the story. When Burgoyne returned to Boston in 1777 as a prisoner after his defeat at Saratoga, an old woman sitting on a shed above the crowd cried out in a shrill voice: "Make way, make way—the general's coming! Give him elbowroom!"

The orders from Sandwich to Captain Chads of the *Cerberus* and to Admiral Graves are from Adm. 2/99, Orders & Instructions, 16 April 1774 to 28 June 1775.

Henry Clinton's description of the crossing is in his letter of June 9, 1775, to the sisters of his late wife. The letter is in the Clinton Papers at the William L. Clements Library.

Howe, Clinton, and Burgoyne—the three warriors who arrived on the *Cerberus*—are as much the stuff of psychology as of history. (A most interesting study, combining the methods of historian and psychologist, is "Sir Henry Clinton: A Psychological Exploration in History," by Frederick Wyatt and William B. Willcox, in the *William and Mary Quarterly*, Vol. XVI, No. 1, January, 1959.) As Allen French wrote, "There are various critical stages in the American Revolution at which the proper action of these three men could have destroyed the patriot army and wrecked the rebel cause." That each man failed at one or more crucial moments is one of the more fascinating "ifs" of the war, and has led some writers to conclude that the battle for Bunker Hill left an indelible mark upon all three, the memory of those grisly slopes affecting their decisions ever afterward. French's *First Year* has a good description of the major generals and their activities in Boston. Belcher, Vol. II, pp. 142 ff., has some interesting commentary on William Howe—that "inert, pleasure-loving man"—and his brother; and Partridge's book, *Sir Billy Howe*, is useful. Henry

Clinton's sensitivity is the subject of a witty and revealing essay in Murdock's *Bunker Hill.*

The British commander-in-chief is in many respects a more appealing subject than any of the major generals, and Alden's *General Gage in America* is an excellent, fair-minded study of the man who "stood between antagonistic forces, whose clash he could not avert." Arthur Tourtellot discusses Gage's temperament and problems sympathetically in *William Diamond's Drum,* as do Allen French in *The Day of Concord and Lexington,* and Harold Murdock in *The Nineteenth of April, 1775.* For Gage's earlier career Alden is especially good, and there is a fine account of Braddock's defeat in McCardell's excellent *Ill-Starred General.* (The latter book is also my source for that unsympathetic adage of the sailors: "A messmate before a shipmate . . ." etc.)

For information on eighteenth-century Boston, I relied heavily upon Justin Winsor's *Memorial History of Boston,* an indispensable and endlessly interesting guide to the town and its inhabitants. Shurtleff's *Topographical and Historical Description of Boston* is helpful but lacks the charm and style and depth of Winsor's work. Esther Forbes's *Paul Revere* contains some good descriptive material on the town at this period.

The eighteenth-century British footsoldier is described at some length in Belcher's *First American Civil War,* in French's *First Year,* and in Ward's *War of the Revolution,* and it is not a pretty picture. The plight of Boston's loyalists is reflected in countless letters written at this time. Among the best are those of Anne Hulton, which appear in *Letters of a Loyalist Lady* and which show the gradually rising feelings of fear and resentment on the part of the King's supporters. To the best of my knowledge, Richard Reeve's illuminating letters have not been published before. They are in the County of Buckingham Record Office, Aylesbury, Buckinghamshire, England, and are quoted by kind permission of the owner, Major General Sir Richard G. H. Howard-Vyse, K.C.M.G. The letter quoted in this chapter is dated May 14, 1775.

Some of the material on the Lorings and their estate comes from the article "Jamaica Plain by Way of London," by Eva

Phillips Boyd. One of the most interesting sidelights to that story is the "Acct. of Sundry Stores, farming utencils and household furniture" abandoned by the Lorings when they were forced to flee—a catalogue, including values, of what the well-appointed Massachusetts country estate contained.

The saga of Lady Frankland and her household effects may be traced in the proceedings of the Provincial Congress and the Committee of Safety, quoted in Force: IV: II: pp. 758, 791, 792, 810, and 811. Esther Forbes's *Paul Revere* describes the lady's origins as Agnes Surriage, as do French's *Siege of Boston* and Tourtellot's *The Charles*.

Burgoyne's feelings regarding the situation in Boston are drawn from several of his letters to friends in England, some of which are reprinted in *A Memorial of the American Patriots who fell at the Battle of Bunker Hill* . . . Excerpts from others may be found in French's *First Year*.

Chapter II

The warning from the New Hampshire Committee of Safety to the Massachusetts Provincial Congress regarding British plans to seize Dorchester Heights and Charlestown appears in Force: IV: II: p. 979. French's *First Year*, p. 209, lists several American sources of information about British plans.

Joseph Warren's letter to Arthur Lee appears in Frothingham's *Warren*, p. 489.

The portents of trouble between England and the colonies may be found throughout the pages of Force: IV: II. I have selected only a few of the many such examples reported during the months prior to April 19, 1775.

An orderly discussion of those chaotic days after Lexington and Concord appears in French's *First Year*, especially pp. 22 through 87. The author sheds much light on an extremely confusing subject—the composition of the various New England armies besieging

Boston between April 19 and June 17—and my discussion of the military owes a great deal to French's study.

The description of Ward is drawn from Martyn's biography of the general. Until recently the only useful biography of Dr. Joseph Warren was that written by Richard Frothingham, and it was the source of most of my information on this neglected leader of the Revolution. John Cary has written a good modern study of Warren, but I was not aware of it until too late to be of much use. Warren and Samuel Adams were the most important revolutionary figures in Massachusetts, and of the two Warren is the more attractive personality—a dedicated man who stood at the top of his profession and who, at the same time, gave all he had of sincerity, honesty, and idealism to the Whig cause. His great popularity, combined with his tragic death at the age of thirty-four, succeeded in making him a near-legendary figure for many years; but the fact that he died too soon to participate in the forming of a new government has deprived him of a reputation today. He deserves much better.

Two recurring themes run through the proceedings of the Provincial Congress: the fear of a standing army and a growing reliance on the Continental Congress in Philadelphia. (Typical of both is this excerpt from the Provincial Congress letter of May 16 to the Continental Congress: "We tremble at having an army, although consisting of our own countrymen, established here without a civil power to provide for and control it.") The majority of references to these subjects, and to the whole desperate matter of clothing, powder, ammunition, weapons, money, and food for the army, are based on documents reproduced in Force: IV: II.

Some of the most interesting personalities involved in the siege were stationed over in Roxbury—among them John Thomas, Nathanael Greene, and that delightful diarist Samuel Haws—but regrettably none of these men figured significantly in the main events covered by this work. Haws, a minute man from Wrentham, kept a journal, and his wry, curiously spelled comments on camp life make entertaining reading. The journal, which runs only to February 1776, was printed in *The Military Journals of Two Private Soldiers, 1758–1775*, compiled by Abraham Tomlinson.

Useful information on Roxbury at the time of the siege appears in the *Memorial History of Boston*, Vols. II and III.

The quotations from Joseph Hodgkins come from a fine book on two Ipswich soldiers, *This Glorious Cause*, by Wade and Lively. These company officers turned out for the Lexington alarm, fought at Bunker Hill, and stayed with the Continental Army through the victory at Saratoga. They lived long enough to attend the fiftieth anniversary of the battle for Bunker Hill, and the papers that constitute their service records make fascinating and occasionally inspiring reading.

John Stark's complaints are catalogued in a letter he wrote to the New Hampshire Congress, reproduced in Force: IV: II: p. 739.

French's *First Year* has much valuable material on the interim skirmishes which occurred between April 19 and June 17. Lieutenant Barker's comments on the Grape Island affair are in *The British in Boston*; Abigail Adams's are from the *Familiar Letters . . . ;* and Amos Farnsworth's diary, published in the Massachusetts Historical Society *Proceedings*, 32:80, is quoted extensively in French's *First Year*.

Material on Israel Putnam, "that Thunderbolt of War," appears in all the books on Bunker Hill. Richard Reeve's letter of May 14, 1775 contains his description of the Connecticut officer. Freeman's *Washington*, Vols. III and IV, is also useful on Putnam.

The chain of events sparked by Gage's Proclamation of June 12 is recorded in Force: IV: II: pp. 1352 ff., where the deliberations and decisions of the Provincial Congress are detailed.

Descriptions of the Hastings house appear in the *Memorial History of Boston*, Vol. III, p. 108, and in *The Cambridge of 1776*, edited by Arthur Gilman. Perhaps this is as good a place as any to record, for the unwary, that "The Diary of Dorothy Dudley," which appears in this little book about Cambridge, is a spurious document. Gilman, in the preface to the second edition, states: "A second edition of this book being demanded, the editor embraces the opportunity to confess that 'The Diary of Dorothy Dudley' was written expressly for *The Cambridge of 1776* by Miss [Mary William] Greely."

In Dawson's *Historical Magazine* for June, 1868, p. 322, there is a discussion of American plans to fortify Charlestown Heights in May—following a recommendation made by a Joint Committee of the Committee of Safety, which was voted down as being too warlike.

The Committee of Safety resolution of June 15, ordering a force to Bunker Hill, is quoted in full in Frothingham's *Siege*, pp. 116–117.

Elizabeth Tyler's late recollection of Joseph Warren is quoted from *Grandmother Tyler's Book*, edited by Frederick Tupper and Helen Tyler Brown.

Chapter III

Computing a timetable for the events that began on the afternoon of June 16 is rather difficult. Most accounts put the departure of the troops from Cambridge at 9 P.M. Peter Brown said his company was "ordered to parade at six o'clock" (Peter Brown's letter of June 28, 1775 to his mother, quoted in Frothingham's *Siege*, pp. 392–393, and in Commager and Morris, p. 123), and that was the time set for other units, according to various orderly books. Taking these hours—6 and 9 P.M.—as the terminal points, I assumed a certain amount of time for the untrained companies to form at the beginning and end of the three-hour period, and arrived at a rough estimate of 7 P.M. for President Langdon to join them on the green. Langdon's prayer was almost certainly a long, drawn-out affair. His sermons were notoriously long, and Sibley's *Harvard Graduates* tells how children in his congregation "remembered to the ends of their lives the length of his sermons and the bitter gloom of the unheated meetinghouse on winter afternoons." Apparently the soldiers liked him better than the Harvard undergraduates did: a group of students once went to Langdon with a petition and said: "As a man of genius and knowledge we respect you; as a man of piety and virtue we venerate you; as a President we despise you."

An excellent description of the Cambridge of 1775 appears in the *Memorial History of Boston,* Vol. II, pp. 105 ff., and I relied mainly on that work and on the excellent Henry Pelham map of Boston—an essential contemporary source of information on this area—for the location of college buildings, dwellings, and roads, and for my subsequent description of the topography between Cambridge and Charlestown. *The Cambridge of 1776* is also helpful, as are Frothingham's *Siege* and Freeman's *Washington,* Vol. III, p. 480 (in July of 1775 Washington made a tour of inspection over much the same route covered by the marchers on June 16).

Examples of the army's supply and sanitation difficulties are drawn·from many scattered references in Force: IV: II, chiefly from minutes of the Massachusetts Provincial Congress.

James Coggswell's letter concerning the moral state of the camp, quoted in French's *First Year,* p. 177, is in the Boston Public Library *Bulletin* for November 1900, p. 390. There are frequent references in the minutes of the Provincial Congress to violations of the Sabbath; those cited here are in Force: IV: II: pp. 1409, 1415.

There was great concern in Cambridge and Watertown for the Harvard library, and the documents from which my discussion comes are Force: IV: II: pp. 1004–5, pp. 1409–10.

The resolution permitting generals to draw on the commissary for liquor is in Force: IV: II: p. 1414.

Several orderly books and journals were useful for this chapter. Experience Storrs's excellent diary, full of homely, human details, may be found in *The New England Quarterly* for March 1955. Storrs is a wonderful example of the solid, responsible citizen-soldier who was not quite up to soldiering but who knew that was where his duties lay. His is the diary of a gentle man who loved home and farm, but who, when the need was great, gave his energies unreservedly to his local Committee of Safety, militia company, and colonial legislature. He lived until 1801, and the inscription on his tombstone reflects the man of the diary: "He was portly in figure, friendly in disposition . . . A lover of order, a respectable professor of the Christian Religion . . ." Frothingham's "Battle-Field of Bunker Hill" also contains the Storrs diary, but in my opinion the version cited above is better.

My information regarding Colonel Frye comes from Frothingham's *Siege*, and that on his brother from Swett's *History of Bunker Hill Battle*.

One of those knotty and probably insoluble questions is how many men made up the detachment under Prescott. There is much conflicting data on this point, as Bernhard Knollenberg makes clear in his "Bunker Hill Reviewed . . .", and as Mr. Knollenberg has done, I have used Prescott's own total of "about a thousand men" (in his letter to John Adams, dated August 25, 1775, printed in Frothingham's *Siege*, p. 395), which is substantiated by the Massachusetts Committee of Safety report of July 25 (in Frothingham, *Siege*, p. 382). Despite considerable effort, I was unable to arrive at a completely satisfactory breakdown of that thousand-man total, but my attempt is shown below for the benefit of anyone interested in pursuing the matter further.

Unit	Estimated strength
Col. William Prescott's regiment	300 (a)
Col. James Frye's regiment	350 (b)
Col. Ebenezer Bridge's regiment	210 (c)
Connecticut force	200 (d)
Total	1060 (e)

(a) Prescott states in his letter that he had "three hundred of my own regiment."

(b) A return of June 9, cited by Frothingham, *Siege*, p. 118, gives the strength of this regiment as 493. Having no more reliable figures, I have used 350 as a purely arbitrary estimate, to allow for normal attrition, companies which may not have been included in the orders (Prescott's letter reads, "with a detachment of" Bridge's and Brickett's regiments, implying that they were not at full strength. See also *c*, below), and so on. Frye, incidentally, did not march with his regiment on June 16, because he was suffering from gout. As a result, the men were led by Lieutenant Colonel James Brickett, who was wounded in the battle. Frye did rejoin his regiment the next day.

(c) According to the return of June 9, Bridge's regiment had a total strength of 315, and a return of June 23 showed only nine companies belonging to the regiment. This would be an average of thirty-five men per company. Frothingham's *Siege*, p. 176, states that three companies—or 105 men, using the thirty-five-man average—did not go out with Prescott on the night of June 16. Ford's company arrived on Bunker Hill just before the action began; Major Brooks, with two companies, was en route to the hill when the retreat commenced. Subtracting these 105 men from the 315 total leaves the figure of 210 used in my estimate.

(d) Prescott's letter says "and two hundred Connecticut forces, commanded by Captain Knowlton."

(e) This total may or may not include Captain Samuel Gridley's company of artillery (forty-nine men, by a return of June 16). My guess is that Prescott did not include the artillery in his round-number estimate of one thousand.

The colorful description of the troops assembled on Cambridge Common comes from Ward's *War of the Revolution*, Vol. I, p. 78.

Winsor's *Memorial History of Boston*, Vol. III, has much useful information on the houses of Tory Row and their occupants. The latter are fully covered in Sabine.

Joseph White's brief, poignant description of the prayer and the departure is taken from his "Narrative of Events . . ." in the collection of the Library of Congress. White had enlisted in Gridley's artillery regiment at the beginning of May, to serve for eight months as "a bombardier," but the minute the adjutant discovered that White was "a good speller," White was invited to become assistant adjutant.

Frothingham's *Siege*, p. 122, depicts the column marching out of Cambridge with Prescott and two sergeants in the lead. The description of Prescott came from his son, Judge William Prescott, and appears in "Judge Prescott's Account of the Battle of Bunker Hill," printed in Frothingham's "Battle-Field of Bunker Hill."

Fairfax Downey describes Colonel Richard Gridley at some length in *Sound of the Guns*, and there are several allusions to the artillery and its command problems in Force (see IV: II: pp. 1410, 1415, for example).

The postscript to a letter of June 21, 1775 (in Force: IV: II: p. 1056) contains a reference to the drought.

The Inman house and family are discussed in *Memorial History of Boston*, Vol. III, p. 106, which is also the source of my statement regarding the swords of Prescott and Linzee finding their way to the historian's mantel. Putnam's son Daniel is quoted in Samuel Swett's *History of Bunker Hill Battle*. Statements concerning the Connecticut troops and their quarters may be found in Frothingham's *Siege* and "Battle-Field of Bunker Hill."

As noted earlier, the *Memorial History of Boston* contains excellent descriptions of the terrain. Here, and in Esther Forbes's *Paul Revere*, mention is made of Charlestown Common and the remains of the Negro Mark.

Chapter IV

Montresor's redan, remnant of the British retreat from Concord, is mentioned by French, *First Year*, p. 213. This little fortification formed the basis for the much larger and stronger work constructed by the British after the battle. Montresor's own drawing of the later fort is reproduced with "A Survey of Charles Town shewing the three Posts now garrison'd by His MAJESTY's Troops for the Winter. 10th Dec^{ber}. 1775."

Samuel Gray's report of the discussion held en route to Breed's Hill is in a letter reproduced in Frothingham's *Siege*, pp. 393–395.

Descriptions of Charlestown peninsula appear in French's *First Year*, Frothingham's *Siege*, and Freeman's *Washington*, Vol. III. Mention of the fences dividing the fields is made in several British accounts of the battle. Mauduit's criticism of Howe and his conduct of the attack contains this statement (p. 39): ". . . knowing nothing of the ground, [Howe] attempted to march the troops in a part where they had ten or twelve rows of railings to clamber over; the lands between Charlestown and the beach being, for the convenience of the inhabitants, divided into narrow slips, not more than from ten to thirty rods over." This was one of the most graphic descriptions I encountered of the fences which ran down to the water's edge. Several maps are helpful, too, notably the one published in 1777 by Thomas Hyde Page, Howe's aide, who lost a leg in the battle and was invalided home. Page's map, based on an actual survey by Montresor, is particularly valuable for the topography. (Included in picture insert in this book.) John Trumbull's view of Charlestown peninsula, showing Bunker and Breed's Hill, Morton's Point, the village of Charlestown, the Neck, and the causeway, appears on page 83.

Amos Farnsworth noted in his diary that he and about sixty others went with Captain Nutting into Charlestown. The excerpt is in Commager and Morris, p.122.

The Committee of Safety report puts the size of the redoubt at eight rods square. Peter Brown's letter to his mother describes it as "about Ten Rod long, eight wide, with a Breast Work of about Eight more." The fort is shown in Page's and De Berniere's maps.

Bolton, pp. 152–153, has a useful description of the eighteenth-century technique of constructing earthworks, and it was tempting to think that Gridley may have employed gabions and fascines in building the redoubt. However, there is no mention of any such devices in the contemporary accounts, and Clinton's statement that the redoubt was "neither picketted pallasaded or ditched" also convinced me that it was a crude affair, made entirely of earth.

Although some accounts of the battle state that the *Somerset* was at anchor in the Charles with the other British vessels, it is my conclusion that she was not. The *Somerset's* log has no mention of her participation in the action; furthermore, in correspondence of June 16, Graves states that he shifted the big ship to a safer anchorage off Hancock's wharf, replacing her at the ferry position with the *Lively*. His letter of June 22, listing the vessels that covered the British landing, includes no mention of the *Somerset*.

That both Clinton and Howe knew, on the night of June 16, of the American activity on Breed's Hill, is a fairly recent discovery, discussed by French, *First Year*, in a note on p. 210. Clinton's knowledge of the fact is noted in his letter of June 13, 1775, in the Clinton Papers, William L. Clements Library.

Captain Bishop's court-martial and suspension for neglect of duty and disobedience of orders are mentioned in a letter of June 14, from Admiral Graves to Philip Stephens (in Adm. 1/485. North America. 1774 to 1777).

The logs of the *Lively* and *Falcon* both confirm the fact that *Lively* began firing on the rebel works at 4 A.M.

In his letter to John Adams (Frothingham's *Siege*, pp. 395–396), Prescott mentions the necessity of adding the breastwork to the redoubt. This addition is clearly visible on the De Berniere map (see picture insert).

Asa Pollard's death is recorded by Swett, p. 22; this soldier is identified by Frothingham, *Siege*, p. 126, as a Billerica man in Bridge's regiment.

The sources of statements about the weather are Paul Litchfield's diary, for June 16, 17, and 18, in the Massachusetts Historical Society Collection; and various ships' logs.

David How's diary has the statement that without Prescott there would have been no fight.

Clinton's observations about the American redoubt and his pleas for an immediate, two-pronged attack to take the rebels in front and rear are contained in a memorandum quoted by French, *First Year*, p. 221.

The best contemporary description of artillery fire I have seen is in James Thacher's *A Military Journal during the American Revolutionary War, from 1775–1783*, in which he describes the siege of Yorktown. The cannon balls, he wrote, "are clearly visible in the form of a black ball in the day, but at night they appear like a fiery meteor with a blazing tail . . ." Thacher also noted how, "When a shell falls, it whirls around, burrows, and excavates the earth to a considerable extent . . ."

Bickerstaff's Boston Almanac for 1775, in the Massachusetts Historical Society Collection, lists high tide on June 17 as 3:03 P.M.

The British orders, giving the composition of the assault force and the order of embarkation, are quoted in full in French's *First Year*, Appendix 19, p. 740.

A description of the impractical British uniforms, with appropriately acid comments, is in Belcher, Vol. I, pp. 322–327, as is a full discussion of loading and firing the eighteenth-century musket.

All ship movements mentioned in this and subsequent chapters are taken from the respective logs (see full note on the ships' logs in the Notes for Chapter V).

The statement that the rebels fell down when they saw the flash of a cannon and resumed work as soon as the ball had landed is made in an enclosure to a letter of June 22, from Richard Reeve to Sir George Howard (in the County of Buckingham Record Office, Howard-Vyse deposit).

The conversation between Gage and Abijah Willard is reported in Frothingham's *Siege*, p. 126.

William Heath tells, in his *Memoirs*, p. 19, how Putnam urged Prescott to send the entrenching tools to a safe place.

Numerous references to the shortage of powder appear in letters and documents of this period; for example, see Force: IV: II: p. 1017, for the state of affairs on the day of battle.

A typical problem in trying to construct a timetable for the confusing events of June 17 was met in the story of Captain John Chester. In his letter of July 22 to the Reverend Joseph Fish of Stonington, Connecticut (quoted in full in Frothingham, *Siege*, pp. 389–391) Chester says he got word of the British landing "Just after dinner," then ran to collect his arms and ammunition and hurried to join his company, which was "nearly ready to march." There was only a brief delay: "We soon marched," Chester stated. However, they did not arrive at Bunker Hill until "near the close of the battle." The best estimate of the battle's end is about 5 P.M. (see note on chronology, with the Notes for Chapter V); presumably Chester finished his midday dinner about 1 P.M. If both times are accurate, it means that it took his company nearly four hours to march the three and a half miles from Cambridge to Breed's Hill. How is this possible? Let us work backward, from the end of Chester's account. He states that he and his company arrived at Bunker Hill, where he had an altercation with another officer, whose company was retreating. It must have taken Chester some little time to convince the cowardly officer (by threatening to shoot him and his men) to return to action. Then Chester and his troops had to make their way through the idlers and skulkers on the slopes of Bunker Hill and march down the hill toward the American breastwork ("on the right of the centre, just by a poor stone fence, two or three feet high, so that the bullets came through"). Here, loading and firing as fast as possible, they "fought standing about six minutes," Chester and his men estimated. Thus, if the battle ended at five o'clock, we could safely give Chester an hour to make his way from the Neck to the breastwork, allowing time for all those events. Assuming a substantial amount of confusion along the road between Cambridge and Charlestown Neck, it is not unlikely that he and his men took an hour and a half to march the three and a half miles. That puts the time back to 2:30 P.M. Giving Chester's men half an hour after he joined them to change their clothes (covering those bright uniforms) and muster; and Chester half an hour to go to his own quarters, pick up his gear, and join his men; the time is back to one thirty. Somewhere, these rough calculations are half an hour off, but this is about as close to an accurate reckoning as I was able to come.

Stark's difficulties in getting to the battlefield were related by Henry Dearborn in 1818. Dearborn's account is obviously inaccurate in certain particulars, but the story of the ammunition shortage seems entirely plausible, and I can see no reason for Dearborn to have invented it. Stark's own account, which is laconic in the extreme and contains little information beyond the fact that he received orders at 2 P.M., is in his letter of June 19 to the New Hampshire Congress (Force: IV: II: p. 1029).

Chapter V

The various ships' logs make it clear that all the vessels were firing on the redoubt. According to the *Somerset* log, "the New Battery at the N° end of Boston began to fire" at 9 A.M. This was the Copp's Hill battery built and equipped by Admiral Graves.

During the early stages of research on this book it became evident that no previous studies had made use of the logs of British ships in the harbor. It occurred to me that these logs, kept as they were by men accustomed to recording events in close conjunction with a timepiece, might throw new light on the battle, for the chronology of events during the engagement has always been a puzzle. As Allen French wrote, "In all the story of Bunker Hill, the hours are almost impossible to determine. Competent observers put Howe's landing, and indeed almost every incident of the day, at different times." The National Maritime Museum in Greenwich, England, has certain material—mostly duplicate ships' logs—and I received from that institution extracts from the log of the Somerset kept by Captain Edward LeCras, and from that of the Glasgow kept by Captain Tyringham Howe. I also learned, through V. Lindray-MacDougall of the Manuscript Department at the National Maritime Museum, this most important fact concerning the logs of eighteenth-century British naval vessels: "The dates may appear confusing at first, as these logs are kept according to the nautical day which was twelve hours ahead of civil time, and started at midday." (In all records of the battle mentioned herein, the ships' time has been corrected.)

My next source was the Public Record Office, where I was able to obtain excerpts from the logs of the Glasgow, Lively, Falcon, and Somerset—all present off Boston at the time of the battle—as well as the log of the Cerberus, on which Howe, Clinton, and Burgoyne sailed to America. The Public Record Office also had certain useful correspondence from Admiral Graves and Captain Linzee of the Falcon (Linzee was the man who married one of Mrs. Inman's daughters). In addition to supplying interesting background information and a valuable record of the ships' movements prior to and during the action, these logs provide what I consider the most accurate timetable yet available on the course of the engagement. For example, Glasgow, Lively, and Somerset all record Lively's opening shots on the redoubt at 4 A.M. on June 17. According to the Somerset log, the Copp's Hill battery opened fire at 9, and the Falcon at 10. During the morning the transport Symmetry and the sloop Spitfire fired on rebels who were marching into Charlestown—a rare confirmation of the fact that the Americans were moving troops into the town at this time.

"All the boats of the Squadron, & all the Transport Boats," the *Somerset's* log reads, were "employed taking in the troops"—i.e., ferrying them—during the amphibious assault, and "at 2, the Troops, under the Cover of the *Lively & Falcon,* landed at Charles town without opposition." Just after discovering this evidence that the landing had taken place at 2 P.M., I was as suddenly confronted with a contradictory statement: the *Lively's* log put the landing at 11 A.M.! The only other mention of a specific hour in the *Lively's* log was 2 P.M., which was the time recorded by the watch officer for the burning of Charlestown. This, however, was contradicted by all the other ships' logs and by virtually all other information available to me. For example, the Reverend Andrew Eliot (an objective bystander) told a friend that the battle began about 3 (and of course the town was not fired until later); the Massachusetts Provincial Congress report to the Continental Congress put the landing at about 2; Prescott said the enemy began landing about 2; and so on. In other words, if the *Lively* log was correct on the time of the landing and the time Charlestown was set ablaze, every other piece of information had to be wrong. Therefore, I accepted the times listed by the *Somerset,* many of which were confirmed by other records of the day. A further point favoring acceptance of the times as set down in the *Somerset* log was that she was Graves's flagship and not actively engaged in the fighting, and thus more likely to have accurate record-keeping. The other hours listed in the *Somerset* log are these: 3 P.M., when "the field Pieces began to fire" [Howe's artillery]; "¼ before 4 a warm Engagement began"; and "½ past 5" when "the firing Slackened," after which the *Somerset's* boats were busy ferrying the wounded over to Boston.

Working back from the 2 P.M. hour for the landing, I set the British embarkation at 1:30 for the following reasons: The distance from the North Battery to Morton's Point was approximately three-quarters of a mile. The tide was with the barges (high tide at 3:03 P.M. meant that it was coming in); so if the barges made two miles per hour, it would have taken about twenty-two to twenty-five minutes for the one-way trip between North Battery and Morton's Point. On this basis, the first wave of barges must have left North Battery shortly after 1:30 in order to land at 2.

My reasons for setting the time of the alarm in Cambridge at 1 P.M. were these: Those redcoats whose staging area was the North Battery could be seen by the rebels out on Breed's Hill. A substantial number of British troops were involved in this amphibious operation, so by all military logic, the first units marched to the wharves well in advance of the scheduled departure time— possibly an hour to an hour and a half before 1:30, or between noon and 12:30. Now, the distance from Breed's Hill to Cambridge was about three and one half miles, or ten to fifteen minutes' ride on a horse; thus news of the imminent British assault, seen by the men on Breed's Hill at 12:30 (or earlier) would have reached Cambridge headquarters by 12:45, and the alarm would have sounded by 1 P.M. (This would seem to jibe with Captain Chester's statement that he heard the drums beating to arms and the bells ringing "Just after dinner.")

We know that Ward was playing his hand very cautiously, and he may have received the news as early as 12:15 and waited for further confirmation from a later courier. He wanted to be certain that the main British attack was directed at Charlestown, and not at Roxbury. Allowing a decent interval for arguments to be made, decisions reached, and orders issued at headquarters, this timetable makes it reasonable for John Stark, off in Medford, to have received his marching orders about 2 P.M., which is when he said he got them.

Howe is the source for the statement that the British formed into three lines on Morton's Hill. His letter to General Gage, dated 21 June 1775 and sent from "Camp upon ye Heights of Charlestown," is in the Gage Papers in the William L. Clements Library. The three lines of infantrymen are also visible on the De Berniere map. When the attack began, however, the troops formed into two lines, for Howe stated that "these troops formed in two lines," and Clinton wrote: "our disposition on the 17th was one long stragling line two deep" [by "stragling" he meant the line as he remembered it at the end of the attack].

Clark's description of waiting in formation on the Mystic beach appears in a letter of June 21 to his brother, Robert Clark of Edinburgh, and is in the Dartmouth Papers, pp. 380–381.

Prescott's account of the landing is taken from his letter to John Adams.

One of the most enigmatic aspects of the engagement is the story of the American artillery. The literature has numerous references to the guns and the artillery officers, but many are contradictory and few are helpful. I have placed four guns in the redoubt (a letter of June 19 written by Captain John Chester and Lieutenant Samuel Webb, in Frothingham's *Siege*, pp. 415–416, refers to "four guns fired by General Putnam after the gunner quitted the field-pieces"). As for two guns at the rail fence, a late statement by Captain Samuel Trevett (Dawson, p. 415) describes moving forward to the fence "to select a station for my *pieces*" [italics mine]. We know there were six guns in all, of which Trevett brought off one (French, p. 252). As for the others, Howe's letter to Gage says: "Five of their cannon are in my possession." Fairfax Downey's *Sound of the Guns* is very helpful regarding artillery in the battle, and Martyn's *Ward*, p. 131, is my source for the statement that Scarborough Gridley never even troubled to cross the Neck from the mainland.

Lieutenant Dana's description of the rail fence appears in Captain John Chester's letter of July 22 to the Reverend Joseph Fish, in Frothingham, *Siege*, pp. 389–391, and in Dawson, pp. 386–387. The three flèches appear on the De Berniere map and are discussed at some length by French, *First Year*, Appendix 23.

The story of Stark ordering "his boys" to throw up a breastwork between the steep bank and the water's edge was told by General James Wilkinson. Although it was written long after the battle, it was based on notes Wilkinson made while walking over the battlefield with Stark on the day the British abandoned Boston. Wilkinson's letter appears in *History of the Battle of Breed's Hill*, by Charles Coffin.

Martyn's *Ward*, p. 131, has a note concerning various regiments that did not or would not join those in the front lines. Discussing the difficulties of estimating the number of Americans in the fight, Swett wrote: "Great allowance must be made for those unable, and those unwilling, to go on: the men went on or off as they pleased, and when they pleased." The composition of the rebel line is drawn from Dawson, pp. 340–343, and from Ward, Vol. I, p. 87.

The critical letter on the American command was written to Samuel Adams by James Warren on June 20, and is quoted in Martyn's *Ward*, p. 162.

Words of praise for Trevett's guns come from Ensign Studholme Brownrigg's letter to General Hodgson, in the Dartmouth Papers.

My information on Warren is derived largely from Frothingham's *Life and Times of Joseph Warren*, pp. 513 ff. French, *First Year*, p. 229, has a footnote concerning the "various conflicting stories" about Warren; on the same page French cites the story about Pomeroy.

Curiously enough, considering all the literature that exists on the subject, the question of who commanded the American forces did not concern me overmuch. In my opinion it was an informal, *ad hoc*, and completely practical arrangement. Prescott was in charge of the men in the redoubt, as he had been since the previous night, and probably assumed responsibility for those behind the breastwork and those in Charlestown. Obviously Putnam outranked him, but neither of the two men, in my estimation, had time or inclination to put rank to the test, and there was no particular reason for any dispute about it anyway; they were much too busy getting things done.

Howe's request to Graves that he set fire to Charlestown is related by the latter in his *Conduct of Admiral Graves*, and is quoted by French, p. 231. The description of the fire comes from Henry Hulton's letter of June 20, printed in *Letters of a Loyalist Lady*, pp. 98–99.

Howe's plans and order of battle are in his own words, in his letter of June 21 to Gage. The letter is now in the Gage Papers in the William L. Clements Library.

A letter of July 5, 1775, written by a British surgeon in Boston, is the source for the quotation about the oversize cannon balls. It appears in Dawson, p. 368. Downey's *Sound of the Guns*, pp. 25–27, has further data on Colonel Cleaveland.

A British critic, writing of the pesky fences, said, "These posts and rails were too strong for the columns to push down." Next morning someone looked at them and discovered that they were studded with bullets "not a hand's breadth from each other." The statements are in Mauduit, p. 39.

Numerous American accounts, contemporary and later, speak of the slow advance of the redcoats; the deliberate, ominous approach made a lasting impression. The Committee of Safety report speaks of "a very slow march"; Israel Potter, writing years afterward, still recalled that "slow step."

Burgoyne's dramatic description of the scene appears in many sources, among them Scheer and Rankin, p. 59, and Commager and Morris, pp. 133–134.

Mr. Edward Mills kindly referred me to a letter describing the engagement, and there I found the only contemporaneous statement I have encountered indicating that the rebels had orders to aim at the British officers. Allen French wrote: "All the late tales give stories of the setting of marks and the measuring of distances, and the warning to hold the fire until the men could see the whites of the eyes, or the buttons, or the gaiters appearing over a rise in the ground. The British officers were easily distinguished by their uniforms. The crossing of the shoulder belts in the middle of the breast gave a perfect and deadly target. But none of these things are told in contemporary stories." The letter to which I refer is from Thomas Bridgen Attwood, writing on June 30, 1775 from New York to Walter Rutherfurd; it is printed in Rutherfurd's *Family Records and Events*, pp. 123–124. Attwood had just received a letter from a New London friend, Captain Tilley, who gave him news of the battle—including quite accurate figures on British casualties. Tilley wrote "from the Provincial Camp," and informed Attwood that "a choice party of our best shots under cover were appointed to fire at none but the Reddest Coats!"

The Reverend Peter Thacher's account of the light infantry retreat is from the Committee of Safety report on the battle, which Thacher wrote.

Knowlton's orders to his men to hold their fire comes from Captain Elijah Hide's report on the battle, in Dawson, p. 379. Hide apparently watched the fighting from Winter Hill.

Chester's letter to Fish, cited above, has the account of Lieutenant Dana's activities.

The British officer's description of the American fire and the losses suffered by the grenadiers and light infantry is in Dawson, p. 367.

Howe's confession of near-panic is from a letter, probably written to the British Adjutant General, printed in Commager and Morris, pp. 131–133.

French, in *First Year*, p. 168, discusses Colonel Abercromby, his reconnaissance trip, and the taunts that greeted him during the battle. The story is also mentioned in a letter of June 25, 1775, written by an unknown British officer, and cited in Dawson, p. 366.

William Prescott's story of the battle is part of his letter to John Adams, cited earlier.

An account of Howe's request for reinforcements and Clinton's actions is in French, *First Year*, pp. 242–243.

Gerrish's conduct is related by an unknown Newbury man, writing on June 21. This excerpt from the letter appears in Wade and Lively, p. 22.

Chester's letter is quoted in French, *First Year*, p. 245; Webb's comments are contained in that portion of a letter written jointly by him and Chester, dated June 19, and printed in Frothingham, *Siege*, pp. 415–416.

Hodgkins is one of the two Ipswich soldiers who are the subject of *This Glorious Cause*. This selection is from his letter of June 23, from pp. 170–171 of that volume.

The story of Robert Steele's expedition for rum and water appears in Scheer and Rankin, pp. 59–60, and on p. 25 of Swett's Notes. Charles Martyn, writing of the men's need for liquid refreshment, states that what they wanted was not water, but "their rum, beer, or cider." He argues that they could have obtained all the water they needed from Charlestown, that morning (Martyn's *Ward*, p. 130).

Reports of individual British casualties appear in several sources, among them the enclosure to Richard Reeve's letter of

June 24, 1775, to Sir George Howard (in County of Buckingham Record Office, Howard-Vyse deposit); and a list in George Washington's Headquarters letter book. The latter, at the Morristown National Historical Park, was brought to my attention by Francis Ronalds.

For years no historian doubted the accepted story of the three British attacks. Then in 1927 Mr. Harold Murdock published his *Bunker Hill, Notes and Queries on a Famous Battle*, in which he questioned the familiar tale on grounds that it was not supported by contemporary evidence. Murdock's arguments must be considered seriously by anyone writing on the subject; but in my opinion they are convincingly refuted by Allen French, in his *First Year of the American Revolution*, Appendix 23, and my reconstruction of the battle owes much to that work.

Frothingham's *Siege*, p. 199, quotes a "British journal" for the story of Evans, Howe's servant. My source for the statement concerning Howe's orders to the British troops to remove their packs is Judge Prescott's manuscript, in Frothingham's "Battle-Field of Bunker Hill," p. 21.

The Ipswich soldier's recollection of the approaching British comes from Wade and Lively, p. 20, and the other American writer's comments on how the British were shot down appear in Dawson, p. 390.

George Harris told his story in his diary, later published as *Life and Services of General Lord Harris*, quoted in S. A. Drake's *Bunker Hill*, pp. 37–38. Lord Rawdon's comments are in French, *First Year*, p. 247.

Samuel Webb's account of the fighting is in his letter of July 11 to Silas Deane, printed in Frothingham's "Battle-Field of Bunker Hill," pp. 31–33.

The account of the boy shouting from behind the wall is from *The Stranger in America*, by Charles William Janson.

Ebenezer Bancroft's story of the battle appears in Hill's *Bi-Centennial of Old Dunstable*. Bancroft commanded the Dunstable company of Bridge's regiment.

A description of the murky interior of the breastwork at the battle's climax is in Dawson, pp. 389–390.

At least two Negroes—Salem Poor and Coffee Whittemore—

are mentioned as participants in various accounts. Both were free-men, the Committee of Safety having resolved that slaves would not be admitted into the army on grounds that it was "inconsistent with the principles that are to be supported" (Force: IV: II: p. 762).

Reuben Dow was one of the Hollis minute men who arrived a little too late for the affair at Concord, and then were mustered into Prescott's regiment. They were in the digging detail on the night of June 16 and suffered heavy casualties in the battle. Information on Dow is taken from Hill's *History of the Town of Mason, N.H.*

Clinton's description of Howe at the close of the battle appears in French, *First Year*, p. 251, and the comments of Rawdon and Burgoyne on the American retreat are from the same work, p. 252.

Several sources describe the death of McClary, among them Nathaniel Folsom, writing to the New Hampshire Committee of Safety on June 22 (his letter is printed in Force: IV: II: p. 1063), and, much later, Swett, in his *History of Bunker Hill Battle*, pp. 48–49.

Although I have not used it in this work, there is, in the Gage Papers in the William L. Clements Library, an interesting, if baffling letter from Robert Carr to Gage, written from the "lines, 25 minutes past 4 o'clock." Since this is certainly one of the very few communications which dates to the action itself, it is well worth investigation. This is the full message:

"Sir - The Rebels have advanced some Field Pieces on the rising ground to the left of Brownes House, I have given Capt. Farrington orders to endeavor to make them remove - I am Sir
Your Excelly. Most Obed^t
  Humble Servt
    Robert Carr
      Lt. Col^o 35 Foot"

Aside from the fact that there are just half as many words in the signature as there are in the message—a nice commentary on

British military protocol, even under fire—this communiqué raises a number of puzzling questions. Unfortunately I have not been able to discover where "Brownes House" was; but presumably it was a reasonably well-known landmark near Charlestown—otherwise why should Carr refer to it by name? I assume it was not *in* Charlestown, since the town, by 4:25 P.M., must have been almost totally consumed by flames. The only buildings which are indicated on Montresor's survey of Charlestown peninsula, done in December, 1775, are on either side of the main road running from the Neck to the ruined town, and about halfway between these two locations. Montresor shows two buildings at the corner of this road and the road leading up toward the redoubt on Breed's Hill; this is the location of a barn, cited by De Berniere on his map, from which some rebels were firing during the action. Whether one of these buildings was "Brownes House" I do not know.

The only units of the 35th to fight in the battle were two flank companies which participated in the attack along the beach. According to Murdock's *Bunker Hill*, note, p. 16, these companies were virtually annihilated; and we know, from a list of killed and wounded sent to England by Richard Reeve (see note on British casualties, page 208), that the 35th lost three captains and two lieutenants in that assualt. If it is true that "Brownes House" was one of the buildings on the southwest side of the peninsula, I think it is reasonable to assume that Carr did not participate in the attack along the Mystic beach, for it is hard to imagine him leaving those badly mauled, nearly officerless units behind and racing around to get into the fight on the other side.

This leaves unanswered the question of what rebel fieldpieces these might be. It is a matter of considerable surprise to discover rebel cannon still fighting at this late hour in the day at this particular location (assuming once again that the site was one of the houses along the main road), and it must be assumed that these were guns abandoned by Gridley and Callender, which were still being served by volunteers.

Finally, the time—"25 minutes past 4 o'clock"—would seem to confirm the accuracy of the *Somerset's* log. Carr's dispatch indicates that the battle is still raging (the rebels have *advanced* the fieldpieces), which leads one to conclude that the 5 P.M. hour for the cessation of hostilities is probably correct.

Chapter VI

Descriptions of the aftermath of battle appear in numerous letters of the period, including Ann Hulton's correspondence in *Letters of a Loyalist Lady*; the quotation from Clarke, in French, *First Year*, p. 257; and Oliver's letter, in Frothingham's *Siege*, p. 194.

Surgeon Grant's angry report about the nails and bits of iron fired by rebels at Breed's Hill is in a letter reprinted in Dawson, p. 361. The enclosure to Richard Reeve's letter of June 24, 1775 (in County of Buckingham Record Office, Howard-Vyse deposit) contains the shocked reference to the "poisonous mixture" with which the Americans coated their ammunition. This rumor must have been current in Boston on June 24; another letter of that day repeats it, in Force: IV: II: p. 1079.

Gage put in the request for "carefull sober Women" to tend the wounded (French, *First Year*, p. 262).

Isaac Lothrop is quoted in Dawson, p. 375, and the dying John Randon's letter appears in the same volume, p. 358.

The Boston merchant's visit to the battlefield is cited by Emmons. Figures turned in by the burial detail show the totals by rank and regiment, where known; the list is in the Gage Papers at the William L. Clements Library.

Margaret Gage's divided loyalties are discussed by John Alden in his *General Gage in America*, p. 248. Weighing the charge that Gage's American wife was disloyal to him and his cause, Alden concludes that she was not, since he finds no evidence whatever in support of the claim.

On the subject of British casualties, I have used Gage's report of June 25—226 killed or died of wounds, and 828 wounded—printed in Force: IV: II: pp. 1098–1099, and in Frothingham's

Siege, pp. 386–389. The names of officers killed and wounded appear in an enclosure to Richard Reeve's letter of June 24, 1775 to Sir George Howard; the American source cited is George Washington's Headquarters letter book, now at the Morristown National Historical Park. The quotation supporting the argument that the rebels were ordered to fire at the British officers is cited above, in the notes for Chapter V, p. 208–209.

There are several sources for Gage's remarks on the rebel army and his predicament in Boston: two letters to Dartmouth, and one to Barrington—all cited in French, *First Year,* pp. 258–259.

George Clark's comments appear in a letter to his brother, found in the Dartmouth Papers.

Francis Ronalds is my source for the letter from Roxbury stating that Gage finally had to order the funeral bells silenced.

The severe punishment meted out to the unfortunate Winifred McCowen is in Howe's Orderly Book, September 26, 1775, quoted in *Sir Billy Howe,* p. 27.

According to Winsor (*Memorial History of Boston,* Vol. III, pp. 112–113), many of the American wounded were taken to the Vassall mansion in Cambridge, where they were treated by Dr. William Eustis (later governor of Massachusetts), a handsome, twenty-two-year-old who had studied under Joseph Warren. Other medical men present were John Warren, William Gamage, Jr., and Andrew Craigie—later apothecary general of the Continental Army. Thomas Oliver's house was another dwelling used as a temporary hospital. In Frothingham's *Siege,* p. 194, other doctors are listed: Thomas Kittredge, Walter Hastings, Thomas Welsh, Isaac Foster, Lieutenant Colonel Brickett, David Townsend, and John Hart. According to Frothingham, many soldiers who died of wounds were buried in a field in front of the Oliver house.

American casualties were the subject of widely varying estimates, but there is no reason to doubt the figures cited in Washington's letter to his brother, especially since the total is substantiated by Ward's orderly book. Frothingham, in his *Siege of Boston,* p. 193, shows the loss by regiment, as closely as he could compile it from letters, official returns, and a Providence newspaper article. His totals are 140 killed, 271 wounded, and thirty captured, but I am more inclined to accept the estimates given by

Washington and Ward. Ebenezer Huntington, in a letter of June 25, says twenty-three Connecticut men were wounded and thirteen missing; seventy-four wounded and nineteen missing from New Hampshire; but he was unable to secure figures on the Massachusetts losses.

Informers for both sides were active these days. The statement regarding the amount of powder that remained in the American camp on the night of June 17 comes from a spy's letter reprinted in Belcher, Vol. I, p. 208.

Samuel Haws's record of events on the day after the battle is in his diary. His regiment, after keeping a rather nervous watch in Roxbury all day on the seventeenth, was ordered to Cambridge "to assist our forces," and arrived there at about midnight. They spent the night in the town and next morning marched to Prospect Hill. Barker's statement that all the houses beyond the Neck were burned appears in *The British in Boston*, p. 61.

The Provincial Congress's minutes on the matter of Joseph Warren's probable death appear in Force: IV: II: p. 1424. Captain Laurie's tale of finding Warren's body appears in the *New England Quarterly*, XXV, No. 3 (September 1952), p. 367. Esther Forbes, pp. 315 and 477, tells of Paul Revere's role in identifying the skull of his old friend by means of the false teeth.

French relates part of the story of the oversized British cannon balls in *First Year*, Appendix 24. The best source of information on the Lovells, father and son, is in Jenks, *Catalogue of the Boston Public Latin School*. Seybolt, *The Public Schools of Colonial Boston*, has some further details. French, pp. 339 ff., is a good source of information on the other American civilians jailed in Boston.

Numerous eyewitnesses recounted the burning of Charlestown. Dr. Eliot's letter is reproduced by Dawson, pp. 369–370, and other descriptions are on pp. 385, 389, 441; Emmons, p. 150, has a reference to the burning of the Mather library, and another account on p. 138.

The rebels were woefully deficient in clothing after the battle. As late as September 21, George Washington wrote the Continental Congress that there were men "in a state of nakedness." Many, he said, "have been without blankets the whole campaign and those which have been in use during the summer are so much worn as to be of little service." (Freeman, Vol. III, pp. 486 and 543).

Ward's letter requesting spears appears in Force: IV: II: p. 1028. Samuel Webb's letter of July 11 to Silas Deane, printed in Frothingham's "Battle-Field of Bunker Hill," pp. 31–33, reports that there were "several thousands of Pikes, with 12 feet handles, which are placed along our Lines." Ward's doleful commentary on the rain and what effect it would have on the men's powder is in Martyn's *Ward*, p. 146.

Joseph Trumbull's letter to Eliphalet Dyer, dated July 11, 1775, is in the collection of the Morristown National Historical Park.

Peter Oliver's colorful description of the siege after the battle for Bunker Hill is quoted in French, *First Year*, p. 344.

Paul Litchfield's diary is in the Massachusetts Historical Society Collections.

I learned of Benjamin Guild's diary through Bernhard Knollenberg, who quotes it in his paper "Bunker Hill Re-viewed . . ." According to Mr. Knollenberg, the unpublished diary is in the Massachusetts Historical Society Collections; the author was a Wrentham schoolmaster in 1775, a tutor at Harvard from 1776 to 1780, and subsequently a Boston bookseller and Fellow of the American Academy.

James Warren, who was no friend to Artemas Ward, wrote to John Adams on June 20—a communication cited in Frothingham's *Warren*, p. 512. The letter from the spy is reproduced in Belcher, Vol. I, p. 208: Samuel Adams's cautionary note to James Warren is in Martyn's *Ward*, p. 163.

Samuel Gray's criticism of the American command is quoted in Dawson, p. 385; and Captain Chester's comments appear in his letter of July 22 to the Reverend Joseph Fish, Frothingham's *Siege*, p. 390.

The proceedings of James Scammon's court-martial are in Force: IV: II: p. 1662. Callender's dismissal by Washington and his subsequent reinstatement for valor at Brooklyn Heights are discussed by French, *First Year*, p. 302.

Jonathan Trumbull's letter carrying the tidings of Bunker Hill to the Continental Congress is reproduced in Force: IV: II: p. 1035. Freeman, Vol. III, pp. 458 ff., describes the arrival of the news in Philadelphia and Washington's receipt of the dispatch at Colonel Lispenard's in New York. This document, which carried the signature of James Warren, the new President of the Massachusetts Provincial Congress, is printed in Force: IV: II: pp. 1039–1040.

Murdock, in his *Bunker Hill*, pp. 83 ff., discusses fully the Committee of Safety report and the authorship of the Reverend Peter Thacher. The original of this interesting document underwent much alteration and editing, and Thacher's manuscript is reprinted in full (with the emendations indicated) in Dawson, pp. 381–384.

Thayer's biography of Nathanael Greene, p. 62, is the source of the quotation from the dying Abercromby. From Dawson, pp. 357, 366, and 368, come the comments by other British officers. A letter of June 25, 1775, reproduced in Historical Manuscripts Commission, Fourteenth Report, Appendix, Part I, contains the comment reminiscent of Burgoyne's elbowroom remark made only one month earlier.

The arrival of General Gage's wife at Plymouth was vividly described in the *Annual Register* for 1775, quoted in French, *First Year*, pp. 323–324.

Sir James Oughton's crusty commentary is quoted at some length by French, p. 562. Samuel Ward's letter appears in French, *First Year*, p. 550, as does the excerpt from Pownal's letter to Clinton, p. 553.

The record of Henry Knox's extraordinary efforts in hauling the guns of Ticonderoga to Boston is in the former bookseller's own hand in the Henry Knox Papers in the Massachusetts Historical Society Collections. An article by Clay Perry on this subject is in *American Heritage*, Vol. VI, No. 3, April 1955. It was Benedict Arnold who first suggested the idea of bringing the cannon from the captured fort on Lake Champlain.

There is a revealing passage in Howe's *Narrative* of his conduct of the war, read in Parliament in 1779, and quoted in *Sir Billy Howe*, pp. 282–283: ". . . if I could by any manoeuvre remove an enemy from a very advantageous position, without hazarding the consequences of an attack . . . I should certainly adopt that cautionary conduct."

Allen French's *First Year*, pp. 657–678, contains an excellent account of how the Americans fortified Dorchester Heights, the British reaction, and the final days of the siege until the time of Howe's departure. Many of the sources quoted here are also cited in French.

Benjamin Hallowell's earlier difficulties with the Liberty Boys are discussed by Esther Forbes in *Paul Revere*, pp. 104, 137, and 184.

The list of loyalists "proscribed as enemies of the new State" in 1778 is printed in *Winsor's Memorial History of Boston*, Vol. II, p. 563. It contains 143 names, among them such eminent ones as John Amory, Thomas Brattle, Benjamin Faneuil, Jr., Thomas Flucker (secretary of the province, and Henry Knox's father-in-law), Harrison Gray and his son, Thomas Hutchinson and his son, the Hallowells, Sir William Pepperrell, and Justice Samuel Sewall. Forty-five of the lot were termed "esquires," nine were "ministers and doctors," and thirty-six were merchants. As Winsor states, "a far greater number left Boston quietly, and never arrived at the dangerous distinction of being publicly denounced." Generally speaking, this was a list of the families which had prospered most during the preceding century, a cross-section of the most important names of pre-Revolutionary Boston, which had gradually been forming a local aristocracy. A list of those loyalists who departed with the British in March 1776 appears in *Memorial History of Boston*, Vol. III, pp. 175–180.

Allen French relates the amusing incident of the Irish lieutenant Adair and the crow's feet in his *First Year*, p. 670, citing the *Journal of Sir Martin Hunter*, p. 15, as his source.

John Sullivan's activities on this St. Patrick's Day are recorded in Freeman, Vol. IV, p. 52.

An account of the Boston boys running to Roxbury with their news is printed in Massachusetts Historical Society *Proceedings*, 27: p. 360.

Heath's *Memoirs*, p. 52, has an account of the dummy sentinels.

The quotations from George Washington, reflecting his concern over Howe's failure to depart, are from Freeman, Vol. IV, pp. 54–59.

Joseph Hodgkins' touching letter to his wife appears in Wade and Lively, p. 195. It was written from camp on Prospect Hill on March 20, 1776.

The order to officers of the Fort Ticonderoga garrison, instructing them to have their men aim and fire at close range, is from the Deputy Adjutant General's orderly book, October 27, 1776, quoted in "The Bulletin of the Fort Ticonderoga Museum," Vol. III, No. 13, July 1933.

Samuel Downing was the old veteran who remembered burning thirteen candles in every hut (one for each state) when peace was declared. The quotation is from the Reverend E. B. Hillard's *The Last Men of the Revolution*, which consists of interviews with six survivors of the Revolution. At the time of the interviews each of the men was over one hundred years of age.

BIBLIOGRAPHY

ADAMS, CHARLES FRANCIS, Editor. *Familiar Letters of John Adams and His Wife Abigail Adams, During the Revolution.* With a Memoir of Mrs. Adams. New York and Cambridge, 1876.
———. "The Battle of Bunker Hill From A Strategic Point of View." American Antiquarian Society *Proceedings*, Vol. 10, pp. 387–389, 1895.

ADMIRALTY RECORDS (Public Record Office, London).
 Captains' Letters
  Adm I/2053. John Linzee. 1772–1775
  Adm I/1610. James Chads. 1772–1775
———. Vice Admiral Samuel Graves—Correspondence.
  Adm. 1./485. North America. 1774 to 1777
———. Orders & Instructions (Earl of Sandwich, First Sea Lord)
  Adm 2/99—pp. 260–261, 285, 286, 327
———. Ships' Logs
  Adm. 51/398—A Journal of the Proceedings of His Majesty's Ship "Glasgow," Tyringham Howe Esq. Commander, commencing 21 April 1775 & Ending 30 Aug. 1776.
  Adm. 51/546—A Journal of the Proceedings of His Majesty's Ship "Lively," Captain Thos. Bishop. 4 Feb. 1775–25 Aug. 1777.
  Adm. 51/336—A Journal of the Proceedings of His Majesty's Sloop "Falcon." Jno Linzee Esq. Commander between 21 Oct. 1774 & 31 Oct. 1776.
  Adm. 51/906—A Journal of the Proceedings of His Majesty's Ship "Somerset." Captain Edward Le Cras. 15 Sept. 1774 & 17 Feb. 1776.
  Adm. 51/181—A Journal of the Proceedings of His Majesty's Ship "Cerberus." Captain James Chads.

ALDEN, JOHN RICHARD. *General Gage in America—Being Principally A History of His Role in the American Revolution.* Louisiana State University Press, Baton Rouge, 1948.

———. *The American Revolution, 1775–1783.* Harper & Brothers, New York, 1954.

AMERICAN HERITAGE PUBLISHING CO., INC. *The American Heritage Book of the Revolution.* Editor, Richard M. Ketchum. Narrative by Bruce Lancaster. New York, 1958.

ANTHONY, KATHARINE. *First Lady of the Revolution: The Life of Mercy Otis Warren.* Doubleday & Co., Inc., New York, 1958.

BAKELESS, JOHN. *Turncoats, Traitors and Heroes.* J. B. Lippincott Co., Philadelphia and New York, 1959.

BARKER, JOHN. *The British in Boston.* "Being the Diary of Lieutenant John Barker of the King's Own Regiment from November 15, 1774 to May 31, 1776; with Notes By Elizabeth Ellery Dana." Harvard University Press, Cambridge, 1924.

BELCHER, HENRY. *The First American Civil War* (2 vols.). The Macmillan Co., Limited, London, 1911.

BLAKE, JOHN B. *Public Health in the Town of Boston, 1630–1822.* Harvard University Press, Cambridge, 1959.

BOLTON, CHARLES KNOWLES. *The Private Soldier Under Washington.* George Newnes, Limited, London, 1902.

BOSTON TOWN RECORDS. 1770 through 1777. Report of the Record Commissioners of the City of Boston. Vol. 18, at Massachusetts Historical Society.

BOWEN, CATHERINE DRINKER. *John Adams and the American Revolution.* Atlantic, Little, Brown, Boston, 1950.

BOYD, EVA PHILLIPS. "Jamaica Plain by Way of London" in *Old-Time New England.* Vol. XLIX, No. 4—April–June, 1959.

BROOKS, NOAH. *Henry Knox, A Soldier of the Revolution.* G. P. Putnam's Sons, New York & London, 1900.

BUNKER HILL CENTENNIAL, Rand, Avery & Co., Publishers, Boston, June 17, 1875.

CARRINGTON, HENRY B. *Battles of the American Revolution.* A. S. Barnes & Co., New York, 1876.

CARY, JOHN. *Joseph Warren—Physician, Politician, Patriot.* University of Illinois Press, Urbana, 1961.

CLARKE, JOHN C. *An Impartial and Authentic Narrative of the Battle Fought on the 17th of June, 1775 Between His Britannic Majesty's Troops and the American Provincial Army, on Bunker's Hill, Near Charles-Town, in New England.* London, 1775.

CLINTON, SIR HENRY. Papers. William L. Clements Library.
———. *The American Rebellion,* Edited by William B. Willcox. Yale University Press, New Haven, 1954.

COMMAGER, HENRY STEELE, and MORRIS, RICHARD B., Editors. *The Spirit of 'Seventy-Six.* The Story of the American Revolution As Told by Participants. (2 vols.) The Bobbs-Merrill Company, Inc., Indianapolis and New York, 1958.

CRICK, B. R. and ALMAN, MIRIAM, Editors. *A Guide to Manuscripts Relating to America in Great Britain and Ireland.* Oxford University Press, New York, 1961.

DARTMOUTH, THE EARL OF. Manuscripts. Historical Manuscripts Commission. Eleventh Report, Appendix, Part IV— 1887—pp. 379-380.
    2 letters: Studholme Brownrigg, Ensign 38th Reg't. to Lieut. Genl. Hodgson.
    George Clark to Robert Clark, Edinburgh.

DAVIDSON, MARSHALL B. *Life in America* (2 vols.) Houghton Mifflin Co., Boston, 1951.

DAWSON, HENRY B., Editor. *The Historical Magazine,* Vol. III, Second Series—June, 1868—No. 6 (pp. 321-442).

DORSON, RICHARD M., Editor. *America Rebels.* Pantheon Books, Inc., New York, 1953.

DOWNEY, FAIRFAX. *Sound of the Guns.* David McKay Co. Inc., New York, 1955.

DRAKE, FRANCIS S. *Life and Correspondence of Henry Knox.* Samuel G. Drake, Boston, 1873.
———. *Memorials of the Society of the Cincinnati of Massachusetts.* Boston: Printed for the Society, 1873.

DRAKE, SAMUEL ADAMS. *Bunker Hill: The Story Told in Letters From the Battlefield by British Officers Engaged.* Nichols and Hall, Boston, 1875.

ELLIS, GEORGE E. *History of the Battle of Bunker's (Breed's) Hill* Lockwood, Brooks, and Company, Boston, 1875.

EMMONS, CHARLES P. *Sketches of Bunker Hill Battle and Monument.* Charlestown, 1843.

FARNSWORTH, AMOS. Diary. Edited by Samuel A. Green. In Massachusetts Historical Society *Proceedings* XXXII (1897, 1899) pp. 74–107.

FISHER, ELIJAH. "Journal of Elijah Fisher" (May 5, 1775 to 1785) in The Magazine of History, Extra No. 6, 1909.

FITCH, JABEZ, JR. "Diary of Jabez Fitch, Jr." in Massachusetts Historical Society *Proceedings*. May 1894.

FORBES, ESTHER. *Paul Revere & The World He Lived In*. Houghton Mifflin Co., Boston, 1942.

FORBES, HARRIETTE MERRIFIELD. *New England Diaries* (1602–1800). Privately printed, 1923.

FORCE, PETER. *American Archives*. Fourth Series, Volume II. Washington, 1839.

FREEMAN, DOUGLAS SOUTHALL. *George Washington*. Vol. III and Vol. IV. Charles Scribner's Sons, New York, 1951.

FRENCH, ALLEN. *The Day of Concord and Lexington*. Little, Brown & Co., Boston, 1925.
———. *The First Year of the American Revolution*. Houghton Mifflin Co., Boston and New York, 1934.
———. *The Siege of Boston*. The Macmillan Co.; New York, 1911.
———. "General Haldimand in Boston." Massachusetts Historical Society *Proceedings*, No. 66, 1936–41.

FROTHINGHAM, RICHARD. "The Battle-Field of Bunker Hill, with a Relation of the Action by William Prescott, and Illustrative Documents." Boston 1876.
———. *History of the Siege of Boston, and of the Battles of Lexington, Concord, and Bunker Hill*. Little, Brown & Co., Boston, 1873.
———. *Life and Times of Joseph Warren*. Little, Brown & Co., Boston, 1865.

GILMAN, ARTHUR, Editor. *The Cambridge of 1776* . . . Cambridge, 1876.

GIPSON, LAWRENCE H. *The Coming of the Revolution, 1763–1775*, Harper & Brothers, New York, 1954.

GREENE, EVARTS BOUTELL. *The Revolutionary Generation, 1763–1790* (A History of American Life—Vol. IV). The Macmillan Co., New York, 1956.

HAMILTON, CHARLES, Editor. *Braddock's Defeat*. University of Oklahoma Press, Norman, 1959.

HAWS, SAMUEL. "A Journal for 1775," in *The Military Journals of Two Private Soldiers, 1758–1775*. Compiled by Abraham Tomlinson. Poughkeepsie, 1855.

HEATH, WILLIAM. *Memoirs of the American War* (Reprinted from the original edition of 1798). A. Wessels Co., New York, 1904.

HEITMAN, FRANCIS B. *Historical Register of Officers of the Continental Army during the War of the Revolution, April 1775 to December, 1783*. The Rare Book Shop Publishing Co., Inc., Washington D.C., 1914.

HILL, JOHN B. *Bi-Centennial of Old Dunstable . . . Also Colonel Bancroft's Personal Narrative of the Battle of Bunker Hill. . . .* E. H. Spalding, 1878.

———. *History of the Town of Mason, N.H. from the First Grant in 1749, to the Year 1858*. Lucius A. Elliot & Co., Boston, 1858.

HILLARD, REV. E. B. *The Last Men of the Revolution*. Moore, Hartford, 1864.

HOW, DAVID. *A Private in Colonel Paul Dudley Sargent's Regiment of the Massachusetts Line . . .* Morisania, New York, 1865.

HULTON, ANN. *Letters of a Loyalist Lady*. "Being the Letters of Ann Hulton, Sister of Henry Hulton, Commissioner of Customs at Boston, 1767–1776." Harvard University Press, Cambridge, 1927.

HUNTINGTON, EBENEZER. Letters, 1774–1781. Reprinted in American Historical Review, No. 4, July 1900—pp. 702–729.

JAMESON, J. FRANKLIN. *The American Revolution Considered as a Social Movement*. Beacon Press, Boston, 1956.

JENKS, HENRY F. *Catalogue of the Boston Public Latin School*, Boston Latin School Association, 1886.

KNOLLENBERG, BERNHARD. "Bunker Hill Re-viewed: A Study in the Conflict of Historical Evidence," in Massachusetts Historical Society *Proceedings*, Vol. 72, October 1957 to December 1960.

KNOX, HENRY. Papers. At Massachusetts Historical Society, Boston.

LANCASTER, BRUCE. *From Lexington to Liberty*. Doubleday & Co., Inc., New York, 1955.

LAVER, JAMES. *British Military Uniforms*. Penguin Books, London, 1948.

LUNT, PAUL. Diary. May–December, 1775. Edited by Samuel A. Green, M.D., Boston, 1872.

LUSHINGTON, S. R. *The Life and Services of General Lord Harris.* London, 1840.

MACKENZIE, FREDERICK. A *British Fusilier in Revolutionary Boston.* "Being the Diary of Lieutenant Frederick Mackenzie, Adjutant of the Royal Welch Fusiliers, January 5–April 30, 1775." Edited by Allen French. Harvard University Press, Cambridge, 1926.

MANUCY, ALBERT. *Artillery Through the Ages.* A Short Illustrated History of Cannon, Emphasizing Types Used in America. U. S. Govt. Printing Office, Washington, D.C., 1949.

MARTYN, CHARLES. *The Life of Artemas Ward.* New York, 1921.

MAUDUIT, ISRAEL. *Three Letters to Lord Viscount Howe, with Remarks on the Attack at Bunker Hill.* 2nd Edition. London, 1781.

MCCARDELL, LEE. *Ill-Starred General: Braddock of the Coldstream Guards.* University of Pittsburgh Press, 1958.

MILLER, JOHN C. *Origins of the American Revolution.* Little, Brown & Co., Boston, 1943.
———. *Sam Adams, Pioneer in Propaganda.* Little, Brown & Co., Boston, 1936.

MOORE, FRANK. *Diary of the American Revolution* (2 vols.) Charles Scribner's Sons, New York, 1860.

MORGAN, EDMUND S. *The Birth of the Republic.* University of Chicago Press, Chicago, 1956.

MORRIS, RICHARD B. *The American Revolution, A Short History.* D. Van Nostrand Co., Inc., Princeton, New Jersey, 1955.

MORSE, JEDIDIAH. *Annals of the American Revolution.* Hartford, 1824.

MURDOCK, HAROLD. *Bunker Hill: Notes and Queries on a Famous Battle.* Houghton Mifflin Co., Boston, 1927.
———. *The Nineteenth of April, 1775.* Houghton Mifflin Co., Boston, 1925.

MURRAY, SIR JAMES. *Letters from America, 1773 to 1780,* Being the letters of a Scots officer, Sir James Murray, to his home during the War of American Independence. Edited by Eric Robson, Barnes & Noble, Inc., New York (No date of pub., editor's preface 27 July 1950).

PARTRIDGE, BELLAMY. *Sir Billy Howe.* Longmans, Green & Co., Inc., London and New York, 1932.

PECKHAM, HOWARD. *The War for Independence.* University of Chicago Press, Chicago, 1958.

PLUMB, J. H. *England in the Eighteenth Century.* Penguin Books, Baltimore, 1950.
————. *The First Four Georges.* The Macmillan Co., New York, 1957.

POTTER, ISRAEL RALPH. "Life and Adventures of Israel Ralph Potter (1744–1826)." Providence, 1824.

PUTNAM, ISRAEL. *Memoirs of the Life, Adventures, and Military Exploits of Israel Putnam.* Evert Duyckinck, New York, 1815.

ROBERTS, OLIVER AYER. *History of the Ancient and Honorable Artillery Company of Massachusetts—Vol. II—1738–1821.* Alfred Mudge & Son, Boston, 1897.

ROBSON, ERIC. "The War of American Independence Reconsidered," *History Today,* Vol. II, No. 5, May 1952.

ROMAINE, LAWRENCE B. *From Cambridge to Champlain* "March 18 to May 5, 1776—A Manuscript Diary." Weathercock House, Middleboro, Mass., 1957.

RUTHERFURD, LIVINGSTON. *Family Records and Events.* New York, 1894.

SABINE, LORENZO. *Biographical Sketches of Loyalists of the American Revolution, with an Historical Essay* (2 vols.). Little, Brown & Co., Boston, 1864.

SARGENT, WINTHROP. *The Life and Career of Major John André, Adjutant-General of the British Army in America.* Ticknor and Fields, Boston, 1861.

SCHEER, GEORGE F. and RANKIN, HUGH F. *Rebels and Redcoats.* The World Publishing Company, Cleveland and New York, 1957.

SHURTLEFF, NATHANIEL B. *A Topographical and Historical Description of Boston* (3rd ed.). Rockwell and Churchill, Boston, 1891.

SIBLEY, JOHN LANGDON, *Biographical Sketches of Those Who Attended Harvard College—1736–40.* Massachusetts Historical Society, Boston, 1958.

SIZER, THEODORE, Editor. *The Autobiography of Colonel John Trumbull.* Yale University Press, New Haven, 1953.

SPENCER, JOSEPH, Brig. Genl. Orderly Book, in "A Memento of the Siege of Boston, Massachusetts." New Bedford, Mass., July 1887.

STORRS, EXPERIENCE, Col. "Connecticut Farmers at Bunker Hill: The Diary of Colonel Experience Storrs." *The New England Quarterly*, March 1955, pp. 72–93.

SWETT, S. *History of Bunker Hill Battle*. Munroe and Francis, Boston, 1827.

THACHER, JAMES, M.D. *Military Journal During the American Revolutionary War*. Silas Andrus & Son, Hartford, 1854.

THAYER, THEODORE. *Nathanael Greene: Strategist of the American Revolution*. Twayne Publishers, New York, 1960.

TOURTELLOT, ARTHUR BERNON. *The Charles*. Farrar & Rinehart, New York, 1941.

————. *William Diamond's Drum*. Doubleday & Co., Inc., New York, 1959.

TYLER, MARY PALMER. *Grandmother Tyler's Book—The Recollections of Mary Palmer Tyler*. 1775–1866. Ed. by Frederick Tupper and Helen Tyler Brown. G. P. Putnam's Sons, New York, 1925.

WADE, HERBERT T. and LIVELY, ROBERT A. *This Glorious Cause*, "The Adventures of Two Company Officers in Washington's Army." Princeton University Press, Princeton, 1958.

WALLACE, WILLARD M. *Appeal to Arms: A Military History of the American Revolution*. Harper & Brothers, New York, 1951.

WARD, CHRISTOPHER. *The War of the Revolution* (2 vols.). The Macmillan Co., New York, 1952.

WATSON, ELKANAH. *Men and Times of the Revolution:* "or, Memoirs of Elkanah Watson, including his Journals of Travels in Europe and America, From the Year 1777 to 1842 . . ." edited by his son, Winslow C. Watson, Dana & Co., New York, 1856.

WHITE, J. *An Narrative of Events as they occurred from time to time, in the Revolutionary War; with an account of the Battles of Trenton, Trenton-Bridge, and Princeton*. Charlestown, October, 1833.

WINSOR, JUSTIN, Editor. *The Memorial History of Boston, Including Suffolk County, Massachusetts*. 1630–1880. James R. Osgood Company, Boston, 1881.

———. *Narrative and Critical History of America* (8 vols.) Vol. VI. Houghton Mifflin Co., Boston and New York, 1887.

WRIGHT, AARON. "Journal of Aaron Wright" (June 29, 1775 to July 4, 1776). In *Historical Magazine*, July 1862—pp. 208–212.

WYATT, FREDERICK and WILLCOX, WILLIAM B. "Sir Henry Clinton: A Pyschological Exploration in History." In *William and Mary Quarterly*, Vol. XVI, No. 1, January 1959.

INDEX

Abercromby, Gen. James, 14, 16, 162, 180, 209

Adams, Abigail, 68, 137, 194, 203

Adams, John, 68, 99, 110, 199, 204, 225

Adams, Samuel, 34, 44, 45, 56, 66, 147, 205

Amherst, Gen. Jeffrey, 14, 18

Arnold, Benedict, 54

Baldwin, Loammi, 78

Ballard, Benjamin, 167–68

Bancroft, Capt. Ebenezer, 137, 176

Bard, Third Officer, 168

Barker, Lt. John, 10, 19, 22, 32, 67, 78, 162, 194, 214

Barrington, Lord, 191

Belknap, Dr. Jeremy, 205

Bernard, Sir Francis, 34

Bishop, Capt. Thomas, 117

Boice, James, 62

Boston, 10–15, 19–22, 29–34, 39–41, 55, 101, 111, 112, 117, 119, 137, 154, 162–63, 183, 192–93, 201, 214, 216, 218–19, 220, 221–22, 224–25

Braddock, Gen. Edward, 14

Brattle, William, 95

Breed's Hill, 78, 106–7, 110, 111, 115, 126, 137, 146, 153, 167, 172, 180, 185, 202, 206, 217, 221, 225

Brewer, Col. Jonathan, 167, 206

Brickett, Lt. Col. James, 93, 99, 150

Bridge, Col. Ebenezer, 99, 176, 206

Brooks, Maj. John, 112, 127–30, 132, 133

Brown, Edward, 173

Brown, Peter, 93, 117, 119, 130, 155, 160, 176

Brownrigg, Ensign Studholme, 150

Bunker Hill, 22, 23, 75–78, 79, 81, 82, 83, 103, 105, 106, 110, 130, 132, 139, 142, 144, 147, 150, 160, 165, 166, 177, 181, 182, 183, 190, 192, 207, 213, 220–21, 222, 225, 226

Burgoyne, Gen. John, 2, 3, 7–9, 41–45, 46, 48, 121, 130, 154, 155, 164, 181, 195, 198, 210

Callender, Capt. John, 127, 142, 206

Cambridge, 39, 45, 55, 56, 64, 79, 81, 82, 85, 90, 95–97, 99, 117, 132, 134, 201

Castle William, 222

Chads, Capt. James, 2

Charles River, 106, 139

Charlestown, 22, 23, 41, 46, 47, 52, 61, 62, 75, 77, 78, 103, 105, 106, 107, 110, 115, 117, 119, 122, 133, 134, 146, 153, 155, 158, 160, 163, 167, 182, 185, 199–201, 226

Chatham, Lord, 24–25

Cheever, David, 132

Chester, Capt. John, 91, 133–34, 135, 159, 165–66, 177, 205

Church, Dr. Benjamin, 74

Clark, Lt. Col. George, 123, 139, 191

Clark, Capt. James, 166

Clarke, John, 186
Cleaveland, Col. Samuel, 153, 197, 218
Clinton, Gen. Henry, 2, 3–4, 6, 9, 41, 44, 46, 115, 120, 121, 122, 164, 181, 182, 183, 192, 201, 213, 217
Coggswell, James, 86
Coit, Capt. William, 166, 177
Collingwood, Midshipman Cuthbert, 152
Committee of Correspondence, Connecticut, 54
Committee of Safety, Massachusetts, 37, 47, 48–49, 56, 58, 59, 62, 67, 68, 71, 74–75, 79, 90, 97, 99, 132, 133, 134, 150, 208, 209
Committee of Supplies, Massachusetts, 61, 202
Concord, Battle of, 6, 10, 19, 24, 25, 51, 56, 73
Continental Army, 207
Continental Congress, Second, 49, 56, 61, 66, 74, 133, 202, 207, 211
Copley, John Singleton, 38, 56
Copp's Hill battery, 107, 126, 130, 139, 152, 153, 155, 164
Council of War, Massachusetts, 74
Cromwell, Oliver, 37
Cunningham, William, 198

Dana, Lt., 142, 159
Dartmouth, Lord, 9, 211
Dawes, Billy, 52, 56
Dealey, James, 51
Dearborn, Henry, 144
Devens, Richard, 75, 133
Dorchester Heights, 23, 41, 46, 47, 75, 78, 79, 115, 119, 134, 192, 201, 216–18, 220, 225
Dow, Capt. Reuben, 177
Drewe, Capt. Edward, 168
Dyer, Col. John, 105, 202

Edes, Peter, 198
Eliot, Rev. Andrew, 199, 201, 202–3
Eustis, William, 150
Evelyn, Capt., 29

Farnsworth, Amos, 59, 68, 69, 78, 90, 98, 110, 112, 176
Farwell, Capt., 177
Febiger, Christian, 165
Foster, Capt. Thomas, 64, 91, 99
Frankland, Agnes Surriage, Lady, 37–38
Frankland, Sir Charles Henry, 37
French and Indian Wars, 69, 121
Frothingham, Richard, 208
Frye, Col. James, 93, 150
Frye, Joseph, 93

Gadsden, Christopher, 50
Gage, Margaret, 190, 210
Gage, Gen. Thomas, 4, 11–22, 25–27, 35, 44, 45, 47, 48, 52, 61, 62, 72–73, 74, 105, 115, 119–20, 121, 126, 127, 139, 162, 164, 180, 190, 191, 192, 197, 198, 203, 210, 213–14
Gardner, Col. Thomas, 166, 180, 181, 206
Garrick, David, 9
George III, 6, 9, 18, 49, 210–11, 213
Germain, Lord George, 6, 9
Gerrish, Col. Samuel, 59, 165, 206
Gill, Moses, 61
Gilman, Col. Israel, 81
Grape Island, 67–68
Graves, Adm. Samuel, 2, 9, 22, 23–24, 69, 72, 112, 117, 120, 126, 151
Graves, Lt. Thomas, 69, 72
Gray, Samuel, 105–6, 205
Great and General Court of Massachusetts, 48

Greene, Gen. Nathanael, 60, 65, 106

Gridley, Col. Richard, 59, 90, 98–99, 105, 110–11, 114, 206, 216

Gridley, Capt. Samuel, 99, 127, 142

Gridley, Maj. Scarborough, 99, 142, 206

Guild, Benjamin, 204

Gunning, John, 168

Hallowell, Benjamin, 219

Hancock, John, 34, 44, 45, 54, 56, 67, 92, 95

Harris, Capt. George, 41, 172, 173

Harvard College, 64, 78, 85, 86, 87

Hastings, Jonathan, 56

Haws, Samuel, 65, 194

Heath, William, 82, 106

Henry, Patrick, 50

Henshaw, Col., 75

Hide, Capt. Elijah, 207

Hodgkins, Lt. Joseph, 65, 166, 224

Hog Island, 68–69

Hopkinson, Francis, 36

Howard, Sir George, 33, 212

Howe, Admiral "Black Dick," 4

Howe, Viscount George Augustus, 4–6

Howe, Maj. Gen. William, 2, 4–7, 36, 44, 45–46, 115, 120, 121, 122, 123, 139, 143, 144, 151, 152–53, 154, 159, 160, 161, 162, 163–64, 168–69, 181, 187, 192, 195, 213, 214, 217, 218, 219, 222, 224

Huger, Isaac, 50

Hulton, Anne, 38–41, 186

Hulton, Henry, 152

Hunt, Shrimpton, 198

Hunter, Ensign, 173

Hutchinson, Thomas, 14, 55

Inman, Mrs. Ralph, 38, 102

Jamaica Plain, 34–35

Jones, Thomas, 36

Jorden, Lt., 121, 169

Kemble, Margaret, 15

Knowlton, Capt. Thomas, 102, 142, 143, 144, 159, 181

Knox, Henry, 60, 214–16

Langdon, Rev. Samuel, 85–87, 97

Laurie, Capt. Walter Sloane, 195

Learned, Col. Ebenezer, 221

Lechmere, Richard, 95

Lechmere's Point, 166

Lee, Arthur, 49

Lee, Gen. Charles, 126

Lee, Joseph, 95

Lexington, Battle of, 6, 10, 19, 24, 51, 52, 54, 71, 73

Liberty Boys, 15, 33, 219

Linzee, Capt. John, 102, 126

Lister, Jeremy, 181

Litchfield, Paul, 203–4

Little, Col., 103, 206

Loring, Elizabeth Lloyd, 35, 36–37

Loring, Com. Joshua, 34–35

Loring, Joshua, Jr., 35, 36, 198

Lothrop, Isaac, 187

Lovell, Benjamin, 197

Lovell, James, 197–98

Lovell, John, 153, 197, 198

Lyon, Capt., 168

McClary, Maj. Andrew, 54, 146, 183

McCowen, Winifred, 192

McDougall, Alexander, 62

McLeod, Donald, 50

Mackenzie, Lt. Frederick, 24

Mann, Capt. Benjamin, 160

Martin, Laughlin, 51

Mason, George, 211

Massey, Lt., 168

Mather, Rev. Cotton, 199

Maxwell, Capt. Hugh, 112, 114, 177

Montresor, Capt., 22, 105, 106

Moore, Maj. Willard, 146, 167

Morton's Hill, 146, 153

Morton's Point, 107, 122, 127, 138, 139, 153

Moultrie, William, 50

Mystic River, 106, 107, 122, 139, 142, 143

Nelson, Adm. Horatio, 152

Nesbitt, Col., 174

Nixon, Col. John, 68, 134, 167, 206

Noddle's Island, 68, 69, 72

North, Lord, 9, 18, 210, 213

Nutting, Capt., 110, 114

Oliver, Peter, 32–33, 85, 186, 203

Oliver, Thomas, 97

Oughton, Sir James Adolphus, 211

Page, Lt. Thomas Hyde, 121, 168

Paine, Thomas, 226

Palmer, Elizabeth, 83

Palmer, Col. Joseph, 73, 79, 83

Parker, Moses, 176, 206

Pelham, Henry, 38

Pepperrell, Sir William, 34

Percy, Lord, 22, 25

Phips, Spencer, 101

Pigot, Brig. Gen. Robert, 22, 123, 152–53, 160, 162, 163, 164, 173, 181

Pitcairn, Maj. John, 174, 180

Plowed Hill, 220

Pollard, Asa, 118, 132

Pomeroy, Gen. Seth, 106, 151, 180

Pownal, John, 213

Prentice, John, 51

Prescott, Col. William, 75, 82, 98, 101, 102, 103, 105, 106, 110, 112, 114–19, 122, 127, 130, 135, 138, 139–42, 143, 147, 160, 162, 163, 165, 174–76, 177, 201, 206

Prescott, William Hickling, 102

Prince, Salem, 174

Provincial Congress, Massachusetts, 34, 37, 44, 47, 48, 49, 50, 56, 59, 61, 62, 65, 66, 67, 73, 74, 82, 85, 86, 87, 97, 98, 99, 132, 150, 187, 199, 205–6, 207

Putnam, Capt. Daniel, 102–3, 133–34

Putnam, Gen. Israel, 69–72, 75–78, 79, 82, 102–3, 106, 110, 114, 130, 132, 134, 142, 144, 147, 150, 160, 161, 165, 183, 206, 221

Randon, John, 187

Rawdon, Lord, 121, 172–73, 177, 181

Reed, James, 79, 81, 143, 146

Reeve, Richard, 33–34, 71, 212

Revere, Paul, 52, 56, 195

Rhode Island Corps, 60, 65

Rochford, Lord, 9

Roxbury, 35, 45, 52, 55, 60, 64, 67, 79, 106, 167, 201, 203

Ruggles, George, 95

Sackville, Lord, 6

Sandwich, Earl of, 2, 10

Scammell, Alexander, 59

Scammon, Col. James, 147, 206

Seven Years' War, 4, 6, 27

Sever, Mr., 73

Shaw, Elijah, 48

Smith, Brig. Gen. Francis, 217

Smith, Gershom, 173

Spaulding, Lt., 138

Spencer, Joseph, 79, 167

Spendlove, Maj., 168

Stark, Gen. John, 65–66, 79, 81, 133, 135, 136, 143–44, 146, 147, 153, 160, 181, 206

Steele, Robert, 167–68

Stockbridge Indians, 50
Storrs, Lt. Col. Experience, 91–93, 132, 134, 135, 147, 167, 183 `
Stow, Nathan, 134
Sullivan, Brig. Gen. John, 220–21

Taylor, Dr., 73
Thacher, Rev. Peter, 158, 208
Thomas, John, 54–55, 60, 68, 79, 106, 134, 135, 167, 216
Tories, 38, 85, 95, 209, 224
Townsend, Dr., 150
Trevett, Samuel, 147, 161, 177, 180
Trisdale, David, 194
Trumbull, Jonathan, 62, 207
Trumbull, Joseph, 65, 202–3

Walker, Capt., 176
Waller, Adjutant, 173–74
Ward, Gen. Artemas, 54–56, 58, 61, 71, 72, 74, 78, 79–82, 86, 91, 93, 106, 127, 130, 132, 133, 135, 166–67, 193, 201, 202, 203, 204–5, 206, 221, 222
Ward, Samuel, 212

Warren, James, 73, 99, 204, 205, 207
Warren, Dr. Joseph, 37, 49, 51, 56–58, 61, 62, 66, 68, 69, 72, 78–79, 82–83, 106, 133, 150–51, 153, 166–67, 177, 194–95, 206
Washington, Gen. George, 95, 193, 206, 207–8, 214, 216, 218–19, 222–24
Webb, Samuel, 166, 173
Wellington, Duke of, 27
Wesley, John, 210
White, Benjamin, 79
White, Joseph, 97–98
Whitney, Silvanus, 51
Whittemore, Coffee, 176
Willard, Abijah, 127
Williams, Maj., 173
Winslow, Benjamin, 35
Winslow, Joshua, 35
Winter Hill, 183, 201, 207
Wolfe, Gen. James, 4, 98
Wyman, Col., 135

Yorke, Sir Joseph, 16

ABOUT THE AUTHOR

RICHARD M. KETCHUM is the author of a number of books of American history, including *The Winter Soldiers*, *Faces from the Past*, *The Borrowed Years 1938–1941*, and biographies of George Washington and Will Rogers.

As director of book publishing activities at American Heritage Publishing Company, he edited many of that firm's volumes, including *The American Heritage Picture History of the Civil War*, which received a special Pulitzer Prize citation.

He was the cofounder and editor of *Blair & Ketchum's Country Journal*, a monthly magazine about country living.

Born in Pittsburgh, Pennsylvania, he graduated from Yale University and commanded a subchaser in the South Atlantic during World War II.

He and his wife have a working sheep farm in Vermont and are active conservationists.